PRAISE FOR *FINDING LEO*

"The need for servant leadership has never been greater, but the supply is not meeting the demand. In this book, Philip Mathew lays out an actionable framework for leaders to become givers rather than takers."

—ADAM GRANT, author of *Think Again*

"A remarkably poignant and spiritual book, yet full of personal and practical applications. While the case studies are about well-known and regarded individuals, the fact of the matter is that leadership is everyone's business. The stories emphasize that leadership begins with finding the Leo within each of us in order to care enough about something or someone other than ourselves, to act, and in so doing, to make a difference. A book to be savored rather than devoured."

—BARRY Z. POSNER, Chair, Department of Management & Entrepreneurship, Leavey School of Business, Santa Clara University

"Keep a highlighter handy when you read *Finding Leo*! You will learn something new in every gracefully written chapter. Mathew delivers a compelling blend of history, scholarship, Greenleaf's foundational principles, and moving stories of servant leaders, ranging from Harriet Tubman and Southwest Airlines founder Herb Kelleher to Mahatma Gandhi and Eleanor Roosevelt. . . . Every practicing and aspiring servant-leader should have Finding Leo in their personal libraries."

—DON M. FRICK, author of *Robert K. Greenleaf: A Life of Servant Leadership*

"I have always tried to live my life as a servant leader. After reading about the extraordinary servant leadership highlighted in *Finding Leo*, I am even more committed to continuing the work of encouraging more people to become servant leaders. If you are a new or experienced servant leader, I highly recommend *Finding Leo* because you will be reminded that Buddha said to the bandit, 'Servant leaders help make a hurting world whole.'"

—DAMON A. BELL, Community College Executive Leader

"Philip Mathew has assembled a wonderful collection of insights from some of the greatest leaders out there. Their stories and perspectives truly illustrate what servant leadership is all about. A solid read for those who aspire to lofty levels of servant leadership."

—MIKE FIGLIUOLO, author of *Lead Inside the Box*

Finding Leo

Finding Leo

Servant Leadership as Paradigm, Power, and Possibility

PHILIP MATHEW

*Forewords by Larry C. Spears
and Shann Ray Ferch*

WIPF & STOCK · Eugene, Oregon

FINDING LEO
Servant Leadership as Paradigm, Power, and Possibility

Copyright © 2021 Philip Mathew. All rights reserved. Except for brief quotations in critical publications or reviews, no part of this book may be reproduced in any manner without prior written permission from the publisher. Write: Permissions, Wipf and Stock Publishers, 199 W. 8th Ave., Suite 3, Eugene, OR 97401.

Wipf & Stock
An Imprint of Wipf and Stock Publishers
199 W. 8th Ave., Suite 3
Eugene, OR 97401

www.wipfandstock.com

PAPERBACK ISBN: 978-1-7252-9325-0
HARDCOVER ISBN: 978-1-7252-9330-4
EBOOK ISBN: 978-1-7252-9331-1

02/06/23

To Roshan and Asha
Light and Hope

Contents

Foreword: Larry C. Spears		xi
Foreword: The Essence of Servant-Leaders: Shann Ray Ferch		xix
Introduction		xxv
1	Herb Kelleher: The Servant-Leader and Listening	1
2	Harriet Tubman: The Servant-Leader and Empathy	18
3	Mother Teresa: The Servant-Leader and Healing	32
4	Malala Yousafzai: The Servant-Leader and Awareness	48
5	John Woolman: The Servant-Leader and Persuasion	64
6	Mahatma Gandhi: The Servant-Leader and Conceptualization	91
7	Eleanor Roosevelt: The Servant-Leader and Foresight	111
8	Wangari Maathai: The Servant-Leader and Stewardship	133
9	Viktor Frankl: The Servant-Leader and Commitment to the Growth of People	150
10	Martin Luther King Jr.: The Servant-Leader and Building Community	170
Bibliography		191
Index		207

Foreword

by Larry C. Spears

I AM HONORED TO have been asked to write one of the forewords to Philip Mathew's wonderful book, *Finding Leo: Servant Leadership as Paradigm, Power, and Possibility*. I would like to tell you briefly about servant-leadership, my own journey in servant-leadership, and the powerful significance of this book.

I was first introduced to the servant-as-leader idea in 1982. At that time, I was working with *Friends Journal*, a Quaker magazine based in Philadelphia. One day we received an article submission from Robert K. Greenleaf on the servant-as-leader idea, which we eventually published. All these years later, I still recall the "a-ha" moment that came over me as I read Greenleaf's description of the servant-as-leader for the very first time. I found that he had given a name to an undefined yearning that I felt within me. I knew that I wanted to do what I could to help make the world a little better place in which to live. I was doing what I could to be of service in that goal, and I hoped that I might eventually have an opportunity to provide some leadership. In reading Greenleaf's definition and best test of a servant-as-leader, I began to understand servant-leadership as a personal philosophy that could be developed and practiced. All these years later, I continue in my personal and public efforts to practice servant-leadership.

From 1990 to 2007, I was privileged to serve as President and CEO of the Robert K. Greenleaf Center. In 1990, I had a chance to spend some time with Robert Greenleaf, and I eventually went on to edit or co-edit all five of Robert Greenleaf's available books, as well as a series of popular servant-leadership anthologies. In 2008, I started a new phase of my work in servant-leadership when I was invited to serve as Servant-Leadership Scholar for Gonzaga University, where I teach graduate courses in servant-leadership, and where I serve as Senior Advisory Editor of *The International Journal of Servant-Leadership* (www.gonzaga.edu/ijsl). Also in 2008, I launched the Spears Center for Servant-Leadership (www.spearscenter.org) and, thus, I began to divide my time between these two institutions, which I continue to do.

Who *is* a servant-leader? Greenleaf said that the servant-leader is one who is a servant first. In *The Servant as Leader* he wrote,

> It begins with the natural feeling that one wants to serve, to serve first. Then conscious choice brings one to aspire to lead. The difference manifests itself in the care taken by the servant— first to make sure that other people's highest priority needs are being served. The best test is: Do those served grow as persons; do they, while being served, become healthier, wiser, freer, more autonomous, more likely themselves to become servants? And, what is the effect on the least privileged in society? Will they benefit or at least not be further deprived?[1]

It is important to remember that servant-leadership begins within every one of us. As a lifelong student of how things get done in organizations, Greenleaf distilled his observations in a series of essays and books on the theme of "The Servant as Leader"—the objective of which was to stimulate thought and action for building a better, more caring society.

The servant-leader concept continues to grow in influence and impact. In fact, we have witnessed a remarkable growth of awareness and practices of servant-leadership. In many ways, it may be said that the times are only now beginning to catch up with Robert Greenleaf's visionary call to servant-leadership. The idea of servant-leadership, now in its sixth decade as a concept bearing that name, continues to create a quiet revolution around the world.

The words "servant" and "leader" are usually thought of as being opposites. In deliberately bringing those two words together in a meaningful way, Robert Greenleaf gave birth to the paradoxical term "servant-leader." In the years since then, many of today's most creative thinkers have been writing and speaking about servant-leadership as an emerging paradigm for the twenty-first century. Robert Greenleaf's writings on the subject of servant-leadership helped to get this movement started, and his views have had a profound and growing effect on many organizations and thought-leaders. Organizations like Starbucks, TDIndustries, The Toro Company, Southwest Airlines, The Men's Wearhouse, PieperPower, Synovus Financial Corporation, The Container Store, and many more are recognized today for nurturing servant-led cultures. These and many more organizational

---

1. Greenleaf, *Servant as Leader*, 15.

practitioners have been encouraged and supported by a long list of thought-leaders such as James Autry, Warren Bennis, Ken Blanchard, Peter Block, John Carver, Stephen Covey, Max DePree, Shann Ferch, Don Frick, John Horsman, Joseph Jaworski, James Kouzes, Larraine Matusak, Parker Palmer, M. Scott Peck, Peter Senge, Peter Vaill, Margaret Wheatley, and Danah Zohar, to name but a handful of today's cutting-edge authors and advocates of servant-leadership. And with this book, *Finding Leo*, we add Philip Mathew to this list of crucial thought leaders who are helping to shape our ongoing understanding of servant-leadership in the twenty-first century.

Some organizational leaders have concluded that servant-leadership is the right thing to do and have subsequently embraced it. This has certainly been an important way in which servant-leadership has grown and advanced over the years. However, I think it is vitally important to note that Greenleaf titled his essay, "The Servant as Leader," and not "The Leader as Servant." While encouraging leaders to act as servants was a remarkable idea, asking servants to act as leaders was (and remains) a truly radical idea. It is also an idea that goes against our expectations of contemporary culture. It is this fact that makes servant-leadership such a unique and potent philosophy.

The literature on leadership includes a number of different listings of character traits as practiced by leaders. Much of the leadership literature includes as an implicit assumption the belief that positive traits can and should be encouraged and practiced by leaders, and everyone. Robert K. Greenleaf is someone who thought and wrote a great deal about the nature of servant-leadership and character.

In 1992, I conducted a study of Robert Greenleaf's writings. From that analysis, I was able to codify a set of ten characteristics that Greenleaf wrote about and which he considered as being central to the development of servant-leaders. These include the following:

- Listening: Leaders have traditionally been valued for their communication and decision-making skills. Although these are also important skills for the servant-leader, they need to be reinforced by a deep commitment to listening intently to others. The servant-leader seeks to identify the will of a group and helps to clarify that will. He or she listens receptively to what is being said and unsaid. Listening also encompasses hearing one's own inner voice. Listening, coupled with periods of reflection, is essential to the growth and well-being of the servant-leader.
- Empathy: The servant-leader strives to understand and empathize with others. People need to be accepted and recognized for their special and unique spirits. One assumes the good intentions of co-workers and

- Healing: The healing of relationships is a powerful force for transformation and integration. One of the great strengths of servant-leadership is the potential for healing one's self and one's relationship to others. Many people have broken spirits and have suffered from a variety of emotional hurts. Although this is a part of being human, servant-leaders recognize that they have an opportunity to help make whole those with whom they come in contact. In his essay, "The Servant as Leader," Greenleaf writes, "There is something subtle communicated to one who is being served and led if, implicit in the compact between servant-leader and led, is the understanding that the search for wholeness is something they share."[2]

- Awareness: General awareness, and especially self-awareness, strengthens the servant-leader. Awareness helps one in understanding issues involving ethics, power, and values. It lends itself to being able to view most situations from a more integrated, holistic position. As Greenleaf observed, "Awareness is not a giver of solace—it is just the opposite. It is a disturber and an awakener. Able leaders are usually sharply awake and reasonably disturbed. They are not seekers after solace. They have their own inner serenity."[3]

- Persuasion: Another characteristic of servant-leaders is reliance on persuasion, rather than on one's positional authority, in making decisions within an organization. The servant-leader seeks to convince others, rather than coerce compliance. This particular element offers one of the clearest distinctions between the traditional authoritarian model and that of servant-leadership. The servant-leader is effective at building consensus within groups. This emphasis on persuasion over coercion finds its roots in the beliefs of the Religious Society of Friends (Quakers)—the denominational body to which Robert Greenleaf belonged.

- Conceptualization: Servant-leaders seek to nurture their abilities to dream great dreams. The ability to look at a problem or an organization from a conceptualizing perspective means that one must think beyond day-to-day realities. For many leaders, this is a characteristic that requires discipline and practice. The traditional leader is consumed

---

2. Greenleaf, *Servant as Leader*, 50.
3. Greenleaf, *Servant as Leader*, 41.

by the need to achieve short-term operational goals. The leader who wishes to also be a servant-leader must stretch his or her thinking to encompass broader-based conceptual thinking. Within organizations, conceptualization is, by its very nature, a key role of boards of trustees or directors. Trustees need to be mostly conceptual in their orientation, staffs need to be mostly operational in their perspective, and the most effective executive leaders probably need to develop both perspectives within themselves. Servant-leaders are called to seek a delicate balance between conceptual thinking and a day-to-day operational approach.

- Foresight: Closely related to conceptualization, the ability to foresee the likely outcome of a situation is hard to define, but easier to identify. One knows foresight when one experiences it. Foresight is a characteristic that enables the servant-leader to understand the lessons from the past, the realities of the present, and the likely consequence of a decision for the future. It is also deeply rooted within the intuitive mind. Foresight remains a largely unexplored area in leadership studies, but one most deserving of careful attention.

- Stewardship: Peter Block (author of *Stewardship and the Empowered Manager*) has defined stewardship as "holding something in trust for another."[4] Robert Greenleaf's view of all institutions was one in which CEOs, staffs, and trustees all played significant roles in holding their institutions in trust for the greater good of society. Servant-leadership, like stewardship, assumes first and foremost a commitment to serving the needs of others. It also emphasizes the use of openness and persuasion, rather than control.

- Commitment to the Growth of People: Servant-leaders believe that people have an intrinsic value beyond their tangible contributions as workers. As such, the servant-leader is deeply committed to the growth of each and every individual within his or her organization. The servant-leader recognizes the tremendous responsibility to do everything in his or her power to nurture the personal and professional growth of employees and colleagues. In practice, this can include (but is not limited to) concrete actions such as making funds available for personal and professional development, taking a personal interest in the ideas and suggestions from everyone, encouraging worker involvement in decision-making, and actively assisting laid-off employees to find other positions.

---

4. Block, *Choosing Service*, xx.

- Building Community: The servant-leader senses that much has been lost in recent human history as a result of the shift from local communities to large institutions as the primary shaper of human lives. This awareness causes the servant-leader to seek to identify some means for building community among those who work within a given institution. Servant-leadership suggests that true community can be created among those who work in businesses and other institutions. Greenleaf said, "All that is needed to rebuild community as a viable life form for large numbers of people is for enough servant-leaders to show the way, not by mass movements, but by each servant-leader demonstrating his or her unlimited liability for a quite specific community-related group."[5]

These ten characteristics of servant-leadership are by no means exhaustive. However, they serve to communicate the power and promise that this concept offers to servant-leaders who are open to its invitation and challenge. In *Finding Leo*, Philip provides the world an extraordinary service by fleshing out the meaning and application of these characteristics. And he has done so through emphasizing the actions of some of the world's great practitioners of servant-leadership.

Philip's choices of people to illustrate each of these characteristics are profound and inspiring. They include: Herb Kelleher (1931–2019), founder of Southwest Airlines (*Listening*); Harriet Tubman (c. 1820–1913), American abolitionist and activist (*Empathy*); Mother Teresa (1910–1997), powerful advocate for the sick and poor (*Healing*); Malala Yousafzai (b. 1977), activist for female education and the youngest Nobel Prize laureate (*Awareness*); John Woolman (1720–1772), Quaker minister and abolitionist (*Persuasion*); Mahatma Gandhi (1869–1948), his commitment to nonviolent resistance led to India's independence and helped to inspire the American civil rights movement (*Conceptualization*); Eleanor Roosevelt (1884–1962), driving force behind The Universal Declaration of Human Rights (*Foresight*); Wangari Maathai (1940–2011), founder of the Green Belt Movement and 2004 Nobel Peace Prize laureate (*Stewardship*); Viktor Frankl (1905–1997), noted psychiatrist, Holocaust survivor, and author of *Man's Search for Meaning* (*Commitment to the Growth of People*); and Martin Luther King Jr. (1929–1968), renowned minister, social activist, author, and leader of the American civil rights movement (*Building Community*).

It is helpful to understand that servant-leadership starts within each one of us and that it is primarily a personal philosophy and commitment that we can choose to practice in any environment. Also, servant-leadership

5. Spears, "Tracing the Growing Impact," 6.

is not a leadership style that one puts on and takes off like a coat, depending upon the weather (or situation). Rather, if we understand Greenleaf's best test as the fundamental understanding of servant-leadership, then it becomes clear that the choice to act as a servant-leader is ours to make, and no one else's. Our personally embracing servant-leadership does not require the approval of our supervisor, or our organization's chief executive. We don't need anyone's permission to personally do our best to act as a servant-leader. It is our choice.

Another helpful insight is to state the obvious: there are no perfect servant-leaders and no perfect servant-led institutions. Institutions are led by people—and people are imperfect. Even the most well-intentioned servant-leaders will at some point in time do or say something that they regret. At those times, the best thing to do is to sincerely apologize, and to seek to learn from it. In other instances, someone else may become angry at us for a decision that we are convinced was the right one and which was made with the greater good in mind. When that happens, and if we are aware of it, the opportunity is there to try and promote healing by reaching out to one another. While there are no perfect servant-leaders, through our ongoing development and practice we can become *authentic* servant-leaders. As this book demonstrates, the effective uses of foresight, listening, and other servant-leader characteristics are often at the heart of profoundly positive change in the world.

Servant-leadership isn't pie-in-the-sky kind of work. It requires personal commitment and dedication. Servant-leadership is also a universal concept—one that we can recognize in ourselves, and in others, when we come to understand what it means, and what it looks like in practice.

In *Finding Leo*, Philip has beautifully expanded our understanding of servant-leadership characteristics, and he offers us clear examples of servant-leaders who have helped to change the world for the better. I invite you to read what is contained within this book and to draw strength and inspiration from it for your own servant-leadership journey.

Larry C. Spears
Servant-Leadership Scholar, Gonzaga University
Senior Advisory Editor, *The International Journal of Servant-Leadership*
President, The Spears Center for Servant-Leadership, Inc.
Author-Editor, *Insights on Leadership* and other books
Indianapolis, Indiana
2021

Foreword: The Essence of Servant-Leaders

by Shann Ray Ferch

WHAT A PROFOUND GIFT it was to be introduced to Dr. Philip Mathew many years ago. I was initially struck by three things: Philip's great sense of calm, his willing investment in the heart and spirit of others, and his transcendent, internationally-focused intelligence. In the years since that meeting, my admiration for Philip and his work in servant-leadership has only grown, becoming both more nuanced and more multivalent. Thanks to Philip's book, *Finding Leo: Servant Leadership as Paradigm, Power, and Possibility*, people will find themselves lovingly and wisely encouraged to reach farther into Robert K. Greenleaf's true test of servant-leadership.

As an affirmation of this, I found in Philip's presence people become more wise, more free, more autonomous, more healthy, and better able to serve others. The least privileged are benefitted, or at least not further deprived. Among the ten characteristics of servant-leadership, Dr. Mathew embodies a very uncommon constellation: he listens well, he has rare foresight and prophetic strength, he is empathic and aware, he builds a community committed to the growth of people, and he is a leader in concert with others capable of healing the heart of the world. Professionally, I have always been inspired by Philip's depth, his radiance, and his quiet leadership. Personally, being honored to be called his friend, I've found not only my soul but the souls of others given greater freedom to grow, thrive, and become more whole. Even in the context of disturbing trends worldwide, such as an increasing ascension of fascism, despotism, and human rights abuses, Dr. Mathew works in peaceful unity with others to generate hope and a more graceful and fully envisioned future. This essence, a person willing to serve, devoted to the center of life, and capable of healing communities, systems, and individuals, is the essence of the servant-leader.

In *Finding Leo*, Dr. Mathew has written a pathway to understand more about the essence of the servant-leader. Philip's choice of many of the world's most revered leaders, balanced by women and men with great social gravity and fierce conceptualizations of just how to build community, is stunning. The feminine and the masculine in concert heals the world, and in Philip's book we find a glorious harmony between Harriet Tubman, American abolitionist; Mother Teresa, servant of the poor; Herb Kelleher, founder of Southwest Airlines; Malala Yousafzai, champion of education for girls and women amidst patriarchal supremacy; John Woolman, the great Quaker genius of enduring persuasion; Mahatma Gandhi, proponent of soul force toward social transformation; Eleanor Roosevelt, wisdom-seeker who shepherded The Universal Declaration of Human Rights; Wangari Maathai, founder of the Green Belt Movement; Viktor Frankl, revered doctor of the soul, Holocaust survivor, and world-changer; and Martin Luther King Jr., a voice and sacrificial presence of the highest dreams of humanity.

In *Finding Leo's* chapters of hard-won beauty and fortitude, I find an authentic connection to my own family history of genocide and reconciliation that has given shape to how I understand what beloved relationships can be. Philip's work is inviting and challenging, loving and met with responsibility to greater life. As I've worked to understand servant-leadership and forgiveness in the face of staggering harm, I've spent crucial time digging into my own generational history. And a strange story has emerged.

It's a simple story, but crucial to my family's well-being. My grandmother Catherine, probably the most beloved member of our family when I was young, immigrated with her family to America from Czechoslovakia. In New York City, she married my grandfather Herbert, whose German parents had also immigrated to America. They wed during World War II—a Czech woman and a German man marrying during the precise time that Germany was making no secret of committing genocide against Czechoslovakians in Europe.

Eventually, I visited the site of the Lidice Massacre. Hitler destroyed an entire Czech town, murdering all the men and boys above 16 years old by firing squad behind a barn. He wanted to make an example of the town in response to the Czech resistance assassinating one of the key architects of the Holocaust, Reinhard Heydrich—the "Butcher of Prague." Heydrich had directly called for the organized killing of all Czechs, and after many months of planning, the resistance took him out with a British-made bomb. Like many egotistical leaders, Heydrich was arrogant. With German precision, he drove his green Mercedes coupe with the top down through the countryside at a regimented time in the afternoon. The resistance simply hid, jumped out into the road and threw the bomb in the car as it came around a bend.

In retaliation, Hitler decided on a spectacle. The town of Lidice had nothing to do with the assassination. But Hitler had the SS kill nearly everyone there and raze the town, placing landfill over it and planting trees in order to make Lidice disappear. They killed the men. The pregnant women were forcibly aborted, some killed, and most of the remaining sent to concentration camps. The children who looked Aryan enough were put in *Lebensborn*, a program where they were adopted into SS families to be raised as good Nazis. The other children, all eighty-two of them, were gassed to death in vans known as "soul killers." All of this is only the barest overview of the unspeakable things done. Yet from that dark backdrop of their immediate national heritage, my grandparents, Catherine and Herbert, enjoyed a loving marriage of more than 50 years. Their gentleness, their toughness, their relationship's combination of love and power, was honest and inspiring. I find this same balance of love and power in Philip Mathew's book.

Servant-leadership, in its impact, reveals a healthy balance of love and power. When leaders or followers or both are inflexibly rosy or glossing over real issues, the community lacks power. Similarly, an overemphasis on power without the nurturing of gentleness inevitably lacks love. Martin Luther King Jr. stated, "Love without power is anemic and sentimental, and power without love is reckless and abusive."[1] This is why there is a need for love and power. King connects forgiveness directly to that balance.

So, how practically do we work toward achieving balance in our own lives and leadership? *Finding Leo* points the way, showing the importance of leaders developing communities that consider how the roles of feminine and masculine are integrated in daily life, family life, professional life, and in the intersections across regions and nations. I believe we need to create room as servant-leaders for our communities to benefit from love and power, from true strength and true, nurturing gentleness. I believe the masculine deeply engaging what it means to be nurturing and the feminine boldly sharing its strength reveals the transformative unity of our shared humanity across all intersectionality. The impact can be long-lasting societal change with regard to diversity, equity, and inclusion across race, gender, sexual orientation, economic status, educational status, and all other forms of communal life. That said, qualities that are more named as feminine often get erased or made invisible in much of the patriarchal dominant-culture leadership world. For example, many of us in the West have often understood God as a distant and demanding father figure. Is there an aspect of unknowable

---

1. King Jr. "Where Do We Go from Here?," 186.

strength in God, and in the beloved other? Of course. But when out of balance with the deep, nurturing love found in true community, authentic servant-leadership is absent.

In my experience, leaders often find it hard to balance authority and rationality with kindness and relationality. Gradually, healthy relationships atrophy when leaders fail to embody a balance of healthy love and power such as the balance we see in each chapter of Dr. Mathew's book. Love and power, power and love: one is to be held with the other. The extent to which we cut off the divinely given feminine or the divinely given masculine qualities in ourselves personally and in our collective lives, determines the extent to which we do harm, the degree to which servant-leadership becomes difficult or impossible.

In the beautifully imperfect lives of each chapter in Dr. Mathew's *Finding Leo*, moral responsibility sings a song of humility—of being willing to learn, willing to accept that we are not automatically in the right. Willing to accept that we may need to ask hard questions of ourselves and others in order to honor a relationship in conflict. Again, if our leadership is predominately rational and linear, add more beauty, circularity, and the honoring of creativity—without losing the gifts of reason. This is shown especially in our long-term relationships and in the kind of enduring resilience needed to effect not only personal, but communal, national, and international change. We cannot be fundamentally defensive and stonewalling, contemptuous or hateful, if we want to find common ground. That kind of person, relationship, or nation-state is going to fracture. Such people, and such systems, are fundamentally brittle, calcified, and rigid, and they break if stressed hard enough.

Research from the Gottman Institute bears out that 80 percent of people who divorce have a four-way set of factors in common—contempt and hatred, defensiveness and stonewalling for the gender qualities of the beloved other.[2] This echoes the nature of strife, war, and trauma throughout the world: people in power holding power over those around them. In *Finding Leo*, servant-leadership is about the ability to accept and receive a way of being that is different from your own. I find this principle true on every level of society. How can we relate as humans if we are dehumanizing the other person or group? How can we relate if we are being dehumanized or dismissed ourselves?

Without the healthy balance of love and power envisioned in servant-leadership, we lose our starting place to seek care, compassion, truth, and a reconciled state.

---

2. Gottman, "Theory of Marital Dissolution and Stability," 62.

So, what do we do? How do we seek something better and more whole?

In the ten magnificent lives of *Finding Leo*, from Harriet Tubman to MLK and each representative in between, Dr. Mathew shows we must consistently be responsible for our own postures and actions in ways that are open and communal, as well as fiercely oriented toward serving the highest-priority needs of the world. When we notice our faults and make legitimate atonement in the eyes of those we've harmed, healing follows. Reconciliation, a hallmark of the servant-led life, can get tense, political, or violent very quickly. But with continued commitment to servant-leadership, when we face conflict, love begins to encompass our relationships in honor, dignity, gentleness, and goodness for one another. Respect for the people that have been harmed and a readiness to take the initiative to respond to the harm defines servant-leadership justice in the world. In a beloved relationship, the one who has done harm comes to the table to listen, ready to ask for mercy and commit to change in order to restore the dignity of the other group or person.

Of course, there's no perfect world. None of these things are easy. But in America, with our history of genocidal tendencies, and in all nations, all humanity, with our infighting, we often pursue life together in backward ways that result in erasure and increasing acts of inhumanity. We put the burden of initiative on the shoulders of those suffering. There is a better, more gentle way. The leaders in *Finding Leo* listened deeply and demonstrated the humility and courage required to change the world. In *Finding Leo* I'm reminded of two passages from the book of Isaiah: "God has given you the garment of praise instead of the spirit of despair" (Isa 61:3), and "Arise, shine for your light has come, and the glory of God has risen upon you" (Isa 60:1). Our times are deeply challenging, but they are calling us to something unforeseen. In listening, we are led by the people closest to the heart of the matter—usually these are the people in our midst, including ourselves, who can be named as the wretched of the earth. Not wretched in shame, but in a sense of holy affirmation. Authentic servant-leaders are often those who have suffered the ills of abusive leadership in business, government, education, religion, and family. Such servant-leaders have emerged more whole through the beauty of being broken and seeking to help others.

Unhealthy leadership generally reflects command and control. According to Greenleaf, a Quaker and a subtle but wise international leader, the true test of servant-leadership is that others around the servant leader become more whole. Servant-leadership reveals itself in the elegant devotion of a leader for the good of others, a lifestyle that shuns the addiction to power.

In *Finding Leo: Servant Leadership as Paradigm, Power, and Possibility*, I see women and men of all backgrounds, in deep embrace, fully reconciled, and with fearless commitment to full atonement—both the atonement that is the result of what we might call divine intervention, and then the physical, day-to-day working out of reparations that rebuild relationships that have been fractured. From here, together, we restore justice, equity, and inclusion throughout the world. This is the vision Dr. Philip Mathew has set forth. May we see this vision internationally, nationally, and in our one-on-one relationships: a vision of unconditional love and positive regard for our neighbor. What a grace it is to read this book. In *Finding Leo*, may we find at the end of our journey new joy, great peace, and vital life.

Introduction

THE TITLE OF THIS book, perhaps reminiscent of a popular movie about a colorful clownfish, is actually inspired by Hermann Hesse's novella *Journey to the East*.[1] Indeed, the story influenced the birth of the modern-day servant-leadership movement. Hesse wrote about a group of pilgrims traveling on a mystical voyage; they belonged to a philosophical order known as the League. Among the adventurous group was a simple laborer named Leo. He accompanied the group as their servant. When grunt work needed to be done, such as carrying the luggage, Leo was your man.

As the journey proceeded, the group noticed something different about Leo. Though he worked quietly in the background, often hardly noticed, he sustained the group with his spirit and song. The group depended on Leo and he soon became everyone's favorite person; even the animals loved Leo! He was a man of "extraordinary presence."[2] The journey was going swimmingly well, until one day, Leo disappeared. Shortly thereafter, things got messy, the group fell into disarray, and they abandoned their quest.

A few years later, a member of the League was traveling alone when he ran into Leo. He invited him to meet the officials who sponsored the journey. While before the august group, the man made a startling discovery. The humble servant Leo was actually the head, spiritual guide, and President of the League! He was stunned by this revelation. Leo's disappearance turned out to be a test of the group's fortitude. Robert Greenleaf, the father of the modern-day servant-leadership movement, was profoundly moved by Hesse's story and paused to consider its deeper implications. As an executive at one of America's largest companies, he had been studying the nature of leadership for many years. To Greenleaf, the discovery of Leo captured the sum and substance of what it means to be a leader,

1. Hesse, *Journey to the East*.
2. Greenleaf, *Servant Leadership: A Journey*, 7.

> ... this story clearly says that *the great leader is seen as servant first*, and that simple fact is the key to his greatness. Leo was actually the leader all of the time, but he was servant first because that was what he was, *deep down inside*. Leadership was bestowed upon a man who was by nature a servant. It was something given, or assumed, that could be taken away. His servant nature was the real man, not bestowed, not assumed, and not to be taken away. He was servant first.[3]

Greenleaf further explained,

> The servant-leader is servant-first—as Leo was portrayed. It begins with the natural feeling that one wants to serve, to serve *first*. Then, when the opportunity arises to serve by leading, the individual makes the conscious choice to lead. That person is sharply different from the person who starts with the desire to lead. The *leader first* may be motivated by a desire for personal power or wealth. It is still possible that he or she will decide later to serve—after becoming a leader. ... The difference manifests itself in the care taken by the servant-first to make sure that other people's highest priority needs are being served.[4]

SERVANT-LEADERSHIP AS PARADIGM, POWER, AND POSSIBILITY

Leo's servanthood challenged the group's assumptions about the nature of leading. Rather than leading from dominance and self-interest, Leo served first. Perhaps this is why finding Leo felt like a shockwave. Leo did not conform to the traditional leader-follower model where the leader sits atop the organizational pyramid and attention is directed up the hierarchy. In an interesting study on the mentality of great leaders, Stanford professor Bob Sutton described how a phenomenon that occurs in nature is often replicated in our workplaces,

> ... followers devote immense energy to watching, interpreting, and worrying about even the smallest and most innocent moves their superiors make. This is something we've long known about animals; studies of baboon troops show that the typical member glances at the alpha male every 20 or 30 seconds to see what he is doing. And although people don't check what their boss is

---

3. Greenleaf, *Servant Leadership: A Journey* 7–8 (italics original).
4. Greenleaf, *Servant Leadership: A Journey*, 13 (italics original).

doing two or three times a minute, this tendency is well documented in human groups, too.[5]

Sutton found that when the leader constitutes the center of a group, an "asymmetry of attention"[6] is created and there becomes an emphasis on approval seeking. Karen Dillon, former editor of the *Harvard Business Review* explained, "We do the same thing when we've been promoted, constantly looking up to make sure our boss is seeing and approving of us, which means we're paying less attention to the people we're now leading."[7] Contrast this with a servant-leadership paradigm where the organizational pyramid is turned upside down and the power dynamic is reversed. Rather than pursuing power, the servant-leader empowers. Instead of seeking to be served, servant-leaders serve *first*, conveying care and concern through their actions. As a result, individuals, organizations, and communities thrive and become "healthier, wiser, freer, more autonomous, and more likely themselves to become servants."[8] When this happens, our world becomes bursting with possibility.

Now, some have misunderstood servant-leadership to mean that employees run rogue within the organization while the leader runs around doing their bidding. Or, they assume that "servant" means "slave." Don Frick, Robert Greenleaf's authorized biographer and servant-leadership authority, clarified the concept,

> For [Greenleaf], a *servant* is not a 'service provider,' a martyr or a slave, but one who consciously nurtures the mature growth of self, other people, institutions and communities. This is done in response to the deepest guidance of spirit, not for personal grandiosity. Servanthood is a function of motive, identity, and right action. . . . For Greenleaf an authentic leader is one who chooses to serve, and serve first, and then chooses to lead.[9]

Leadership scholar Ken Blanchard explained how the relationship between "servant" and "leader" works in practice. When a team or organization embarks on a new endeavor, for example, the focus is on the *leadership* side of the equation. The emphasis is on communicating the mission, vision, and direction so that everyone is on the same page and rowing in the right direction. Once that is established, the leader pivots to the *servant* side, with

5. Sutton, "Of Baboons and Bosses," para. 5.
6. Pink, "Interview with Bob Sutton," para. 3.
7. Dillon, "New Managers Should Focus," para. 4.
8. Greenleaf, *Servant as Leader*, 7.
9. Frick, *Greenleaf*, 5–6 (italics original).

a focus on listening, empathy, awareness, persuasion, and the other characteristics of servant-leadership. The leader's focus is on providing what the people need to fulfill their mission. Thus, servant-leaders lead and serve *at the same time*, flowing seamlessly between leader and servant. By maintaining the integrity of servant and leader, power is distributed throughout the organization, and employees are emboldened and freed to fulfill the mission. Blanchard explained,

> When the organizational pyramid is turned upside down, rather than employees being responsive to management, they become responsible—able to respond—and the manager's job as a servant leader is to be responsive to them. This creates a very different environment for implementation. If a manager works for the employee, as servant leaders do, what is the manager's purpose now? To help their employees accomplish goals, solve problems, and live according to the vision.[10]

In this way of leading, the relationship between people and productivity becomes one of mutual coexistence. Today, companies such as Southwest Airlines, TD Industries, the Toro Company, ServiceMaster, Vanguard, Synovus Financial Corporation, and Starbucks, among others, have proudly and successfully embraced a servant-leadership model.[11] I am hopeful that as you discover the power of servant-leadership you will be inspired to do the same.

In writing this book, I am deeply grateful for the support of two of the most distinguished scholars in the field of leadership studies. My mentor and friend, Dr. Shann Ray Ferch, author, poet, forgiveness researcher, and professor of leadership studies at Gonzaga University, penned one of the forewords for this book. Shann was my advisor during my doctoral studies. He introduced me to the philosophy of servant-leadership and the profound writings of Robert Greenleaf. I have been fortunate to be the recipient of his wisdom, insight, and encouragement over the years. Shann has exemplified the heart and soul of servant-leadership through word and deed in my life.

Since the passing of Robert Greenleaf, one of the scholars most associated with the contemporary servant-leadership movement is Larry C. Spears. Larry has graciously written the other foreword for this book. In his current position as President of The Spears Center for Servant-Leadership, Inc., and in his former role as President and CEO of the Robert K. Greenleaf Center for Servant-Leadership, Larry has done yeoman's work extending the influence of servant-leadership around the globe. His numerous books,

---

10. Blanchard, "Let's Clear Up some Misunderstandings," para. 6.
11. See Rushman, "Servant-Leadership," 124–25.

articles, and teachings communicate the breadth and depth of servant-leadership philosophy with an eloquence and approachability for which I am grateful.

FINDING LEADERS OF EXTRAORDINARY PRESENCE

One of Larry's greatest contributions to the study of servant-leadership is his foundational essay "Ten Characteristics of a Servant-Leader."[12] Based on an exhaustive and penetrating study of Robert Greenleaf's writings, Larry distilled the essence of servant-leadership into ten essential elements. These ten characteristics form the framework for this book as I explore the lives of ten servant-leaders who applied these characteristics and achieved the transformative outcomes envisioned by Greenleaf.

Having studied leadership for a number of years, I have noticed a consistent theme—the people who have changed the world for the better simply started by noticing a problem and then doing something about it. Leadership scholar Richard Daft spoke to this reality when he observed, "Most of us are aware of famous leaders, but most leadership that changes the world starts small and may begin with personal frustrations about events that prompt people to initiate change and inspire others to follow them."[13] The leaders in this book decided to address the problems and issues around them by serving first—and they ended up changing far more than they ever thought possible.

The discerning reader will notice that the leaders described in this book come from all walks of life. They represent a variety of cultures, experiences, and backgrounds. This should inspire you. The path of servant-leadership is open to everyone—all that is required to begin is a desire to serve. If you are new to servant-leadership, it is my hope that this book encourages you to take the first step in a life-changing journey. If you are already on that path, I hope it inspires you to "descend" to greatness.[14] Today, individuals, families, organizations, and communities are looking for leaders who will serve our world through their spirit and song. When we find such leaders, we find Leo.

---

12. Spears, "Ten Characteristics. of a Servant-Leader"
13. Daft, *Leadership Experience*, 27.
14. Matt 23:11; John 13:1–5; Phil 2:5–7.

1

Herb Kelleher: The Servant-Leader and Listening

MOST MULTIMILLION-DOLLAR BUSINESS PLANS aren't sketched on the back of a cocktail napkin.[1] But for Herb Kelleher, co-founder and CEO of Southwest Airlines, business as usual was rarely an option. In 1967, Kelleher's friend Rollin King shared an idea with him that would change the way the airline industry did business. Fortunately for Southwest, Kelleher was all ears. Kelleher and King would shake up the airline business with an unusual plan—operate a low-cost, no-frills airline routed through regional airports to ensure speedy connections and even shorter turnarounds.[2] Fares would begin as low as $10. The "Southwest Effect," a phrase coined by the United States Department of Transportation, would change flying forever.[3] Today, hanging on the wall of a Southwest boardroom, pinned to a wooden plaque, is a cocktail napkin—sketched in the middle is a "golden triangle" connecting the cities of Dallas, Houston, and San Antonio. It was a simple idea that would disrupt an entire industry.[4] A closer look at Southwest Airlines reveals, however, that its success was not based solely on an innovative business model.

1. Freiburg and Freiburg, *Nuts!*, 15.
2. Anthony, "Why It's So Hard," para. 4.
3. Bailey, "How Southwest Pioneered the Low Cost Carrier Model," para. 5.
4. Freiburg and Freiburg, *Nuts!*, 15.

Kelleher's response to King was representative of an organizational culture deeply rooted in the first characteristic of servant-leadership—listening. Robert Greenleaf considered listening to be the foundational characteristic of servant-leadership, for the other nine flow out of this fundamental practice.[5] Larry Spears described it this way,

> Leaders have traditionally been valued for their communication and decision-making skills. Although these are also important skills for the servant-leader, they need to be reinforced by a deep commitment to listening intently to others. The servant leader seeks to identify the will of a group and helps to clarify that will. He or she listens receptively to what is being said and unsaid. Listening also encompasses hearing one's own inner voice. Listening, coupled with periods of reflection, is essential to the growth and well-being of the servant-leader.[6]

Servant-leaders listen first. They listen authentically to the thoughts, feelings, and experiences of others. Kelleher considered listening to be a business advantage. The Dalai Lama echoed this notion, "When you talk, you are only repeating what you already know. But if you listen, you may learn something new."[7] As we examine this first characteristic of servant-leadership, let us begin with a look at Kelleher's formative years to see how they set the stage for a listen-first model of leadership.

LISTENING AS A CORE VALUE

Born on March 12, 1931, Herb Kelleher was the youngest of four children. His mother, Ruth Moore, served as his first role model. She explained that leadership begins with an attitude of care and concern for others. He recalled,

> She was very ethical. . . . We'd sit up and talk to two, three and four o'clock in the morning when I was quite young, about how you should behave, the goals that you should have, the ethics that you should follow, how business worked, how politics can join with business, and all those sorts of things.[8]

---

5. Ferch, *Forgiveness and Power*, 129.
6. See Spears, "Introduction: Understanding the Growing Impact of Servant-Leadership," 16–17.
7. Egan, *3000 Astounding Quotes*, 27.
8. Yeh and Yeh, *Art of Business*, 236.

Ruth modeled the core values that Herb would carry into the business world. As described by leadership researchers Yeh and Yeh,

> Kelleher attributes his fundamental value of 'doing good for others' to his mother, who taught him that a person's essential worth comes from the contribution that he or she makes. It's not surprising, then, that throughout his life Kelleher has never been concerned about position or title and stands out as one of the few great American CEOs truly without ego.[9]

After graduating from New York University's school of law, Kelleher opened a firm in San Antonio, Texas. It was there that he would meet Rollin King, one of his clients. When Kelleher first heard King's proposal, he actually thought it was a bit crazy, but he was willing to hear him out. In all likelihood, King's idea would have failed to germinate if Kelleher had engaged in what leadership consultant Stephen Covey described as "autobiographical listening."[10] An autobiographical listener enters a conversation with his or her own frame of reference (e.g., "Oh yes, that reminds me of the time that I . . ."). It has been said that the opposite of talking is not listening, but waiting to talk![11] This attitude blocks our ability to listen to others.[12] A more effective way is the practice of active listening.

Rather than waiting to reply, an active listener responds by "restating a paraphrased version of the speaker's message, asking questions when appropriate, and maintaining moderate to high nonverbal conversational involvement."[13] According to Covey, great leaders seek first to understand and then to be understood.[14] In my work as a counselor, active listening became the center of my practice and laid the foundation for successful client outcomes. Likewise, listening can transform individuals, families, organizations, and society itself. Later, we look at the skills involved in active listening.

LISTENING AS A BUSINESS VALUE

Kelleher's commitment to listening was evident in his role as Southwest CEO. In the high-stress world of airline customer service, Kelleher placed people

---

9. Yeh and Yeh, *Art of Business*, 237.
10. Covey, *Seven Habits*, 245.
11. Aldag and Kuzuhara, *Creating High Performance Teams*, 152.
12. Worthington, *Marriage Counseling*, 240.
13. Weger et al., "Relative Effectiveness of Active Listening," 13–31.
14. Covey, *Seven Habits*, 235–60.

at the center of his company. Southwest hired first for attitude and then for skill—welcoming those who could handle pressure with a positive attitude and empathy. Kelleher rechristened the Human Resources department as the "People Department."[15] Rather than organizing around a traditional hierarchy, Kelleher placed responsibility and authority for problem-solving in the hands of employees. He encouraged them to listen to customer needs and then empowered them to respond quickly. At Southwest, there was no need to wait for a green light from a supervisor because Kelleher believed the people closest to the problem could be trusted to solve it.[16] He noted,

> We've tried to create an environment where people are able to, in effect, bypass even the fairly lean structures that we have so we don't have to convene a meeting of the sages in order to get something done. In many cases, they can just go ahead and do it on their own. They can take individual responsibility for it and know they will not be crucified if it doesn't work out.[17]

When it came to managing workplace conflicts, Kelleher placed listening at the center as well. He replaced a traditional conflict reporting system with face-to-face dialogue sessions. Framed as information-gathering meetings and learning experiences, he encouraged people to come together to resolve their differences. The goal was to discover and learn, rather than assign blame and find fault. At these meetings, conflicting parties shared their thoughts, perceptions, and feelings in order to gain a more nuanced understanding of the issues at hand.[18] This approach is supported by research on high-performance teams, which indicates that constructive conflict management promotes higher-quality decisions and positive organizational outcomes.[19]

In their extensive study on Southwest Airlines, Freiburg and Freiburg described how listening influenced Kelleher's vision as a servant-leader,

> Lots of assistants and big corporate staffs, for example, promote a 'My people are here to serve me' attitude that is antithetical to Southwest's family philosophy.... Instead of just walking up to the second floor to talk with a colleague, an empire builder communicates through assistants, fostering communication that is

---

15. Freiburg and Freiburg, *Nuts!*, 64.
16. Daft, *Management*, 335.
17. Freiburg and Freiburg, *Nuts!*, 76.
18. Patterson et al., *Crucial Conversations*.
19. Janssen et al., "How Task and Person Conflict," 117.

distant and cold that increases the probability that information will be transmitted inaccurately.[20]

One of Kelleher's favorite mantras was that in order for a company to grow big, it must think "small"; thinking big would result in growing small.[21] By "small" Kelleher meant fostering a family-based culture centered on communication up, down, and across the organization. Employees were encouraged to openly share their concerns with managers. One Southwest pilot shared an example,

> I can call Herb today. You don't just call and say there's a problem. He'll say, 'Think about it and tell me the solution that you think will work.' He has an open-door policy. I can call him almost 24 hours a day. If it's an emergency, he will call back in 15 minutes. He is one of the inspirations for this company. He's the guiding light. He listens to everybody. He's unbelievable when it comes to personal etiquette. If you've got a problem, he cares.[22]

Gary Barron, an executive at Southwest, followed this approach as well,

> I tell people, and mean it, you don't have to have an appointment to see me. The only reason to even call is that I may be out of the office. When I got out of a contract negotiation meeting last week, I got a call from a ground equipment mechanic in Houston. I had never met him before and he just picked up the phone because he wanted to know what was going on with the negotiations. So I explained to him what was going on to the extent that I could.[23]

Kelleher encouraged listening at every level of the company, including the C-suite. For example, Kelleher implemented a scenario-based approach to strategic planning rooted in the discipline of listening. In order to facilitate effective planning, he encouraged his executive team to ask "What if?" questions during their meetings—and then asked them to listen to one another. Potential scenarios included the emergence of new flight hubs, competition from other airlines, and changes in the number of aircraft. A robust belief in the power of brainstorming, diverse perspectives, and healthy dissent encouraged collaboration and sharing. By fostering a listening culture, Kelleher helped reduce the impact of sneaky cognitive biases

20. Freiburg and Freiburg, *Nuts!*, 77.
21. Freiburg and Freiburg, *Nuts!*, 78.
22. Gittell, *Southwest Airlines Way*, 13.
23. Freiburg and Freiburg, *Nuts!*, 83.

such as groupthink, selective perception, overconfidence, and an overreliance on concurrence seeking.[24] These listening-based strategic planning sessions substantially impacted the direction of the company: "The result of these discussions is a set of multiple plans. Future scenario generation enables Southwest to prepare for the future in a way that provides direction for the company, yet allows it to maneuver on many fronts."[25]

Like many companies, Southwest was not immune to the problem of organizational silos that result in teams isolating from one another. In the airline industry, this can be especially problematic:

> One significant obstacle has been a tradition of deep divisions among the functions that are involved in air travel: pilots, flight attendants, gate agents, ticketing agents, ramp agents, baggage transfer agents, cabin cleaners, caterers, fuelers, freight agents, operations agents, and mechanics. Much like relationships between physicians and nurses, or between design engineers, production managers, and sales reps, their relationships typically lack shared goals, shared knowledge, or respect for the roles played by the others.[26]

Research indicates that an emphasis on relational coordination can help mitigate this tendency. Gittell, in an extensive study on silos within the airline industry, described how a flight attendant manager practiced this approach:

> We are encouraged to intervene if there is a problem between employees. If a problem emerges between a flight attendant and a provisioner, for example, we will have a team building meeting. We investigate the problem, but it's not a whodunit. Just get the two to sit down and face each other. Each will give their perception of what happened.[27]

In order to encourage relational coordination, Southwest created the "Cutting Edge" program. Employees in roles as diverse as pilots, ticket agents, and ramp agents visited one another on the job so they could experience challenges faced by fellow team members; they also met to discuss and troubleshoot issues. These "cultural exchanges," as they were dubbed, resulted in deeper empathy, higher levels of trust, systems-thinking, and

---

24. Aldag and Kuzuhara, *Creating High Performance Teams*, 173.
25. Freiburg and Freiburg, *Nuts!*, 86.
26. Gittell, *Southwest Airlines Way*, xi.
27. Gittell, *Southwest Airlines Way*, 121.

cross-functional learning. Gittell noted that by listening to one another, employees began sharing knowledge across organizational boundaries:

> By contrast, interviews with Southwest frontline employees revealed that they understood the overall work process—and the links between their own jobs and the jobs performed by their counterparts in other functions. When asked to explain what they were doing and why, the answers were typically couched in reference to the overall process. These descriptions by Southwest employees typically took the form, 'The pilot has to do A, B, and C before he can take off, so I need to get this to him right away.' Rather than just knowing what to do, Southwest employees knew why, based on shared knowledge of how the overall process worked.[28]

The culture exchanges sparked innovation as well. For example, a group of employees from departments as varied as ground operations, systems, finance, customer service, and marketing "... met on their own initiative without seeking permission from anyone to pursue the project."[29] As a result, Southwest Airlines became the first major carrier to offer a ticketless travel option in 1995.[30] Not only was their plan ready within four months, but it was sketched on a cocktail napkin! It was another example of how deeply listening was embedded in the culture of Southwest.

A discussion of Southwest Airlines culture would not be complete without mentioning Colleen Barrett. The much-loved CEO and attorney started her career with Southwest in 1978, serving as legal counsel. She worked her way up to president and CEO in 2001. Barrett particularly embodied Kelleher's attitude of listening and servant-leadership. She created the well-regarded Culture Committee, a company-wide initiative led by employees with at least ten years experience. The committee reviews strategic decisions to ensure they align with the company's values, facilitates the onboarding and training process, and plans social and community events.[31] According to Barrett, "The airline looks for 'listening, caring, smiling, saying "thank you" and being warm' in accounting hires as much as in reservation agents and flight attendants."[32]

Freiburg and Freiburg recounted an incident involving a Southwest customer service agent who had been receiving poor customer service

---

28. Gittell, "Relational Coordination," 50.
29. Freiburg and Freiburg, *Nuts!*, 136.
30. Freiburg and Freiburg, *Nuts!*, 136.
31. Yeh and Yeh, *Art of Business*, 49–50.
32. Peters, "Air Travel's Greatest Show," para. 9.

surveys. It was an uncharacteristic blip that deviated from her typically glowing reviews. When Barrett met with the employee, she began the conversation by asking, "Is everything okay?" The question encouraged the employee to share how she was facing a number of problems in her personal life, including relationship issues and financial stress. According to Freiburg and Freiburg, "Barrett listened and consoled her. A few hours later, the employee received an envelope with $1,800 cash from Barrett's personal account. There was no note; it simply had the employee's name written on it in Barrett's handwriting."[33]

Through Kelleher's example, which encouraged other employees such as Barrett, he modeled listening at every level of the company. Freiburg and Freiburg described how this focus on listening influenced the company's culture:

> People who are curious listen more attentively, ask more questions, and display genuine interest in what others know. They suspend judgment until they have a firm grasp on the issues they are trying to understand. They listen to gain information, not to validate or confirm their own ideas. All of Southwest's officers bring curiosity to their jobs. In their unique ways, each of them balances inquiry and advocacy. As a result, Southwest employees feel that their ideas count. When an officer of the corporation says to an employee, 'I don't know; what do you think?' that employee feels respected, and in turn, becomes more open to learning.[34]

Rather than taking a "know it all" stance, Kelleher and company embraced a "learn it all" mindset.[35] For Kelleher, listening was a two-way street. He realized that he did not have all the answers and that great ideas can come from anywhere. Because he listened to his employees, they in turn listened to him. This approach translated into real economic value for Southwest in terms of greater operational efficiency, fiscal discipline, and a stronger customer service culture.[36]

In a *Fortune Magazine* interview, Kelleher explained, "You have to treat your employees like customers. When you treat them right, then they will treat your outside customers right. That has been a powerful competitive weapon for us."[37] This unpretentious attitude fostered employee engagement

33. Freiburg and Freiburg, *Nuts!*, 227.
34. Freiburg and Freiburg, *Nuts!*, 113–14.
35. Dweck, *Mindset*, 124–132.
36. Freiburg and Freiburg, *Nuts!*, 113.
37. Nocera, "Sinatra of Southwest," para. 9.

and ownership; the very act of listening conveys ultimate respect to others as "it is one thing to be heard, but quite another to be heard empathetically."[38] According to Freiburg and Freiburg,

> People in the field, for example, are less resistant to change and more open to new ideas that come from the executive offices because they know that Herb, Colleen, and others will *listen* to what they have to say. More importantly, these people know that the company's executives will be influenced by what they hear. Listening that evokes some type of action or emotional response essentially shows people that they have been influential. People who feel heard are more willing to hear others.[39]

THE ART OF LISTENING

W. Charles Redding, widely acknowledged as the "father of organizational communication,"[40] asserted that the majority of organizational dysfunction can be traced back in some way to human communication behavior. Redding made this powerful statement:

> In every instance of organizational malaise that comes to mind, at some time and in some way, human communication behavior has been significantly involved. Indeed, there are scholars who have persuasively made the case that a communication failure is at least one of the basic sources underlying every organizational failure.[41]

Organizational leaders would do well to consider the implications of Redding's findings. He stated it plainly: "A lot of basic management is simply knowing how to actively listen."[42] One CEO estimated that about 80 percent of his job depends on the ability to listen to others—as well as others listening to him.[43]

The ability to communicate effectively is consistently rated by employers as one of the most important skills for career success at all levels and stages of employment. Communication falls under a category of business skills often referred to as "soft skills." I believe the term is really a misnomer.

38. Copeland et al., "Listening Skills," 5.
39. Freiburg and Freiburg, *Nuts!*, 308 (emphasis original).
40. Buzzanell, "W. Charles Redding," 310.
41. DeWine, *Consultant's Craft*, xxiii.
42. Redding, *Communications within*, 34.
43. Nichols and Stevens, "Listening to People," para. 2.

As noted by business guru Tom Peters, soft skills are actually the hard skills. They consistently turn out to be the top reason why new employees and senior leaders will succeed or flounder.[44] The old adage that we are hired for "what we are" and fired for "who we are" speaks to this truth. Listening remains the foundational skill in communication.

A fatal mistake is assuming that because we have transmitted a message, communication has taken place. Transmission, however, does not equal communication. Actual communication requires an effective exchange of meaning between speaker and listener. The word "communication" comes from the root word *communis*, which means to have "in common." Effective communicators ensure their message is not only transmitted, but also understood. This begins with an attitude of listening.

Communication scholar Phillip Clampitt, in his research on communication strategies, found that that senior leaders typically choose one of five strategies when communicating with employees:

1. *Spray & Pray:* Executives shower employees with all kinds of information, hoping that employees will be able to sort out the significant from the insignificant.

2. *Tell & Sell:* Executives communicate a more limited set of messages, first telling employees about the key issues, then selling them on the wisdom of their approach.

3. *Underscore & Explore:* Executives focus on developing a few core messages clearly linked to organizational success, while actively listening for potential misunderstandings and unrecognized obstacles.

4. *Identify & Reply:* Executives identify key employee concerns and then reply to them.

5. *Withhold & Uphold:* Executives withhold information until necessary. Secrecy and control are the implicit values of this strategy.[45]

According to Clampitt et al.,

> Many organizational leaders gravitate toward the "Spray and Pray" and "Tell & Sell" strategies for admirable reasons. The "Spray and Pray" strategy creates the illusion that everyone is informed. Some executives will go to meetings armed with their "deck" of 100 PowerPoint slides, delivering the message in rapid-fire fashion. Employees often have difficulty interpreting

---

44. Peters, *Little Big Things*, xxii; Longenecker, "Causes and Consequences of Managerial Failure," 145–55.

45. Clampitt et al., "Leaders as Strategic Communicators," 51–55.

or making sense out of the information thrust at them. The "Tell & Sell" strategy demonstrates the (cheer)leader's enthusiastic endorsement of an initiative. Yet, no one ever asks for employee feedback or checks to see if the message was understood. The "Underscore & Explore" strategy resolves that problem by addressing fewer issues and then exploring employee interpretations. It has the added benefit of creating dialogue around a few core concepts that have the greatest potential to transform the organization.[46]

Similarly, Adam Grant, author, organizational psychologist, and professor at the University of Pennsylvania's Wharton School, in his bestselling book *Give and Take: Why Helping Others Drives Our Success*, challenged the popular notion that a dominant communication style is the most effective way for a leader to get things done. Rather, he found that in many situations, instead of speaking forcefully, being physically dominant, raising one's voice, and engaging in self-promotion, an opposite tact, which he described as "powerless communication,"[47] often turns out to be more effective. Indeed, he found it to be a differentiator in the outcomes between givers and takers. According to Grant, "Powerless communicators tend to speak less assertively, expressing plenty of doubt and relying heavily on advice from others. They talk in ways that signal vulnerability, revealing their weaknesses, and making use of disclaimers, hedges and hesitations."[48] Grant is careful to note that this does not mean that credibility and competence are not essential, but rather, effective communicators understand the power of vulnerability in particular contexts.

Shortly after earning his doctorate, Grant was asked to speak to a group of senior military leaders on the topic of motivating soldiers. He was twenty-six years old. His first presentation was before twenty-three Air Force colonels, most of whom were in their forties and fifties, with decades of flight and combat experience. Grant began his presentation by establishing his expertise on the subject—something he rarely does in a university setting as he has a full term to connect with his students. Given that he only had four hours, rather than four months, he tried a different tact. He noted, "I had started my presentation to the colonels with powerful communication: I talked confidently about my credentials. . . . Deviating from my typical vulnerable style I adopted a dominant tone in describing my qualifications. But the more I tried to dominate, the more the colonels resisted. I

---

46. Clampitt et al., "Leaders as Strategic Communicators," 51–55.
47. Grant, *Give and Take*, 126.
48. Grant, *Give and Take*, 130–31.

failed to win their respect, and I felt disappointed and embarrassed."[49] The post-session feedback suggested the presentation was not as effective as he had hoped.

Reflecting on what he could do differently before his next session with another set of colonels, Grant adapted his communication style. This time, the youthful professor practiced powerless communication. He began his presentation,

> 'I know what some of you are thinking right now: What can I possibly learn from a professor who's twelve years old?' There was a split second of awkward silence, and I held my breath. Then the room erupted with bursts of laughter. A colonel named Hawk piped up, 'Come on, that's way off base. I'm pretty sure you're thirteen.'[50]

While Grant presented the same information, the feedback turned overwhelmingly positive. Through humor and vulnerability, he connected with his audience. Instructively, research indicates that givers lead with humility and respect, often expressed by asking questions, talking tentatively, and sincerely seeking advice and ideas from others. Grant noted "... although group members perceive takers as more effective leaders, takers actually undermine group performance. Speaking dominantly convinces group members that takers are powerful, but it stifles information sharing, preventing members from communicating good ideas."[51]

As we see in the example of Herb Kelleher and Southwest Airlines, authentic listening, rooted in humility and relational respect, enables a leader to see, hear, and understand what is happening within and around their organization. Indeed, listening lies at the center of a range of intrapersonal and interpersonal competencies known as "emotional intelligence," or EQ. It consists of four core skills: self-awareness, self-management, social awareness, and relationship management.[52] In the next chapter, we delve more deeply into the nature of EQ.

---

49. Grant, *Give and Take*, 132.
50. Grant, *Give and Take*, 132–33.
51. Grant, *Give and Take*, 147.
52. Goleman, *Emotional Intelligence*.

SERVANT-LEADERSHIP AND LISTENING

Robert Greenleaf maintained that the "first step in good communication is listening.[53] He believed that many leaders underestimate the value of listening, "A great deal must be gotten by listening. I have a hunch that most managers are poorer listeners than observers."[54] He asserted that a lack of listening "may be the most costly of the human relations skills to be without"[55] and noted, "Of all the work I did in management training in listening, I think I accomplished more with teaching managers how to listen than with anything else."[56] EQ expert Daniel Goleman described poor listening as the "common cold" of leadership.[57] Likewise, organizational consultant Ram Charan noted that one out of every four leaders suffers from a listening deficit.[58]

To Greenleaf, listening was more than a technique. Rather, it was an "attitude toward other people and what they are attempting to express."[59] In Greenleaf's view, a servant-leader approaches listening much like an effective therapist—attending to thoughts and feelings, withholding value judgments, empathizing with the speaker (which is not the same as agreement), and responding constructively in order to understand the "total expression" of the person.[60] Akin to Martin Buber's "I-Thou" dialogical framework, Greenleaf believed that authentic listening is based in mutuality and respect: ". . . [It] begins with attention, both the outward manifestation and the inward alertness."[61]

Indian philosopher Jiddu Krishnamurti described two ways of listening: "[T]here is the mere listening to words, as you listen when you are not really interested, when you are not trying to fathom the depths of a problem; and there is the listening which catches the real significance of what is being said."[62] As demonstrated in the example of Herb Kelleher, servant-leaders begin by listening first. They seek first to understand and then to be understood. They diagnose before prescribing. By the way, have you ever noticed

---

53. Greenleaf, *On Becoming a Servant Leader*, 211.
54. Greenleaf, *On Becoming a Servant Leader*, 212.
55. Greenleaf, *On Becoming a Servant Leader*, 71.
56. Greenleaf, *On Becoming a Servant Leader*, 303.
57. Goleman, "Curing the Common Cold of Leadership," para. 6.
58. Charan, "Discipline of Listening."
59. Greenleaf, *On Becoming a Servant Leader*, 70.
60. Greenleaf, *On Becoming a Servant Leader*, 70; see also Greenleaf, *Servant-Leader within*, 164, 180–81.
61. Greenleaf, *On Becoming a Servant Leader*, 70.
62. Bhargava, "Importance of Listening Well," para. 14.

that the word *listen,* when rearranged, forms the word *silent*? True listening begins by self-silencing.

Leaders hold a particular responsibility to be attentive to the voices of those they serve. Leadership consultant Gina Burgess asserted, "Listening is deciding that the other person is important and what that important person is saying is more important than what you are doing at that precise moment."[63] Greenleaf recommended that leaders engage in a practice of intentional listening,

> Everyone who aspires to *strength* should consciously practice listening, regularly. Every week, set aside an hour to listen to somebody who might have something to say that will be of interest. It should be conscious practice in which all of the impulses to argue, inform, judge, and "straighten out" the other person are denied. Every response should be calculated to reflect interest, understanding, seeking for more knowledge. Practice listening for brief periods too. Just thirty seconds of concentrated listening may make the difference between understanding and not understanding something important.[64]

According to servant-leadership scholar Linda Belton, listening is indispensable in today's world:

> Listening is a strategic advantage to the servant-leader, never more so than in today's cacophonous world of work. With so many aural images bombarding us, listening judiciously can help the leader tune out the extraneous and ferret out the essential. Wisdom often comes in whispers.[65]

Such listening facilitates depth of understanding out of which emerges greater creativity.[66]

Alongside listening to others, it is also important to listen to one's inner voice as well. Listening helps us discover "true north," that is, our life's calling and mission. Attending to our innermost thoughts and feelings, often displaced by the urgency of the present, requires carving out space for stillness. Educator Parker Palmer offered an interesting analogy when he compared inward listening to how a person might encounter a deer in the wild. Rarely, if ever, can we hope to catch a glimpse of a shy deer by

---

63. Burgess, "Listening Is an Attribute," para. 8.
64. Greenleaf, *On Becoming a Servant Leader,* 70.
65. Keith, *Contemporary Servant as Leader,* 40.
66. See Young, "Foresight," 252.

stomping through a forest and loudly beckoning it to reveal itself. Patience and stillness, however, offer hope for a different outcome.

Our former home in the Pacific Northwest is bordered by a green belt—a portion of preserved forest within a neighborhood. We had several occasions where deer wandered into our backyard. If we were absolutely still, they even came up to the patio. The sight was not just awe-inspiring, but instructive. Parker observed,

> Like a wild animal, the soul is tough, resilient, resourceful, savvy, and self-sufficient; it knows how to survive in hard places.... Yet despite its toughness, the soul is also shy. Just like a wild animal, it seeks safety in the dense underbrush, especially when people are around. If we want to see a wild animal, we know the last thing we should do is go crashing through the woods yelling for it to come out. But if we will walk quietly into the woods, sit patiently at the base of a tree, breathe with the earth, and fade into the surroundings, the wild creature we seek might put in an appearance.[67]

In an essay on finding personal purpose, Juana Bordas noted that in an age of continuous connection, leadership requires stillness. Bordas recommended a process to find it naturally:

> We open the doors to greater self-perception by periodically re-examining our course through the art of withdrawal. By constantly reflecting on questions such as, 'How can I use myself to serve best?' and 'What am I meant to do?' servant-leaders reach out to their personal purpose.[68]

Bordas suggested that we find a sacred place, such as a favorite chair, garden, or a place of natural beauty and make time for insight and inspiration. Soon enough, one's soul, much like a shy deer, will emerge in the stillness.

Greenleaf believed that an attitude of listening opens up a world of possibilities, "It is openness to communication—openness within the widest possible frame of reference—openness to hear the prophetic voices that are trying to speak to us all the time."[69] Similarly, leadership professor Shann Ferch described servanthood as "a conscious choice to listen, to discern, and

---

67. Palmer, *Hidden Wholeness*, 58–59.
68. See Bordas, "Power and Passion," 185.
69. Greenleaf, *Servant Leadership: A Journey*, 300.

to respond . . ."[70] The benefits extend to both the leader and the served as a healing balm.[71]

LISTENING TO ONE ANOTHER

If there was ever a time our world needs listeners, it is now. I recall a conversation I once had with a fellow mental health therapist. My colleague made the interesting observation that if he were to set aside his professional credentials and simply hang a shingle on his door that read, "Professional Listener," he would have the same number of clients. His insight speaks to how listening remains the deepest need of the human heart—and the most fundamental way of showing respect for another person.[72] As one writer described it,

> Listening is more than just an auditory function. It is more than what is actually being verbally communicated. Seeing and accepting, not judging what is expressed, is listening. Listening requires a great awareness of the self, internally and externally, of words, facial expressions, body language, tone of voice, and eye contact. Listening is not the act of hearing alone, it is the combination of hearing, seeing, expressing, and feeling. The process of listening is of such significance that it can be termed a cornerstone of an effective helping relationship.[73]

On an interpersonal level, a few basic practices can help us to become better listeners. It begins with the mindset we carry into a conversation. Are we there to argue, point out mistakes and reply, or are we open to listen for understanding? Do we listen for the other person's main idea with the goal of gaining information, or do we tune out because we disagree or devalue what the other person is saying? Awareness of nonverbal language is also critical. Most people do not express how they feel in words, but through body language. Thus, attention to facial expressions, posture, and gestures is important, which requires actively focusing on the totality of the speaker.[74]

Listening can also help heal our fractured and fragmented society. In the mid to late 1990s, Bishop Desmond Tutu visited some of the most

---

70. Ferch, *Forgiveness and Power*, 24.

71. Greenleaf, *On Becoming a Servant Leader*, 71; See also, Ferch, *Forgiveness and Power*, 131.

72. Covey, *Seven Habits*.

73. Copeland et al., "Listening Skills," 6.

74. Bete, *How to Improve Your Listening Skills*.

divided places in the world. His travels took him to post-genocide Rwanda, Nigeria, Liberia, Angola, Dublin, and Belfast. He noted,

> [W]e are experiencing a radical brokenness in all of existence. Times are out of joint. Alienation and disharmony, conflict and turmoil, enmity and hatred characterize so much of life. Ours has been the bloodiest century known to human history. . . . We are not quite at home in our world, and somewhere in each of us there is a nostalgia for a paradise that has been lost.[75]

As exemplified in the servant-leadership of Herb Kelleher, listening is an invitation to change the world—one conversation at a time. Before doling out strategies and solutions, what if we listened first? Leadership scholar Meg Wheatley suggested that such a return to listening would prove transformative:

> Human conversation is the most ancient and easiest way to cultivate the conditions for change—personal change, community and organizational change, planetary change. If we can sit together and talk about what's important to us, we begin to come alive. We share what we see, what we feel, and we listen to what others see and feel. . . . [W]hen we begin listening to each other, and when we talk about things that matter to us, the world begins to change. . . . Simple conversations held at kitchen tables, or seated on the ground, or leaning against doorways are powerful means to start influencing and changing our world.[76]

FINDING: LISTENING

The first and foundational characteristic of servant-leadership is the willingness to listen. Servant-leaders listen sincerely, actively, and authentically. Listening effectively is one of the most difficult things a leader will do. Make time to listen to what others see, think, and feel. Listening also means stepping out of our familiar spaces and actively seeking different perspectives. Ask questions. Seek advice. Within the space of those conversations lies power and possibility.

---

75. Hill, *Theology of Martin Luther King, Jr.*, 178.
76. Wheatley, *Turning to One Another*, 3, 9.

2

Harriet Tubman: The Servant-Leader and Empathy

ONE MORNING IN 1834, twelve-year-old Araminta "Minty" Ross was ordered to visit the grocery store. It was an order because Minty was enslaved. Her enslaver, Edward Brodess, had loaned her to his friend Mr. Barrett. Along with Minty's other responsibilities, she was charged with shopping for the family's groceries. Barrett was in a foul mood that particular morning because one of his field hands had fled the plantation. Furious, he went in search of the man and found him hiding in the general store. By the time Minty arrived, the two were in a standoff. What happened next would change her life forever.

In an attempt to escape, the man dashed for the door. Barrett yelled for Minty to stop him. She refused. Enraged, he hurled a two-pound metal weight at the fugitive. The projectile missed its target and brutally hit Minty in the head. She collapsed instantly from the blunt force trauma. With a cruel callousness, Barrett sent Minty back to Brodess in a severely injured state; neither man provided the medical attention she needed. Later, she shared details of the incident:

> [It] broke my skull and cut a piece of [my] shawl clean off and drove it into my head. They carried me to the house all bleeding and fainting. I had no bed, no place to lie down on at all, and

they lay me on the seat of the loom, and I stayed there all that day and the next.[1]

Minty's family prayed fervently for days as she drifted in and out of consciousness. Miraculously, she survived the brutal event.

Troubled by his financial losses, Brodess attempted to sell Minty. When his efforts failed, he hired her out once again. She recalled how she was sent to work the fields with "blood and sweat rolling down my face until I couldn't see."[2] As a result of the vicious blow, Minty suffered from epileptic seizures and nightmares—signs of a traumatic brain injury. She also experienced vivid dreams for years after the event. Later in life, as a free woman, Minty returned to her childhood home to help the enslaved escape their bonds via the Underground Railroad. She believed that God was guiding her through the visions that resulted from her childhood trauma.[3]

Today, we know Minty as abolitionist, activist, soldier, and servant-leader Harriet Tubman. Araminta means "protective"—a name she lived up to that fateful morning in the store and later in life as the Underground Railroad's most famous conductor. The Underground Railroad was a clandestine effort—sometimes spontaneous, sometimes highly organized—by African-Americans and their allies to help lead the enslaved to freedom.[4] Despite the risk of capture and death, Tubman executed a number of daring and dangerous missions to free the enslaved. What led her to engage in such selfless service? Historical and personal accounts lead us to believe she was driven by the power of empathy, the second characteristic of servant-leadership. In this chapter we explore this characteristic through the servant-leadership of Harriet Tubman.

Historians estimate that Tubman rescued between seventy and 300 people from the bonds of slavery over her lifetime. Respected Tubman scholars McGowan and Kashatus spoke directly to the role of empathy in Tubman's life as emancipator, protector, and activist:

> Harriet's position could be better understood by her own experience with slavery. She had suffered the evils of the peculiar institution. Her family had been separated because of it. She had been beaten, repeatedly, by the hand of the master. For her, slavery was *real* and *personal*; not an abstract concept to be debated in the halls of Congress...[5]

---

1. Clinton, *Harriet Tubman*, 22.
2. McGowan and Kashatus, *Harriet Tubman*, 10.
3. McGowan and Kashatus, *Harriet Tubman*.
4. Pinsker, "Vigilance in Pennsylvania."
5. McGowan and Kashatus, *Harriet Tubman*, 98 (emphasis original).

Larry Spears described the connection between empathy and servant-leadership as follows:

> The servant leader strives to understand and empathize with others. People need to be accepted and recognized for their special and unique spirits. One assumes the good intentions of coworkers and colleagues and does not reject them as people, even when one may be forced to refuse to accept certain behaviors or performance. The most successful servant leaders are those who have become skilled empathetic listeners.[6]

We begin this chapter with an overview of Tubman's life and her personal journey to freedom; then we consider how empathy shaped her servant-leadership as "The Moses of Her People."[7] Finally, we examine the vital role of empathy for servant-leaders today.

HARRIET TUBMAN'S PATH TO FREEDOM

Harriet Tubman was born around 1820 in Maryland's Dorchester County. Her parents, Ben Ross and Harriet Green, had eleven children. Born into enslavement, Tubman was chopping wood, hauling timber, pulling barges, and plowing fields as early as six years old. Later in life she leveraged these experiences to her advantage. According to McGowan and Kashatus,

> The work allowed her to develop the great physical strength and endurance for which she would later be known. She also learned the healing power of plants and herbs from the swamps and marshlands of Dorchester County. This knowledge would later prove beneficial in aiding runaways who were injured on the secret journey to freedom.[8]

Despite her difficult start in life, Tubman was resilient and mentally strong. She believed that while the body might be enslaved, the human spirit was free. When religion was used to justify slavery, she found refuge in Old Testament stories of deliverance and redemption.

Tubman sought to obtain her freedom legally for years.[9] Each time, Brodess stepped in or tried to sell her. He even prevented her emancipation after her marriage to John Tubman, a free man, around 1844. Finally, upon

---

6. See Spears, "Introduction: Understanding the Growing Impact of Servant-Leadership," 17.
7. Bradford, *Harriet Tubman*, 13.
8. McGowan and Kashatus, *Harriet Tubman*, 9.
9. McGowan and Kashatus, *Harriet Tubman*.

Brodess's death, there emerged a glimmer of hope. It was soon snuffed out, however, when his widow, Eliza Ann, made plans to sell her enslaved workers to pay family debts. Tubman decided that it was time to take destiny into her own hands:

> 'There was one of two things I had a right to—liberty or death . . . If I could not have one, I would have the other.' On September 17, 1849, Harriet and her two brothers, Ben and Henry, made an escape attempt.[10]

The trio's arduous journey was unexpectedly cut short. As they made their way to Pennsylvania, they were overcome by feelings of fear, compounded by their lack of familiarity with the route. They worried about the fate of family members left behind. The siblings decided to return to the plantation.

Around the fall of 1849, Tubman made another escape attempt. Eliza Brodess posted a notice in the *Cambridge Democrat* offering a $50 reward for Tubman's capture in Maryland. She then offered $100, later raised to $500, if she was caught outside the state.[11] Tubman biographer Catherine Clinton described her journey:

> The first time out in the open, Tubman must have dreaded the baying of bloodhounds signaling a posse in pursuit. Would she have known to rub asafetida (a foul-smelling herb) on her feet to elude tracking dogs? She knew to follow the North Star, but what if clouds filled the autumn night sky? It must have been a terrifying experience for her, leaving behind loved ones and familiar terrain.[12]

Tubman's flight was an especially bold move at a time when most fugitives were young men—women rarely tried to escape alone. A loose network of safe houses, churches, and farms provided assistance during her journey. By the 1840s, this "web of assistance" included the unofficial route known as the Underground Railroad.[13] Fugitives were assisted by a complex series of signs and signals, often in the form of code (e.g., *stations, stationmasters, agents, cargo*) and auditory signals (e.g., the call of a hoot owl) borrowed from the railways.

Tubman's journey took at least ninety days, most of it occurring at night. Despite the various dangers on the route, including bounty hunters,

---

10. McGowan and Kashatus, *Harriet Tubman*, 21.
11. Clinton, *Harriet Tubman*.
12. Clinton, *Harriet Tubman*, 34.
13. Clinton, *Harriet Tubman*, 36.

Tubman safely reached Wilmington, Delaware, where Quaker abolitionist Thomas Garrett stood ready to greet her. He entrusted her to the care of an agent who helped her cross into Pennsylvania. The state had abolished slavery in 1780, largely through the influence of John Woolman, a Quaker abolitionist and servant-leader whose story is told later in this book. Tubman described her first steps on freedom's soil:

> When I found I had crossed that magic line separating the land of bondage from the land of freedom I looked at my hands to see if I was the same person. There was such a glory over everything. The sun came out through the trees, and over the fields, and I felt like I was in Heaven.[14]

THE MOSES OF HER PEOPLE

Tubman settled in Philadelphia where she found work and friendship. With its free Black population and faith community, the city proved to be an ideal place to start a new life. While it might have been tempting for Tubman to pursue her own interests as a free woman, she joined the city's abolitionist movement. As a part of this effort, she decided to return to her former home to help guide her family and others to freedom. Her courageous decision was complicated by the passing of the 1850 Fugitive Slave Law, which provided enslavers full authority to repossess anyone they had enslaved, regardless of state law and without the benefit of trial by jury. It even legalized the enslavement of free Blacks through kidnapping. Abolitionists tried in vain to fight the law in the courts.

Tubman's first rescue mission was an operation to free her niece Kessia and her young children. Tubman and Kessia's husband, John Bowley, a free man, devised the plan. Tubman made her way to the town of Cambridge where the Brodess family was auctioning Kessia. Bowley participated in the auction as was his right and won using a counterbid strategy. While the auctioneers drafted the paperwork, Bowley helped Kessia and the kids escape under cover of night. The family made their way to Baltimore where Tubman was waiting in a nearby town. She guided the family to freedom in Philadelphia.[15] It would be the first of many missions.

Interestingly, as Tubman embraced her calling as a liberator, she was plagued by periods of self-doubt. Much like Moses, who delivered his people from bondage, she pleaded with God to send someone who was more

---

14. McGowan and Kashatus, *Harriet Tubman*, 32.
15. McGowan and Kashatus, *Harriet Tubman*.

educated and more equipped for success. Despite her doubts, she moved forward, feeling led to serve as a guardian of freedom.

After the successful rescue of Kessia, Tubman made several trips back to Maryland to free a number of other families. She was in charge of the Chesapeake Route, a passage running through the Midwest and Eastern part of the United States. In 1851, after Tubman helped her brothers escape, she helped liberate her husband John. In 1857, she guided her elderly parents, Ben and Harriet, to Canada. Some of her most famous journeys included assisting the Dover Eight, guiding a group of thirty-nine people to freedom, and leading the successful Combahee River Raid that liberated more than 750 enslaved people in 1863.[16] With each trip, Tubman placed herself at greater risk. McGowan and Kashatus described the impetus for her selfless actions:

> What began as a personal desire for freedom quickly became a lifelong mission to free enslaved members of her own family, as well as other slaves who sought passage to the north. Historians speculate that the number of trips Tubman made to the South range between 10 and 19, and the number of runaway slaves she guided, between 70 and 300. In addition, she is said to have commanded a reward estimated at between $12,000 and $40,000. Regardless of the actual numbers, Tubman's place in American history as the predominant African American agent of the Underground Railroad was established by contemporaries who equated her with Moses, the Old Testament emancipator of the Hebrews.[17]

By 1860, Tubman had traveled the Underground Railroad at least nineteen different times. She was proud that she never veered off track or lost a passenger.[18] Frederick Douglass recognized Tubman's heroic efforts, "Excepting John Brown—of sacred memory—I know of no one who has willingly encountered more perils and hardships to serve our enslaved people than [Harriet Tubman]."[19]

Tubman's servant-leadership extended well beyond leading the enslaved to freedom. As part of her work as an abolitionist, she provided food, medical care, and clothing for the rescued. She joined the war effort, serving as a nurse and soldier in the Union Army, becoming the first woman to carry

---

16. "Combahee Ferry Raid."
17. McGowan and Kashatus, *Harriet Tubman*, xiii.
18. Donnelly, "In Praise of Harriet Tubman," para. 2.
19. Bradford, *Moses of Her People*, 135.

out a military operation.[20] Tubman was asked by the federal government to assist Black soldiers in Massachusetts by organizing medical care and dignified burials. During this critical period in the nation's history, Tubman served as an advocate for African-American soldiers. She was instrumental in drawing attention to the deplorable conditions they faced in the wake of their service to the nation. After the war, Tubman moved to Auburn, New York where she established a residential care home. She served there until her death in 1913.

As a conductor in the Underground Railroad, Tubman was the ultimate servant-leader. Much like Leo in Hesse's novel, Tubman guided her passengers to freedom through selfless service. She lifted their morale and served as the glue that held each group together along their journey to freedom. Tubman was well acquainted with the brutality of bondage. Despite the potential costs, she willingly risked her own freedom on behalf of others. She had skin in the game. Greenleaf explained that a servant-leader is a servant *first*—such was Tubman's character.

We now consider the force that compelled Tubman to act so selflessly. Why would she undertake such missions amidst great personal risk? Why was she willing to lay down her life for others? I believe the answer is found in the servant-leadership characteristic of empathy.

UNDERSTANDING EMPATHY

Empathy is "feeling what another person feels."[21] The word has its etymological roots in the Greek word *empatheia*, which means to "feel into." An empathic person is willing to enter into the emotional world of another person to achieve a shared understanding. The English word comes from a German psychological term, *einfühlung*, which literally means "feeling-in."[22] According to developmental psychologist Martin Hoffman, empathy can be triggered by a variety of mechanisms, including a sincere effort to see the world through another's eyes. Direct association is another source of empathy, "When the observer sees the target's emotional expression or situation, it reminds the observer of her own past emotional experiences ... you re-experience the original fear from the memory."[23] Tubman could empathize particularly well because she had been enslaved. She could "feel into" the circumstances of those seeking freedom at the deepest level.

20. Harriet Tubman Biography, "Harriet Tubman Myths and Facts."
21. Wondra and Ellsworth, "Appraisal Theory of Empathy," 411.
22. Lanzoni, "Short History of Empathy," para. 4.
23. Wondra and Ellsworth, "Appraisal Theory of Empathy," 411.

In a seminal *Harvard Business Review* article, leadership scholars Warren Bennis and Robert Thomas explored the notion of a "crucible" experience—an intense, unplanned, often-traumatic event that has a transformative impact upon one's life.[24] The metaphor comes from the Middle Ages, where alchemists attempted to turn base metals into gold. The authors explain how painful experiences can be transformed into a life-giving leadership path.

Crucibles take many forms—from periods of self-doubt to life-threatening events. Bennis and Thomas noted that they include experiences of prejudice and hate, during which a person is confronted with inaccurate pictures of the self. Feelings of anger, confusion, and abandonment are common. "For all its trauma, however, the experience of prejudice is for some a clarifying event. Through it, they gain a clearer vision of who they are, the role they play, and their place in the world."[25] They described the transformative power of the crucible thusly:

> It is the combination of hardiness and ability to grasp context that, above all, allows a person to not only survive an ordeal, but to learn from it, and to emerge stronger, more engaged, and more committed than ever. These attributes allow leaders to grow from their crucibles, instead of being destroyed by them—to find opportunity where others might find only despair. This is the stuff of true leadership.[26]

Tubman emerged out of her crucible with a renewed sense of self and a mission to rescue those who were in bonds, just like she had been.

EMPATHY AND EMOTIONAL INTELLIGENCE

As noted in chapter 1, leadership requires emotional intelligence (EQ). A central aspect of emotional intelligence is empathy. Social psychologist Daniel Goleman is largely credited with popularizing the concept in contemporary leadership studies. He describes emotional intelligence as a set of skills that enables a person to recognize emotions and then manage them for effective personal and social outcomes.[27]

The first component of emotional intelligence, self-awareness, is characterized by an ability to recognize emotions (positive or distressing)

---

24. Bennis and Thomas, "Crucibles of Leadership."
25. Bennis and Thomas, "Crucibles of Leadership," para. 9.
26. Bennis and Thomas, "Crucibles of Leadership," para. 41.
27. Goleman, *Emotional Intelligence*.

as they happen. The second component, self-management, involves the management of those emotions. Leaders strong in this capacity are able to experience their feelings while simultaneously keeping them in check. Social awareness, the third component, refers to the ability to tune in to the feelings, needs, and concerns of others. The critical skill in this domain is empathy. The fourth component, relationship management, involves the ability to leverage social awareness in order to inspire and influence others toward positive outcomes.[28] Goleman, in his Emotional and Social Competency Inventory (ESCI), measured EQ through seven qualities: empathy, attunement, organizational awareness, influence, developing others, inspiration, and teamwork. According to Goleman, empathy is a skill that can be developed with time, intention, and listening.

Empathy allows us to discern the emotional undercurrents that ebb and flow around us. It enables leaders to accurately read the room and "pick up on emotions in other people and understand what is really going on with them. This often means perceiving what other people are thinking and feeling even if you do not feel the same way."[29] Leaders who exercise empathy are able to understand what motivates others, including those whose backgrounds are different than their own, and are sensitive to the needs of others.[30]

The Atlantic magazine explored the topic in an article titled "A Short History of Empathy." The article referenced the work of social psychologist C. Daniel Batson, who described eight dimensions of empathy:

1. knowing another's thoughts and feelings,
2. imagining another's thoughts and feelings,
3. adopting the posture of another,
4. actually feeling as another does,
5. imagining how one would feel or think in another's place,
6. feeling distress at another's suffering,
7. feeling for another's suffering, and
8. projecting oneself into another's situation.[31]

Contrast this with a leadership style where the needs, wants, and interests of others go unnoticed. *New York Times* columnist Nicholas Kristof

28. Goleman, "How Emotionally Intelligent Are You?"
29. Bradberry and Greaves, *Leadership 2.0*, 156.
30. Goleman and Boyatzis, "Social Intelligence."
31. Lanzoni, "Short History of Empathy," para. 9.

referred to this as the "empathy gap, a self-absorption centered around one's personal needs and concerns in mind."[32] Leading with empathy means acknowledging the emotions of others, being thoughtful of their needs, and then making decisions that takes their feelings into consideration. Leadership scholar James Autry insightfully noted, "Leadership, like life, is largely a matter of paying attention."[33] According to emotional intelligence coach Jennifer Williams,

> Feeling understood is not only a basic human need, but it is also how we connect, help, and support one another. If we can't recognize someone in pain, how can we support them? If we are unable to accept and empathize with our own emotions, it is difficult to be present to people around us. And for this reason, empathy is crucial for our interconnectivity.[34]

The business world is beginning to acknowledge the power of empathy as a powerful and hidden source of innovation. Microsoft CEO Satya Nadella in particular has boldly endorsed empathy as a lever for organizational change. In his book *Hit Refresh: The Quest to Rediscover Microsoft's Soul and Imagine a Better Future for Everyone*, Nadella described his personal journey toward empathy. His son Zain suffered from cerebral palsy due to asphyxia *in-utero*; physically, he was visually impaired, limited in communication, and confined to a wheelchair. The joys and challenges of raising Zain, in partnership with his wife Anu, transformed Nadella to the core: "Being a husband and father has taken me on an emotional journey. It has helped me develop a deeper understanding of people of all abilities and of what love and human ingenuity can accomplish."[35]

Nadella discovered the power of empathy in an unexpected way. He was searching for ways to improve Zain's quality of life through technology. One day, three high school students studying computer science heard about Zain and the difficulty he was having in choosing his favorite music. Desiring to help, the young men developed a sensor that attached to the side of Zain's wheelchair. Through the marvels of technology, he was now able to flip through his music collection with just a tap of his head. Nadella recognized this breakthrough would not have been possible without empathy—it literally changed Zain's life.

Inspired by the transformative power of empathy, Nadella encouraged employees at Microsoft to embrace it as a source for ideas and innovation.

32. Kristof, "Where's the Empathy?"
33. Autry, "Love and Profit," 47.
34. Williams, "What is Empathy?," para. 3.
35. Nadella, *Hit Refresh*, 8.

He challenged them to begin by reflecting on the unarticulated needs of people around the world. The results at Microsoft have been striking. For example, to assist people with ALS, a progressive neurodegenerative disease, Microsoft employees developed eye-gaze tracking technology. This breakthrough happened during a company hackathon where the team spent extensive time with former NFL player Steven Gleason, who is confined to a wheelchair, in order to better understand his challenges. He now uses the technology in his daily life.

In an interview with the *Wall Street Journal*, Nadella described the link between empathy and innovation:

> Being hard-core and driven is as essential today as it ever was. But there needs to be humility. The reason why I use the word *empathy* is because the business we are in is to meet the unmet, unarticulated needs of customers. That's what innovation is all about. And there's no way you're going to do that well without having empathy and curiosity.[36]

Nadella's experience echoes the words of Harper Lee, who wrote in the classic *To Kill A Mockingbird*, "You never really understand a person until you consider things from his point of view. . . . Until you climb inside of his skin and walk around it."[37]

HARRIET TUBMAN: THE EMPATHETIC SERVANT-LEADER

Leadership consultant Stephen Covey described empathy as the ability to get inside another person's frame of reference: "You look out through it, you see the world the way they see the world, you understand their paradigm, you understand how they feel."[38] The servant-leader, through empathy, communicates a powerful message:

> I am sensitive to your feelings, values, and experiences. I want to see things from your perspective to understand how you can develop as a person. I demonstrate through my thoughts, words, and actions that I empathize.[39]

---

36. Stevenson, "Rare Joint Interview," para. 5.
37. Lee, *To Kill a Mockingbird*, 36.
38. Covey, *Seven Habits*, 240.
39. See Gunnarson and Blohm, "Welcoming Servant-Leader," 70.

Tubman's own accounts, as well those from historians and biographers, indicate that empathy was the driving force behind her selfless service. McGowan and Kashatus noted,

> Harriet's position could be better understood by her own experience with slavery. She had suffered the evils of the peculiar institution. Her family had been separated because of it. She had been beaten, repeatedly, by the hand of the master. For her, slavery was real and personal; not an abstract concept to be debated in the halls of Congress, as so many white abolitionists viewed it.[40]

History professor Meghan Martinez noted the role of empathy in Tubman's selfless actions as well:

> Her empathy likely led to many of her decisions including the decision to sacrifice her own safety to free others, returning to the South again and again, and her decision to help open the Tubman Home for Aged & Indigent Negroes later in her life. She was always taking care of people.[41]

Scholars at Dalhousie University conducted a study of the social structures that contributed to Tubman's success on the Underground Railroad. They found trust-based empathy enabled Tubman to "bridge structural holes" and gain social capital among other conductors through sheer determination, dedication, and the will to succeed:

> We believe that part of Tubman's success, and the success of the other conductors and their passengers, was made possible by a well-coordinated, secret effort that involved the transfer of *trust*. . . . In essence, it appears that the conductors' decision to help Tubman may have had very little to do with her knowledge of the landscape and more to do with her determination to save her family, her belief in the power of a higher authority to guide her actions, and their recognition that she had the skill and confidence to overcome any obstacle that would prevent her from succeeding with her mission. Taken together, these factors provided the basis for transferring expectations of trust from her colleagues, who in turn, transferred their contacts to her.[42]

Likewise, R. L. Williams, in a study of Tubman's life, noted that her leadership was defined by the pursuit of freedom, energized by love, empathy, and community building:

40. McGowan and Kashatus, *Harriet Tubman*, 98.
41. De La Rosa, "New Harriet Tubman Movie," para. 24.
42. Young et al., "Even Superheroes," 416 (emphasis original).

> Freedom was not a possession to be held but a way of existing in relationship to others. It was for the well-being of community. Tubman enacted freedom as pursuit of liberation for the people of God in bondage to white slavers in the antebellum South. . . . As she saw it, freedom is something for which we are all made. To say otherwise is to slander God's very image, which was given to all human beings.[43]

Robert Greenleaf encouraged servant-leaders to demonstrate empathy in all of their interactions. He likened it to unconditional acceptance,

> These are two interesting words, acceptance and empathy. If we can take one's dictionary's definition, *acceptance* is receiving what is offered, with approbation, satisfaction, or acquiescence, and *empathy* is the imaginative projection of one's own consciousness into another being. The opposite of both, the word *reject*, is to refuse to hear or receive—to throw out.[44]

Greenleaf stressed that servant-leadership arises from the desire to simply serve: "It begins with the natural feeling that one wants to serve, to serve first. Then conscious choice brings one to aspire to lead."[45] He believed "caring for persons, the more able and the less able serving each other, is the rock upon which a good society is built,"[46] and a hallmark of empathy. He stated, "Men grow taller when those who lead them empathize, and when they are accepted for who they are. . . . The servant always accepts and empathizes, never rejects."[47]

Dr. Martin Luther King Jr. believed that leadership requires a "tough mind and a tender heart."[48] Harriet Tubman exemplified such grace. In an essay on the toughness of servant-leadership, Dennis Tarr reflected on the strength of empathy:

> Being empathetic presents a challenge. It is not easy to walk the second or third mile in someone else's shoes. None of us 'likes' to do it. It's much easier to walk away from a problem or unpleasant task. In fact, it takes an exceedingly tough person to be a true listener, to be a person who can empathize with another.[49]

---

43. Williams, "Christ-Centred Concreteness," 127.
44. Greenleaf, *Servant as Leader*, 20 (emphasis original).
45. Greenleaf, "Institution as Servant," 62.
46. Ferch, *Forgiveness and Power*, x.
47. Greenleaf, *Servant as Leader*, 20.
48. King, *Strength to Love*, 13.
49. Spears, *Reflections on Leadership*, 81.

Leadership professor and servant-leadership scholar Shann Ferch described empathy with an elegant word picture: "Empathy is the heartfelt expression of leaders who identify with the humanity of others. Servant-leaders laud the victories of others, but they also share in the sufferings and the immensity of their losses."[50] He added, "Empathy is the compassionate gift of seeing life through the eyes of another, and in seeing clearly, to extend tenderness."[51] Servant-leaders take an active interest in the concerns of others. Empathy shifts interactions from the purely transactional to the transformational. As a conductor on the Underground Railroad, Harriet Tubman did just that as she led others to freedom through a life of sacrificial service.

FINDING: EMPATHY

Empathy requires stepping outside of oneself long enough to enter into the experience of another. Few acts make us more fully human than to be empathetic. The servant-leader notices the soul, struggle, and journey of the beloved other. Often, those who question the role of empathy, caring, and compassion, particularly in business, find themselves longing for these very qualities when the tide turns against them. While the corporate world may speak of pursuing "customer experience," "DEI," "corporate culture," and "outside-of-the-box thinking," the servant-leader recognizes the source of such outcomes is empathy.

---

50. Ferch, *Forgiveness and Power*, xi.
51. Ferch, *Forgiveness and Power*, 140.

3

Mother Teresa: The Servant-Leader and Healing

IN HIS BOOK, *THE Wounded Healer,* Dutch Catholic priest and author Henri Nouwen shared the following story from the Talmud, the ancient Jewish collection of stories and legal writings:

> Rabbi Yoshua ben Levi came upon Elijah the prophet.
> While he was standing at the entrance of Rabbi Simeon ben Yohai's cave... He asked Elijah, "When will the Messiah come?"
> Elijah replied, "Go and ask him yourself."
> "Where is he?"
> "Sitting at the gates of the city."
> "And how shall I know him?"
> "He is sitting among the poor, covered in wounds. The others unbind all their wounds at the same time, and then bind them up again. But he unbinds one at a time and binds it up again, saying to himself, 'Perhaps I shall be needed; if so, I must always be ready so as not to delay for a moment.'"[1]

In Nouwen's story, the Messiah, though rejected, despised, and wounded, is ready to minister healing. While meaningful on many levels, the narrative points to the paradox of servant-leadership. In the midst of our brokenness, or perhaps because of it, each of us is offered an opportunity to

---

1. Nouwen, *Wounded Healer*, 81–82.

extend healing and wholeness to others. Such grace resides not in being perfect, but in love and a readiness to serve. Nouwen described it this way:

> Making our own wounds a source of healing, therefore, does not call for a sharing of superficial personal pains, but for a constant willingness to see one's own pain and suffering as rising from the depth of the human condition which all men share."[2]

Healing is the third characteristic of servant-leadership. Professor Shann Ferch described it as the most rare and needed of the ten characteristics.[3] As in the story about the Messiah, individuals, families, and communities around us suffer wounds of alienation, separation, isolation, and loneliness.[4] How then can servant-leaders help heal the world? Larry Spears described this characteristic of servant-leadership in the following way:

> The healing of relationships is a powerful force for transformation and integration. One of the great strengths of servant leadership is the potential for healing one's self and one's relationship to others. Many people have broken spirits and have suffered from a variety of emotional hurts. Although this is a part of being human, servant leaders recognize that they have an opportunity to help make whole those with whom they come in contact.[5]

Mother Teresa stands as a powerful example of the servant-leader as healer. Often, when we think of her, the image that comes to mind is that of "Saint Teresa"—a larger-than-life figure separated from the rest of humanity. While there is no doubt about the magnitude of her contribution, those who had the privilege to be in the presence of the diminutive nun noticed how ordinary she appeared. She stood four-foot-eleven, weighed less than 100 pounds, and wore a simple cotton *sari* and sandals. Mother Teresa insisted to everyone who met her that there was nothing special about her. She maintained that it was her willingness to serve with love that made the difference. When she reluctantly allowed her life story to be written, she told the biographer to focus on the letter and not the pen.[6] She believed that any person could find a Calcutta in which to serve. Robert Greenleaf reminded us, "The servant-leader is servant first. It begins with the natural feeling that

---

2. Nouwen, *Wounded Healer*, 88.
3. Ferch, *Forgiveness and Power*.
4. Nouwen, *Wounded Healer*, 83.
5. See Spears, "Introduction: Understanding the Growing Impact of Servant-Leadership," 17.
6. Spink, *Mother Teresa*, 143.

one wants to serve. Then conscious choice brings one to aspire to lead."[7] Mother Teresa exemplified this truth.

A CALL TO SERVE

Mother Teresa was born on August 26, 1910, in Skopje, a city in present-day Albania. Her given name was Agnes Gonxha Bojaxhiu; she was the youngest of three children. Her father, Nikola, was a businessman and her mother, Drana, was a homemaker. The family's life was upended when Nikola passed away unexpectedly while attending a political gathering in Belgrade. Soon after his death, his business assets were seized and the family was plunged into financial disaster.

Amidst these difficulties, Drana's spirit of service sustained her family through dark days. Even with limited resources, she prepared meals, mended clothing, and ran errands for the poor and hungry, just as she always had done. Drana's acts of service were not lost on Agnes. Years later, she recounted how her mother's example helped shape core values such as kindness, generosity, compassion, and devotion to God. She frequently remembered her mother's advice, such as, "My child, never eat a single mouthful unless you are sharing it with others," "Some of them are our relations, but all of them are our people," and "When you do good, do it quietly as if you were throwing a stone into the sea."[8]

At around age twelve, Agnes experienced a calling to minister through service. She prayed for discernment and sought counsel. A local priest asked her to consider whether the idea of vocational ministry brought her joy— she affirmed that it did. When she was eighteen, Agnes attended a spiritual retreat where she committed her life to service. While outwardly Drana questioned Agnes's decision, she was secretly testing her daughter's resolve. Upon perceiving her unwavering sincerity, she gave her blessing. Agnes left home to undergo intensive language training at Loreto Abbey in Ireland. Two months later, she was assigned to Calcutta, India, and took the name "Sister Mary Teresa of the Child Jesus."

A Westerner arriving in India for the first time is greeted by a delightful cacophony of sights, sounds, smells, and tastes. Mark Twain, in his journey to the subcontinent, remarked that the air smelled like "dust and spices."[9] Calcutta, known as the City of Joy, jolted young Teresa's senses. As she entered the teeming city, she witnessed a level of poverty she had never

7. Greenleaf, *Servant Leadership: A Journey*, 27.
8. Spink, *Mother Teresa*, 6.
9. Vallance and Mills, *Pole to Pole*.

seen. After her arrival, she was sent to Darjeeling, a city at the foothills of the Himalayas, for her novitiate. There, she studied theology, Indian languages such as Bengali and Hindi, and taught at St. Teresa's school. Authorities at the convent took note of her sincere passion for service.[10] Upon completing her training, she returned to Calcutta to teach at Loreto Entally, a primary school for girls. The school's mission was to tackle poverty through education.[11] She then taught at St. Mary's High School from 1931 to 1948. In 1937, she took vows of poverty, chastity, and lifelong obedience and became "Mother Teresa." While the majority of her students came from middle-class backgrounds, the suffering and poverty she witnessed outside the convent haunted her deeply.

A CALL TO HEAL

In *Captain Stormfield's Visit to Heaven*, Mark Twain told the story of a man who had embarked on a lifelong quest to find the world's greatest general. He died without accomplishing his mission. When he arrived at the pearly gates, he told St. Peter, "I've been looking for the world's greatest general." St. Peter smiled and said, "If you'll look over right over there, you will see him." The man could not believe it, "But that's not the world's greatest general! That's the cobbler from my hometown!" St. Peter replied, "But if he had been a general, he would have been the greatest ever."[12] Don Clifton, an expert in strengths-based leadership, used this story to speak to the importance of discovering one's calling in life:

> Twain's tale points to a painful truth that's echoed in the words of Oliver Wendell Holmes, 'Most people go to their graves with their music still inside them.' There are plenty of perfectly good cobblers out there who could have been great generals, given the opportunity or encouragement. But they also could have pursued completely different, perhaps historic, careers. Give this tale some thought when planning your own career. We want the music that is inside you to be heard![13]

Mother Teresa felt led to leave Loreto Entally to work directly with the poorest of the poor in Calcutta. In 1946, while traveling on a train to Darjeeling, she experienced a "call within the call." She desired to minister in a

---

10. Spink, *Mother Teresa*, 15.
11. Spink, *Mother Teresa*, 16.
12. Clifton, *StrengthsQuest*, 235.
13. Clifton, *StrengthsQuest*, 235.

new way: "I was to leave the convent and help the poor while living among them. It was an order. To fail would have been to break the faith."[14] Mother Teresa again spent time in prayer and sought the counsel of a trusted priest who helped her finalize her decision:

> She was to leave Loreto but she was to keep her vows. She was to start a new congregation. That congregation would work for the poorest of the poor in the slums in a spirit of poverty and cheerfulness. There would be a special vow of charity for the poor. There would be no institutions, hospitals, or big dispensaries. The work was to be among the abandoned, those with nobody, the very poorest.[15]

In this bold step, we see the threads of a personal faith, a mother's influence, and the deep wounds of a hurting world form a cord of three strands in Mother Teresa's life. Unlike the cobbler in Twain's story, Mother Teresa responded to the inner call. How she did so is instructive as we seek to understand how servant-leaders can become a healing force. Notice how she sought the guidance of trusted others and tuned in to her inner voice. Educator and leadership consultant Parker Palmer noted that the word *vocation* comes from the Latin for "voice." Discovering one's vocation is a matter of listening to that voice:

> Before I can tell my life what I want to do with it, I must listen to my life telling me who I am. I must listen for the truths and values at the heart of my own identity, not the standards by which I *must* live—but the standards by which I cannot help but live if I am living my own life.[16]

Through listening, the first characteristic of servant-leadership, we allow our lives to speak. Theologian Frederick Buechner lent further clarity to this notion of calling. In his book, *Wishful Thinking*, he noted, "There are all different kinds of voices calling you to all different kinds of work and the problem is to find out which is the voice of God rather than of Society, say, or the Superego, or Self-Interest."[17] One of his most well-known statements about finding one's vocation has helped many find personal clarity:

> By and large a good rule for finding out is this: the kind of work God usually calls you to is the kind of work (a) that you need most to do and (b) that the world most needs to have done. . . .

---

14. Spink, *Mother Teresa*, 15.
15. Spink, *Mother Teresa*, 23.
16. Palmer, *Let Your Life Speak*, 4–5 (emphasis original).
17. Buechner, *Wishful Thinking*, 118.

The place God calls you to is the place where your deep gladness and the world's deep hunger meet.[18]

Mother Teresa discovered this special intersection of calling and need; she decided that the people's wounds would become her wounds.

Mother Teresa needed to navigate a number of complications in order to make her vision a reality. First, she had to secure permission from her spiritual elders. Requesting to leave an order was a highly unusual request. There was also unease about sending a young woman to work alone in an urban center. Finally, the optics of a European woman coming to "rescue" Indian nationals was a risky proposition, particularly as India was just shaking off its colonial past.

After several months of negotiation, Mother Teresa obtained approval to pursue her calling. She received a decree of "exclaustration" which permitted her to work outside the convent on a trial basis for one year. A memo was posted within the Loreto convent, "Do not criticize. Do not praise. Pray."[19] In 1948, Mother Teresa exchanged her Loreto habit for a white *sari* with a blue border (representing the Virgin Mary); it was the most inexpensive one she could find. A cross was pinned to her left shoulder. She then traveled to Patna for medical training. A few days before Christmas 1948, with a personal savings of five rupees, she opened the Missionaries of Charity School in the Motijhil area of Calcutta. The open-air academy, located in the heart of one of the largest displaced communities in India, launched with an inaugural class of twenty-one students.[20]

THE ANGEL OF CALCUTTA

By some estimates, over 2 million indigent and impoverished people lived in Calcutta during Mother Teresa's time, eking out a meager living in an overcrowded and undermanaged city. The poor lived and died on congested streets and railway platforms. Public hospitals were filled beyond capacity. The city's infrastructure proved woefully inadequate to address the overwhelming need.

Mother Teresa experienced moments of self-doubt and loneliness as she took her first steps without the safety net of the convent. She described the first few months as the "dark night of the birth of the Society."[21] Some-

18. Buechner, *Wishful Thinking*, 118–19.
19. Spink, *Mother Teresa*, 30.
20. Terlizzi, *Women of the Nobel*, 119.
21. Spink, *Mother Teresa*, 37.

times, financial support failed to materialize. On other days, even a meal was a luxury. Her spirit of service, however, soon drew likeminded young women to her side. As the charity developed a working constitution, the mission took on a more structured identity. The core values of love, trust, and a cheerful attitude were its hallmarks. Mother Teresa told her fellow nuns "in order to understand and help those who have nothing, we must live like them. . . . The only difference is that these people are poor by birth and we are by choice."[22] She resolved not to solicit funds, but rather trust that the mission would be sustained by the generosity of those who felt led to contribute.

Mornings at the Missionaries of Charity began at 4:40 a.m. The nuns prayed from 5:15 a.m. to 6:45 a.m. Breakfast, when available, consisted of a few *chapatis* and powdered milk; sometimes, a glass of water would have to do. By 8:00 a.m., Mother Teresa and her team headed into the streets, ministering to the needs of the sick, destitute, and dying. After a quick lunch and afternoon tea, they returned to the sweltering streets of the city. Dinner, served at 6:00 p.m., consisted of rice, *dal*, and other vegetables. After evening devotions and some leisure time, the nuns retired for the evening.[23]

One of Mother Teresa's special qualities was her willingness to take on any task with joy. Once, when a new initiate hesitated to clean a dirty toilet, Mother Teresa grabbed a broom and pail and cleaned the bathroom herself. One biographer noted, "The visionary fervor that burned in her was not the kind that invited compromise, but she asked nothing of those around her that she was not prepared to do herself."[24] With her innate desire to serve, Mother Teresa reflected the spirit of Leo. Hermann Hesse described him as a ". . . a servant who does menial chores, but also sustains them with his spirit and song. He is a person of extraordinary presence."[25]

In 1952, a benefactor helped Mother Teresa secure an abandoned Hindu temple that had been dedicated to the goddess Kali. Under the auspices of the charity, the building was converted into a hospice known as *Nirmal Hriday*, or the "Place of the Immaculate Heart." It was open to everyone, regardless of caste, creed, or religion:

> Low cots or mattresses were placed on the ledges that ran along either side of the two great rooms, and the almost flesh-less frames of people consumed by disease and maggots were given a place to rest in the cool half-light that fell from the small

---

22. Spink, *Mother Teresa*, 44.
23. Spink, *Mother Teresa*, 46–47.
24. Spink, *Mother Teresa*, 48.
25. Greenleaf, *Servant Leadership: A Journey*, 7.

windows high up in the walls. . . . The sick destitute, the beggar picked up from the streets, the leper rejected by his family, the dying man refused admittance to a hospital—all were taken in, fed, washed, and given a place to rest.[26]

Following city policy, overcrowded hospitals triaged patients and only treated those who had a realistic chance of recovery. Patients at death's door were transferred to *Nirmal Hriday* to die with dignity. To Mother Teresa, every life—and every death—mattered: "A beautiful death is for people who lived like animals to die like angels—loved and wanted."[27] In the early days of the ministry, Mother Teresa transported the sick and dying to the hospice in a wheelbarrow. The Sisters tended to the residents' most basic needs, by providing haircuts, baths, and placing morsels of food in the mouths of the dying. They treated patients with tuberculosis and held the hands of the abandoned. A dying man, uttering his last words, declared, "Now I can die like a human being."[28]

Mother Teresa held a special place in her heart for orphans and babies, especially those who were born prematurely or experienced mental or physical disabilities. She never turned a child away. "I don't care what people say about the death rate. Even if they die an hour later, we must let them come. These babies are not uncared for and unloved, because even a tiny baby can feel."[29] She encouraged her fellow nuns to actively participate in her mission of healing, "Don't just look around like a spectator, really look with your ears and your eyes, and you will be shown what you can do to help."[30] Her depth of love and sacrifice was evident. Children under the care of the convent began to gain weight and thrive. Many enrolled in the city's schools or pursued a vocational trade. The mission was driven by the belief that God was present in every human being and that the beauty of humanity could be found where we least expect it.[31]

Mother Teresa was also eager to serve those afflicted with leprosy. Though not contagious, the fear and social stigma surrounding the malady were almost insurmountable. Facing ostracism and rejection, many patients delayed treatment, even as the disease ravaged their bodies. Once diagnosed, isolation from family and work was all but guaranteed. Many lepers spent their lives alone and seeking alms.

26. Spink, *Mother Teresa*, 55.
27. Spink, *Mother Teresa*, 55.
28. Spink, *Mother Teresa*, 55.
29. Spink, *Mother Teresa*, 60.
30. Spink, *Mother Teresa*, 57.
31. Spink, *Mother Teresa*, 61.

Touched by their struggle, Mother Teresa opened a medical clinic for the city's leprosy patients. When local officials shut it down to make room for a housing unit, she turned an ambulance donated from the United States into a mobile leprosy unit. The pop-up clinic proved to be a clever innovation. Patients could be treated "without removing the patient from his family, his essential source of love, or from his employment, the mainspring of his dignity."[32] Whether it was under a tree or alongside a railway track, a mobile clinic could be set up quickly. Mother Teresa was particular about preserving the dignity of her patients. She instructed her fellow nuns not to wear gloves because they were ministering to Christ himself: "The same kind of reasoning determined that it was not by its efficiency or effectiveness that an action should be judged but by the amount of love that was put into it."[33]

In 1959, the Missionaries of Charity found a more permanent location for their center. Besides attending to patients' medical needs, the charity provided training in skilled trades such as carpentry, sewing, and shoemaking. The Indian government donated thirty-four acres for more housing. In 1964, when Pope Paul VI visited India, he donated his popemobile to the charity. Mother Teresa raffled the Lincoln Continental to build *Shanti Nagar*, "The Place of Peace," where recovering patients could grow rice, raise cattle, and learn how to start their own businesses.

Mother Teresa's efforts began to draw attention outside Calcutta. The Missionaries of Charity were invited to open convents across India. Prime Minister Jawaharlal Nehru inaugurated a Delhi-based convent. The Sisters assisted during natural disasters that hit the subcontinent. Soon, other countries sought to replicate Mother Teresa's model. The first Missionaries of Charity outside of India was established in Venezuela. More charities were opened throughout Europe, Australia, Africa, and the United States. Requests for speaking and fundraising engagements poured in. Mother Teresa graciously declined these offers and encouraged her fellow nuns to live by faith. She reminded them, "I don't want the work to become a business but to remain a work of love . . . joy, peace, and unity are more important than money."[34] By the early 1970s, the Missionary Brothers of Charity and Missionaries of Charities, Contemplative were launched, each with their own unique mission. Mother Teresa welcomed the initiatives. In 1969, the International Association of Co-Workers of Mother Teresa, a lay organization affiliated with the Missionaries of Charity, was established with the blessing of Pope Paul

---

32. Spink, *Mother Teresa*, 65.
33. Spink, *Mother Teresa*, 69.
34. Spink, *Mother Teresa*, 93.

VI. Ten years later, its membership grew to an astounding 800,000 workers across five continents.[35]

In 1962, Mother Teresa received the Magsaysay Award for International Understanding. The *Padma Shri*, India's second-highest civilian honor, followed. In 1973, she received the first-ever Templeton Prize for Progress in Religion. Numerous honors came from countries around the world. In keeping with her vow of poverty, monetary gifts were invested back into the work. In 1979, Mother Teresa was honored with the Nobel Peace prize for "work undertaken in the struggle to overcome poverty and distress, which also constitutes a threat to peace."[36] She attended the regal ceremony in her inimitable cotton *sari* and sandals. She skipped the ceremonial banquet and requested the $192,000 prize money be donated to the poor.[37] In 1980, she received India's highest civilian honor, the *Bharat Ratna*, or Jewel of India.

Despite these tributes, Mother Teresa's work was by no means over. She continued to assist with crises around the world, including the AIDS epidemic after a personal request from President Ronald Reagan. Pope John Paul II reluctantly accepted her resignation as the Superior General of the Missionaries of Charity in April 1990 due to her increasingly poor health. She had served the order for over 35 years. Her retirement was short-lived, however, as she was asked to return to service. She was hospitalized several times as the work began to take a serious toll. In 1997, Sister Nirmala was named as Mother Teresa's successor. On September 5, 1997, the evening before Princess Diana's funeral, Mother Teresa passed away from heart failure. She was eighty-seven years old. As an Indian citizen, she was honored with a state funeral and laid to rest in Calcutta. In October 2003, she was beatified. In September 2016, Pope Francis canonized her as "Saint Teresa of Calcutta."

The Missionaries of Charity continued to grow after Mother Teresa's death. By 1984, the charity's mobile clinics had treated over 4 million leprosy patients.[38] At the time of her death, over 4,000 members of the charity were leading 610 missions, including hospices, homes, orphanages, soup kitchens, and schools, in over 123 countries.[39] In 2013, there were 700 missions operating in over 130 countries.[40]

---

35. Spink, *Mother Teresa*, 134.
36. Odekon, *SAGE Encyclopedia of World Poverty*, 1072.
37. "Mother Teresa," para. 10.
38. Spink, *Mother Teresa*, 203.
39. Odekon, *SAGE Encyclopedia of World Poverty*, 1072.
40. "Mother Teresa," para. 6.

THE SERVANT-LEADER AS HEALER

Mother Teresa believed that internal wounds were just as painful as physical maladies. In order to understand the life and work of Mother Teresa, one must grasp this profound truth. She said, "The only cure for loneliness, despair, and hopelessness is love. It is a mistake to think that poverty is only being hungry, naked, and homeless. The poverty of being unwanted, unloved, and uncared for is the greatest poverty."[41] Her medical and social work among the poor, sick, and dying was the vehicle through which she expressed her belief that people need not only physical care, but also love and compassion.

Consider the story of Dave Roever, a Vietnam-era Purple Heart veteran. In July 1969, Dave was a twenty-one-year-old newlywed and an elite Brown Water Black Beret patroling Vietnam's Vam Co Tay River. One afternoon, eight months into his tour, a phosphorous grenade exploded in his hand, instantly burning him beyond recognition. Dave recalled the horrific incident, "When that grenade exploded it took off half my skin, I looked down and my face was on my boots."[42] The explosion "incinerated his ear, his hair and parts of his scalp. It ravaged his face, destroyed his right eye and eyelid; split his right hand in half and tore a hole in his chest through which he could see his own heart beating beneath the thin layer of flesh that was left."[43]

Dave was hospitalized for over fourteen months, undergoing a number of reconstructive surgeries and bone grafts. When his wife Brenda visited him in the hospital, Dave feared that she would leave him, just as some of the other soldiers' wives had done. Dave recalled seeing one wife tossing her wedding ring onto the hospital bed and walking out of the room. When Brenda visited him, Dave "apologized that he would never be good-looking again. Brenda quipped, 'You never were that good-looking to begin with.' Roever realized he was one of the lucky ones."[44]

Amazingly, Dave not only recovered, but opened a new chapter in his life as an author, minister, and motivational speaker; he became a wounded healer. I had the privilege of meeting Dave at one of his events. Though he carried significant scar tissue in his body, his message of healing was inspiring, "Everybody has scars. Mine just happen to be on the outside. Not everyone leaves with scars on the outside, but scars on the inside can

---

41. Odekon, *SAGE Encyclopedia of World Poverty*, 1072.
42. Mendoza, "Grenade's Blast," para. 2.
43. Wangrin, "Good Scar," para. 11.
44. Wangrin, "Good Scar," para. 14.

be just as damaging. Everyone has an internal war."[45] Servant-leaders like Dave Roever and Mother Teresa understand that the world needs healing in many forms, not just physical. Through their service they fulfill Robert Greenleaf's hope that we would "reestablish men and women in the role of servants—healers—of society."[46]

Thomas Egnew, a licensed clinical social worker affiliated with the University of Washington, conducted a study on the meaning of healing beyond physiological processes in order to help doctors facilitate more holistic patient outcomes.[47] In his investigation, he examined the lived experience of a group of physicians as they cared for their patients. Egnew observed how the notion of healing in a holistic sense has faded from attention in traditional medicine and is a topic rarely discussed in the literature.[48] In an industrialized model of healthcare, a focus on cure had eclipsed the need for care. "The physician's role became 'curer of disease' rather than 'healer of the sick.'"[49] In the study, healing was defined as "the process of bringing together aspects of one's self, body-mind-spirit, at deeper levels of inner knowing, leading toward integration and balance with each aspect having equal importance and value."[50] Indeed, the word *healing* means "to make whole" which suggests a multidimensional recovery.[51]

Egnew found the notion of healing associated with several themes, including *wholeness, narrative,* and *spirituality*—all of which extend beyond conventional notions of physical cure. Let's take a moment to explore his findings. The theme of healing as *wholeness* was associated with positive physical, emotional, intellectual, social, and spiritual outcomes. Interestingly, participants did not associate wholeness exclusively with physical health or cure. Patients reported experiencing wholeness even when facing an incurable disease and the likelihood of dying. Healing was found "independent of illness, impairment, cure of disease, or death."[52]

Healing as *narrative* was associated with a reinterpretation of life, which included the insight that illness can facilitate deeper connections with others—particularly family, friends, and caregivers. Healing was related to the greater context of a patient's life. "[R]eal persons in connection

---

45. Jones, "Wounded Vietnam Veteran," para. 12.
46. Greenleaf, "On Being a Seeker," 453.
47. Egnew, "Meaning of Healing."
48. Egnew, "Meaning of Healing," 256.
49. Egnew, "Meaning of Healing," 255.
50. Egnew, "Meaning of Healing," 256.
51. Greenleaf, *Servant-Leader within*, 60.
52. Egnew, "Meaning of Healing," 257.

with other real persons . . . to be whole is always to be whole in the presence of others."[53] The continuity of care fostered feelings of connection, relationship, and safety, which helped patients cope with feelings of vulnerability and loneliness. The theme of healing as *spirituality* was associated with meaning-making, reconciliation, and transcendent suffering. Patients reported feeling a sense of meaning even outside of a physical cure. Though facing an uncertain outcome, they reported discovering new perspectives, wisdom, and a sense of peace.

Ultimately, Egnew found that shared suffering and caring relationships is what helped patients heal in a holistic sense. He proposed that a "physician-healer" model—someone who treats heart and soul—could help reconnect modern medicine with its roots as a healing profession. The servant-leadership of Mother Teresa embodied this notion of holistic healing. Through her servant-leadership she attended to the deeper aspects of healing to facilitate wholeness. She recognized the need to care for body, soul, mind, and spirit. As a servant-leader, she was called to "ease the pain of those who are hurting and make whole that which has come apart."[54]

Mother Teresa gave priority to matters of the spirit. In that regard, she ministered to people regardless of their faith tradition. Indeed, in the pluralistic Indian context, she was respected and revered by believers and nonbelievers alike. Her example is a reminder that the character of a servant-leader is anchored in transcendent core values such as kindness, compassion, joy, and love. Mother Teresa emphasized this to the young nuns ministering alongside her. She said that she would rather they "make mistakes in kindness than to work miracles in unkindness."[55] Robert Greenleaf referred to this as the "natural feeling" to serve.[56]

Mother's Teresa's servant-leadership as a healer was also undertaken in a spirit of humility. Eminent English journalist and author Malcom Muggeridge conducted one of the most well-known interviews with Mother Teresa. In his book, *Something Beautiful for God*, Muggeridge pulled back the curtain so we could glimpse Mother Teresa's servant-leadership expressed in her understated, yet elegant manner. Muggeridge believed that Mother Teresa was reluctant to speak much about her early life because her servant-leadership meant the "end of her biography and the beginning of her life."[57]

---

53. Egnew, "Meaning of Healing," 257.
54. See Showkeir and Showkeir, "Clarifying Intention," 162.
55. Spink, *Mother Teresa*, 70.
56. Greenleaf, *Servant Leadership: A Journey*, 13.
57. Muggeridge, *Something Beautiful*, 16.

She preferred that Muggeridge focus on the acts of love, rather than the vehicle through which they were expressed.

A United States Senator once asked Mother Teresa if she ever gets discouraged ministering amidst overwhelming poverty and suffering. She responded emphatically, "God has not called me to be successful. God has called me to be faithful."[58] Similarly, one biographer recalled how Mother Teresa responded when she asked for permission to write her story,

> As always, the focus was deflected from herself. [She wrote], 'No one thinks of the pen while reading a letter. They only want to know the mind of the person who wrote the letter. That's exactly what I am in God's hand—a little pencil. God is writing his love letter to the world in this way, through works of love.'[59]

The biographer noted how Mother Teresa did not want to be placed on a pedestal, because doing so might give others the false impression that a life of service was possible only for the extraordinarily spiritual or saintly, when it was actually available to everyone.

Mother Teresa placed particular value on the life of the individual. I am reminded of the story of a man who was walking along the beach. He noticed a little boy throwing an object into the ocean. He asked the boy what he was doing. He replied, "Sir, I'm throwing this starfish back into the ocean. The tide's going out and if I don't get them into the water, they'll die on the beach." The man replied, "Son, don't you see the miles of beach and the hundreds of starfish? You'll never make a difference!" The boy gently picked up another starfish and tossed it back into the surf and said, "But sir, it made a difference to that one." Mother Teresa spoke to how servant-leaders heal the world by cherishing the worth and dignity of every person:

> I do not agree with the big way of doing things. To us what matters is in the individual. To get to love the person we must come in close contact with him. If we wait till we get the numbers, then we will be lost in numbers. And we will never be able to show that love and respect for the person. I believe in person to person . . .[60]

Someone once said that the only thing worse than being hated is to be ignored. Mother Teresa believed that the deepest human need of the human heart is to be wanted and to be seen. By establishing a home for the dying, for example, she conveyed the message that every individual matters—even

---

58. Spink, *Mother Teresa*, 245.
59. Spink, *Mother Teresa*, 150.
60. Muggeridge, *Something Beautiful*, 118.

if he or she has only a few breaths left. "We want them to know that there are people who really love them, who really want them, at least for the few hours they have to live, to know human and divine love."[61] Mother Teresa was convinced that serving the unwanted and unloved was a healing balm:

> In these twenty years of work amongst the people, I have come more and more to realize that it is being unwanted that is the worst disease that any human being can ever experience. Nowadays we have found medicine for leprosy and lepers can be cured. . . . For all kinds of diseases there are medicines and cures. But for being unwanted, except there are willing hands to serve and there's a loving heart to love, I don't think this terrible disease can ever be cured.[62]

Much like the shepherd in the parable of the lost sheep, servant-leaders seek to serve the highest needs of others through care, dignity, and love. Mother Teresa reminds us of the inherent worth within each person, "Do we look at the poor with compassion? They are hungry not only for food; they are hungry to be recognized as human beings."[63]

Business executive and servant-leadership consultant Helena Judith Sturnick offered a six-stage framework for healing leadership.[64] Stage one is *consciousness of health*. Here, the servant-leader assesses personal and institutional health. Stage two is the *willingness to change*, that is, a focus on inner work and personal healing. The leader faces the possibility that he or she has actively, albeit unconsciously, hurt or diminished others in some way. Within such openness lies the seeds of change. This understanding can be accelerated through the help of a mentor or coach. Stage three is the *teachable moment*. This is facilitated through an experience of vulnerability that transforms the servant-leader into a *wounded healer*.[65] Stage four is a *healthy support system*. Lasting change rarely happens in isolation; support systems may range from a single person to a community. Stage five is *immersion in the duality of our inner lives*. Here is the recognition that we cast shadow and light. Stage six is a *return to service in leadership*. The servant-leader reengages with the unhealthy system in order to serve. Sturnick noted that service, by its very nature, is a healing balm.[66]

---

61. Muggeridge, *Something Beautiful*, 92.
62. Muggeridge, *Something Beautiful*, 98–99.
63. Mother Teresa, *Meditations*, 19.
64. See Sturnick, "Healing Leadership," 185–90.
65. See Sturnick, "Healing Leadership," 208.
66. See Sturnick, "Healing Leadership," 193.

Someone once asked Rabbi Isadore, "How is one to know the precise time when night ends and day begins?" One of his students spoke up, "It is when one can distinguish between a dog and a sheep in the far distance, that is when day begins." Another offered, "It is when you can tell the difference between a fig tree and a date tree, then night is fully gone." The wise Rabbi said, "No, it is neither of those things. It is when you can see your brother or sister in the face of a stranger. Until then, night is still with us."[67] Servant-leaders are called to be healers in a wounded world. Mother Teresa's life reminds us that healing begins with a servant-leader who stands ready to help and then sets out to accomplish small things with great love.

FINDING: HEALING

The story is told of the Buddha, who was once threatened with death by a bandit.

"Then be good enough to fulfill my dying wish," said Buddha. "Cut off the branch of that tree."

One slash of the sword, and it was done! "What now?" asked the bandit.

"Put it back again," said Buddha.

The bandit laughed. "You must be crazy to think that anyone can do that."

Buddha responded, "On the contrary, it is you who are crazy to think that you are mighty because you can wound and destroy. That is the task of children. The mighty know how to create and heal."[68]

Servant-leaders help make a hurting world whole.

---

67. CoursesWeb, "*101 Zen Stories,*" para. 1.
68. De Mello, *Heart of the Enlightened*, 36.

4

Malala Yousafzai: The Servant-Leader and Awareness

THE FINE PARTICLES OF dust flew into the eyes of the girls as they looked out the window of their school bus on a warm afternoon. The vehicle lurched to a halt, as if caught in the stop-and-go traffic of a city center. But this was a quiet road in Pakistan's North West Frontier. The unexpected stop interrupted the universal lightness and laughter that accompanies the end of a school day. A man spoke to the driver and confirmed that the bus belonged to the Khushal School. As they conversed, another man, dressed like a college student, hopped aboard the rear bumper of the bus and carefully looked over the rows of pastel colored *salwar-kameez*. He asked the girls a question: "Who is Malala?" The answer would change the trajectory of a fifteen-year-old girl's life, her friends, and the Swat Valley as he pulled out a gun and started shooting.

Malala Yousafzai was living dangerously. She had defied the ban on female education imposed by the Taliban in northwestern Pakistan. She spoke out against the ban at age eleven, and was told, "Shut up, or else!" When she continued to attend classes, she was warned, "Stay home, or else!" On October 9, 2012, the warnings culminated in a ruthless attack on Malala as the gunman fired three shots from a Colt .45 revolver. One bullet hit her fourteen-year-old friend Shazia in the shoulder; another struck sixteen-year-old Kainat Riaz in the arm. Malala was shot in the head. She collapsed onto the lap of her friend Moniba. The gunman and his accomplice fled the scene, leaving the girls in a pool of blood. But the bullets would not accomplish their devilish mission. Shazia and Kainat survived. And so did Malala.[1]

In this chapter we explore the servant-leadership characteristic of *awareness* through the life of Malala Yousafzai. As a young girl, she fought fiercely for the right of girls to attend school and gain an education. Though her leadership on the issue came at a severe personal cost, she remained undeterred. Here is how servant-leadership scholar Larry Spears described the power of awareness,

> General awareness, and especially self-awareness, strengthens the servant-leader. Awareness helps one in understanding issues involving ethics, power, and values. It lends itself to being able to view most situations from a more integrated, holistic position. As Greenleaf (1977/2002) observed: 'Awareness is not a giver of solace—it is just the opposite. It is a disturber and an awakener. Able leaders are usually sharply awake and reasonably disturbed. They are not seekers after solace. They have their own inner serenity.[2]

In this chapter we explore how Malala applied the characteristic of awareness to advocate for a free, safe, and quality education for girls in Pakistan and around the world. In the pages that follow, I describe her struggle through the themes of light and darkness.

SUN

Malala was born on July 12, 1997, in Mingora, a small town about 100 miles from Islamabad, Pakistan. She was named after Malalai of Maiwand, the daughter of a Pashtun shepherd who courageously led an army against the British. Her bravery and sacrifice turned the tide of the battle, making her a national hero. The Pashtun people are the historic founders of the Afghan kingdom. They reside in Afghanistan and Pakistan's rugged North West Territories. They are renowned to this day for their bravery and code of hospitality. Many Pashtun live in Pakistan's Swat Valley, considered one of the most beautiful places on earth, with its snow-capped mountains, waterfalls, lush landscapes, and rich culture. The area's ancient Buddhist heritage is evident from the many stupas and carvings scattered throughout the valley. Islam came to the land in the eleventh century. The region fell under Taliban rule in 2007.

---

1. Yousafzai, *I am Malala*.
2. See Spears, "Introduction: Understanding the Growing Impact of Servant-Leadership," 17.

Much like the other servant-leaders in this book, Malala's life was shaped by the influence of others, particularly her father, Ziauddin. As a teacher, he considered education vital to personal, social, and national progress. When the Taliban prohibited girls from attending school, his passion turned into activism. Malala followed in his footsteps. She recalled,

> Education had been a great gift for him. He believed that lack of education was the root of all of Pakistan's problems. Ignorance allowed politicians to fool people and bad administrators to be re-elected. He believed schooling should be available for all, rich and poor, boys and girls.[3]

After earning his master's degree in English, Ziauddin taught at a private college for a few years, but his real desire was to open a school that nurtured critical thinking and creativity, skills he felt were missing in Pakistan's educational system. When the time was right, he invested his entire life savings and borrowed money to open an English-language school in Mingora. While Ziauddin started with high hopes, financial difficulties brought the work to a standstill just after a few months; but he was not one to give up on a dream. He soon opened the Kushal School, named after an Afghan warrior who united the Pashtun tribes in the seventeenth century. Kushal opened with a grand total of three students and very little liquidity. Despite a number of obstacles, including local officials demanding bribes (which he refused to pay), a flood that destroyed a large part of the building, and unending cash flow problems, Ziauddin pressed on.

Around this time, the Taliban began to exert their influence in the region outside the Swat Valley. Men were required to grow beards, women had to wear *burqas*, and sports, movies, and music were deemed *haram*. They took their brand of Islam even further by burning down schools for girls. These new regulations, foreign to the Pashtun way of life, crept into the Swat Valley where Malala and her family lived. Reflecting on this sudden turn of events, Malala wrote,

> When I heard stories of the atrocities in Afghanistan, I felt proud to be in Swat. 'Here a girl can go to school,' I used to say. But the Taliban were right around the corner and were Pashtuns like us. For me the valley was a sunny place, and I couldn't see the clouds gathering behind the mountains. My father used to say, 'I will protect your freedom, Malala. Carry on with your dreams.'[4]

---

3. Yousafzai, *I Am Malala*, 33.
4. Yousafzai, *I Am Malala*, 33.

CLOUDS

Amidst these changes, the Kushal School was quickly becoming a respected institution in the area. Ziauddin opened an elementary school and two high schools, serving over 800 students. Despite his financial struggles, he worked with students who could not afford school fees so they could continue their education. Amidst these events, the 9/11 terror attacks took place in the United States. No one envisioned the impact they would have. Malala and her family lived directly under the shadow of the Taliban and Osama bin Laden. Life as they had known it began to change dramatically.

Just as the Kushal School's financial outlook started to improve, a local *mufti*, under the influence of the Taliban, began riling up the locals. He pressured elders to ostracize Ziauddin, claiming that he was breaking Islamic law by not requiring female students to wear a *purdah*, another custom that was foreign to the people of the valley. He tried to get the school's landlord to cancel Ziauddin's lease. Though his efforts failed, they proved to be a preview of the challenges ahead.

When Malala turned ten, the Taliban moved into the Swat Valley. She recalled how their long hair, thick beards, turbans, and camouflage vests stood out, "It seemed to us that the Taliban arrived in the night just like vampires. They appeared in groups, armed with knives and Kalashnikovs . . ."[5] The group was led by Maulana Fazlullah, a charismatic twenty-eight-year-old. He set up a pirate radio station to promote the Taliban's message. He discussed social issues, criminal justice reform (something many in the Frontier felt the national government was ignoring), and envisioned a return to a more "orthodox" and "pure" version of Islam.

Within six months, residents in the valley began disposing of their television sets, DVDs, and other forms of entertainment. Bollywood movies, a favorite pastime, were banned. Women were encouraged to stay at home and a veil was required if they needed to go outside. Barber and beauty shops were closed and shopping in local bazaars was forbidden. The Taliban instituted *Sharia* law. Justice was swift and harsh. Malala, however, found these changes inconsistent with her understanding of Islam.

One day, Ziauddin arrived to find a message posted on his school building. The note declared female education as "un-Islamic" and warned, "Stop this—or you will be in trouble and your children will weep and cry for you."[6] Several teachers, fearful of the consequences, resigned. Despite the threats, he pressed on and Malala continued to attend school. Students

---

5. Yousafzai, *I Am Malala*, 90.
6. Yousafzai, *I Am Malala*, 100.

hid their book bags under their shawls as they walked between home and school. The classroom served as a respite from the complicated and dangerous reality outside the walls. Malala recalled, "When I was in the street it felt as though every man I passed might be a Talib."[7]

The Taliban escalated their campaign and began blowing up schools in the valley, particularly ones where girls attended. A suicide bomber detonated himself in Malala's high school. Malala's father tried to raise awareness by organizing marches and giving media interviews. When Malala asked if he ever felt afraid, he replied, "At night our fear is strong *Jani*, but in the morning, in the light we find our courage again. . . . We must rid our valley of the Taliban, and then no one has to feel this fear."[8]

While still a young girl, Malala began to speak to news organizations to remind people what was at stake. "I was only eleven . . . in my heart was the belief that God would protect me. If I am speaking for the rights of girls, I am not doing anything wrong. It's my duty to do so."[9] Malala even appeared on a BBC debate program hosted by a popular Pakistani journalist. Her opponent was a Taliban representative. During the interview, she advocated for the right of girls to pursue an education. Though she received support from around the country, the situation at home was only getting worse. "Our words were like eucalyptus blossoms of spring tossed away on the wind. The destruction of schools continued."[10] The Taliban escalated their fear campaign by using improvised explosive devices to demolish schools, flattening over 400 by the end of 2007.

SHADOW

In 2008, the Taliban announced that in early January 2009, all educational facilities for girls would be permanently closed. Despite the edict, Ziauddin was determined to continue "until the last room, the last teacher and the last student was alive."[11] Malala stood by her father's decision. "Though we loved school, we hadn't realized how important education was until the Taliban tried to stop us. Going to school, reading and doing homework wasn't just a way of passing time, it was our future."[12]

---

7. Yousafzai, *I Am Malala*, 112.
8. Yousafzai, *I Am Malala*, 114.
9. Yousafzai, *I Am Malala*, 117.
10. Yousafzai, *I Am Malala*, 118.
11. Yousafzai, *I Am Malala*, 120.
12. Yousafzai, *I Am Malala*, 120–21.

The Taliban escalated their violence. They murdered Shabana, one of Malala's closest friends. Despite this, Malala continued to give interviews around the country, speaking out against the Taliban. Ziauddin was threatened with death after he called for military intervention. Fearing for his life, he stayed with friends in case they raided his home. The events in the valley drew worldwide attention and the BBC was searching for a student to write a diary describing life under the Taliban. Finding a volunteer proved difficult. When Malala heard about it, she saw it as an opportunity to bring attention to their cause, "When I heard my father talking about this, I said, 'Why not me?' I wanted people to know what was happening. Education is our right, I said. Just as it is our right to sing and play."[13]

Though she had never kept a diary before, with her father's help, she began to share her experiences. The BBC provided a weekly blog and encouraged her to write in Urdu. The journalist who published the blog told Malala about Anne Frank, another brave young lady who kept a diary. Malala wrote under the pseudonym "Gul Makai," an Afghan folk heroine. Her journal captured the attention of adults and children throughout the Swat Valley. They had no idea that it was their own Malala who was writing the blog. Soon, newspapers around the world printed her diary and excerpts were read over the radio.

By 2009, attendance at the Kushal School dropped to less than thirty. Families pulled their children out of school, while others left the valley altogether. Malala was asked to participate in a *New York Times* documentary about the developments, "I told the documentary makers, 'They cannot stop me. I will get my education if it's at home, school or somewhere else. This is our request to the world—to save our schools, save our Pakistan, save our Swat.'"[14] Malala's family recognized the dangers of speaking out, but assumed the Taliban would not harm children. But her grandmother was not so sure. Malala continued to blog even as her school was shutdown.

When the documentary *Class Dismissed in Swat Valley* was released, even greater attention was brought to their struggle. When the Taliban experienced blowback, they agreed to allow girls under ten years old to attend school. Though Malala did not qualify, she and a few of her friends continued to defy the ban. After a short-lived peace agreement between the government and the Taliban disintegrated, Malala and her family decided that it was time to leave the Swat Valley. The gunfire, bombings, and increasing likelihood of death had become too much. Their decision meant that they

---

13. Yousafzai, *I Am Malala*, 129.
14. Yousafzai, *I Am Malala*, 134.

were designated as "internally displaced persons" by the United Nations; it was the largest evacuation in Pashtun history.

Malala and her family settled in her mother's ancestral village of Karshat. She resumed schooling as a seventh grader. During one of her classes, she read a poem class that included these powerful words, "A diamond must be cut many times before it yields even a tiny jewel."[15] During the unrest, Malala's family shifted among various cities and villages as the government tried to drive out the Taliban. Finally, when they had been cleared from the valley, Malala and her family were able to return. Their once beautiful city looked like a war zone. Pockmarked buildings and burned vehicles were everywhere. The Kushal School had been looted and destroyed. After a lot of hard work and determination, Ziauddin reopened his school a few months after their return. As time passed, however, it became clear that the Taliban were still in the area. Soon, they resumed terrorizing anyone who dared stand against them.

DARKNESS

The death threats against Ziauddin became increasingly specific. They warned that he would pay a heavy price for his defiance. In October 2011, KidsRights, an Amsterdam-based child advocacy, nominated Malala for their international peace prize. South African Archbishop Desmond Tutu personally endorsed her for the award. Though Malala did not win, she was invited to speak at a national education conference in Lahore. At the event, she addressed the education ban and asserted that she would not let fear deter her efforts. The Chief Minister of Punjab donated $4,500 to support Malala's campaign. The Prime Minister personally awarded her Pakistan's first National Peace Prize. Her fight for awareness had reached new heights and people in high places were paying attention. With a higher profile, the death threats escalated and Malala was identified as a personal target. Her parents wondered whether the campaign was worth pursuing if their daughter would be a casualty. When they suggested she pull back, Malala responded,

> I don't know why, but hearing I was being targeted did not worry me. It seemed to me that everyone knows they will die one day . . . it doesn't matter if it comes from a Talib or cancer. So, I should do whatever I wanted to do.[16]

The situation was much more serious than Malala realized, however. The police informed Ziauddin that because of her international profile, the

---

15. Yousafzai, *I Am Malala*, 152.
16. Yousafzai, *I Am Malala*, 188.

Taliban considered his daughter a high-value target and offered the family a security detail. Someone posted a letter at a local mosque decrying the Kushal School as immoral and a few days later Ziauddin's close friend was assassinated. The message was clear—Malala and her family would be next.

October 9, 2012 proved to be the darkest day in Malala's life. It started as any other—she attended school, took an exam, and headed home with friends. Nobody could have anticipated what happened next. Her friend Shazia recalled looking out the window of the school bus, lost in a daydream, when the gunman opened fire.

LIGHT

Malala barely survived the attack as the bullets narrowly missed her brain. With her life hanging in the balance, she was airlifted to a military hospital for emergency surgery. She was then flown to a trauma center in England. News of the shooting spread around the world. The Taliban took responsibility for the shooting and declared that Malala was targeted for "preaching secularism" and "promoting Western culture."[17] They had planned the assassination for two months. Malala's road to recovery included a number of complex surgeries and months of rehabilitation. Her indomitable spirit, the love of her family, and the support of well-wishers from around the world ultimately made the difference between life and death.

Malala was invited to speak to the United Nations on her sixteenth birthday. She addressed 400 world leaders, with millions more watching around the globe. Malala explained how she wanted to speak to "every person around the world who could make a difference. . . . Deep in my heart I hoped to reach every child who could take courage from my word and stand up for his or her rights."[18] She urged her audience, "Let us pick up our books and pens. They are our most powerful weapons. One child, one teacher, one book and one pen can change the world."[19]

Today, Malala continues to be a fierce advocate for education, particularly on behalf of girls. She continues her work as an alumnus of Oxford University. The latest data from UNESCO indicates that over 130 million girls around the world are prevented from pursuing an education. Malala's life has become a megaphone for her message, and her fight is far from over.

17. Yousafzai, *I Am Malala*, 215–16.
18. Yousafzai, *I Am Malala*, 261.
19. Yousafzai, *I Am Malala*, 262.

SERVANT-LEADERSHIP AND AWARENESS: WAKING UP

Much has been written about the importance of awareness for leaders. It can be said that the quality of our leadership is directly proportional to the degree of our awareness. To borrow a phrase from Harvard professor Ron Heifetz, awareness happens when leaders "get off the dance floor and get on the balcony."[20] Malala did just that when she assessed the danger her society faced with a ban on girls' education. Greenleaf described awareness as the "schizoid life" of leadership wherein a servant-leader inhabits the "real world" with its daily concerns and responsibilities, but remains detached enough to grasp the significance of events within the larger sweep of history and for the future.[21] Awareness provides the servant-leader a 30,000-foot view so she is able to see where to focus, while remaining grounded enough to address present realities.

Greenleaf believed that awareness was a prerequisite for a leadership role. "A qualification for leadership is that one can tolerate a sustained wide span of awareness so that one can better 'see it as it is.'"[22] He described it as "opening wide the doors of perception so as to enable one to get more of what is available of sensory experience and other signals from the environment than people usually take in."[23] The Dutch artist Vincent van Gogh said, "I feel that my work lies in the heart of the people, that I must keep close to the ground, that I must grasp life in its depths, and make progress through many cares and troubles."[24] How can we grasp life at its depths? It begins with awareness. Sometimes, it is contained within the events everyone else sees; at other times, it is embedded in the smaller, quieter events that go unnoticed in the world-at-large. Either way, Greenleaf observed that when we lack awareness, "We also miss leadership opportunities."[25]

Awareness provides the perspective we need to navigate the whitewater rapids of leadership. As it has been said, "When you're up to your neck in alligators, it's easy to forget that the goal was to drain the swamp." When we feel the pressure of the present, it is easy to lose sight of the larger picture. Greenleaf asserted that awareness helps servant-leaders clarify priorities:

> The cultivation of awareness gives one the basis for detachment, the ability to stand aside and see oneself in perspective

---

20. Heifetz and Linsky, *Leadership on the Line*, 53.
21. Greenleaf, *On Becoming a Servant Leader*, 322.
22. Greenleaf, *Servant as Leader*, 27.
23. Greenleaf, *Servant as Leader*, 27.
24. Van Gogh, "Letter from Vincent van Gogh, para. 4.
25. Greenleaf, *Servant as Leader*, 27.

in the context of one's own experience amidst the ever-present dangers, threats, and alarms. Then one sees one's own peculiar assortment of obligations and responsibilities in a way that permits one to sort out the urgent from the important and perhaps deal with the important.[26]

It was this level of awareness that helped Malala to stay on track; the little foxes that might have altered her path did not distract her. In *The Seven Habits of Highly Effective People*, Stephen Covey encouraged leaders to assess their life priorities through four quadrants: 1) important, 2) not important, 3) urgent, and 4) not urgent. He encouraged us to live at the intersection of *important but not urgent*. Here, we distinguish between the daily tasks that demand our attention from what truly matters.[27] Professor Cornel West put it this way, "Attend to the things that really matter and turn your back to those things that are distractions. We live in a culture with weapons of mass distraction."[28]

During Halloween season, my wife and I take our kids to a corn maze hosted by a local farm. We are given a map and a friendly "Have fun!" as we start walking down the muddy paths surrounded by green stalks towering over our heads. The first few steps seem fairly obvious. Within a few minutes, however, I feel lost. The clues on the map feel of little use as the scenery blends together. Soon enough my kids are convinced that we are just walking in circles. *"Dad, weren't we just here?"* In those moments I have often wished I had a drone to catch a bird's-eye view of the maze. The view from the ground feels confusing and I am missing the larger perspective. It also does not help that I am directionally challenged! Similarly, awareness provides the servant-leader a glimpse of the big picture and the path to follow.

Greenleaf believed that two individuals could see the same event, but hold differing perspectives because of their levels of awareness. When discussing this notion with my students, I present a series of optical illusions to illustrate my point. While everyone is looking at the same picture, some see a rabbit, while others are sure they are looking at a duck. In another picture, some see a vase, while others see two faces. A third picture presents either a young woman, or a picture of an older woman. The activity drives home a larger point: awareness allows servant-leaders to see a different, but similarly valid reality. When the majority of people saw a hopeless situation, Malala saw a leadership opportunity.

---

26. Greenleaf, *Servant as Leader*, 27–28.
27. Covey, *Seven Habits*.
28. West, "Speaking Truth," 9:43–9:54.

Leadership guru Peter Drucker recounted the story of a man who came across three stonecutters engrossed in their work. His curiosity compelled him to ask what they were doing:

> The first replied, "I'm making living."
> The second kept on hammering while he said, "I'm doing the best job of stonecutting in the entire county."
> The third looked up, and with a gleam in his eye, said, "I'm building a cathedral."[29]

The first stonecutter was doing a day's work for a day's pay. His focus was on the immediate reward. The second stonecutter was driven by ego and personal ambition. The third stonecutter was engrossed in something larger than himself. He embraced a transcendent purpose.[30] While it was the same activity, there existed three different levels of awareness.

Businessman Mukesh Ambani, chairman of India's Reliance Industries, spoke to the role of awareness in leadership at a 2011 World Economic Forum discussion. During a panel on strategies for accelerating India's economic growth, he explained how his business decisions were driven by awareness. He noted that when he encourages people to invest in India, many are quick to point out the problems the country is facing. Ambani, however, saw things differently. "A lot of people think that India is a land of problems. I really think that India is a land of a billion opportunities and not a billion problems."[31] To be clear, awareness does not mean that we maintain a Pollyannaish attitude or deny painful realities. Indeed, Malala was well aware of the risks of speaking up. She understood the costs of awareness.

According to Greenleaf, awareness is about letting "something significant and disturbing develop between oneself and a symbol."[32] Malala allowed the ban on girls' education to disturb her enough to do something about it. Such magnitude of awareness can certainly evoke a sense of fear, "Making a commitment to foster awareness can be scary—you never know what you may discover."[33] Yet Malala's balcony perspective helped her overcome those fears. Greenleaf reminded us that awareness requires an inward journey.[34] He shared how servant-leaders experience "more than the usual alertness, there is more intense contact with the immediate situation, and

---

29. Rosenberg, "Three Stonecutters," para. 10.
30. Rosenberg, "Three Stonecutters," para. 11.
31. Hindu, "Land of [sic] Billion Opportunities," para. 2.
32. Greenleaf, *Servant as Leader*, 316.
33. See Spears, "Understanding and Practice of Servant-Leadership," para. 18.
34. Greenleaf, *Servant as Leader*, 316.

a lot more is stored away in the unconscious computer to produce intuitive insights in the future when needed."[35]

There are many other examples of servant-leaders who changed the world through awareness. Consider Wendy Kopp, founder of Teach for America. Like Malala, she was passionate about the transformative power of education. In 1989, Kopp was a twenty-one-year-old Princeton University student when she founded what has been described as the most successful secondary educational program of the past twenty-five years. Kopp grew up in University Park, a wealthy suburb of Dallas, Texas, known as "The Bubble." Her upbringing was "extraordinarily isolated from reality and the disparities in educational opportunity."[36] Rarely is there trouble in The Bubble. Contrast that with the experience of her roommate, who grew up in the South Bronx, where over half of the students are born into poverty and test scores are often below the national average. During her freshman year, Kopp's roommate, struggling with the rigors of the Ivy League, dropped out of the prestigious university. She felt ill-prepared compared to students who had graduated from private schools.

Disturbed by this unfortunate turn of events, Kopp decided to focus on the issue of educational inequity. She gathered a group of students and business leaders for an education conference. Out of those meetings emerged a vision for a new type of organization that would recruit recent college graduates who were willing to teach for two years in America's most underserved school districts. When Kopp laid out her plans in her senior thesis, her advisor labeled them as "deranged" and wondered why anyone would volunteer for such an assignment. He also doubted that Kopp could raise the estimated $2.5 million needed to get the project off the ground. Undeterred, Kopp pressed on and soon launched Teach for America.

In 2012, when Teach for America invited applicants to join its inaugural core, Kopp received over 48,000 applications. That year, 5,800 college graduates entered the classroom. Kopp reflected on her journey: "I've come to truly believe that leadership is at the heart of every problem we face.... We look for people with perseverance, the ability to motivate others, humility, and people who have high expectations for the kids. We want people who are completely dedicated to the mission."[37] Today, Teach for America has over 50,000 corps members and alumni who have taught over 5 million students across the country.

---

35. Greenleaf, *Servant-Leader within*, 55.
36. George, *Discover Your True North*, 28.
37. "Teach for America," para 4.

Awareness also made a difference in the leadership of Roy Vagelos, former CEO of Merck & Co. Vagelos learned about river blindness (*onchocerciasis*), a dreaded disease that affected more than 20 million people in West and Central Africa, the Middle East, and Latin America. Over 600,000 people had gone blind from the bite of a disease-transmitting blackfly. In the mid-1970s, the disease was so prevalent in some parts of the world that many resigned themselves to catching it as they aged.

In 1985, a team of Merck scientists told Vagelos that they had developed a drug that could be effective against the disease—that was the good news. The bad news was that development costs could soar past $200 million and there was no guarantee it would work. Furthermore, not only would the medicine be of limited use outside of certain parts of the world, those most in need of the drug would not be able to afford it. Going against his advisors' recommendations, Vagelos green-lit the project.

In 1987, Vagelos announced the development of Mectizan (*ivermectin*), a new drug to treat river blindness. Merck would distribute the drug free of charge through the World Health Organization. The medicine proved so effective that farmers returned to their abandoned riverside plots. Senator Edward Kennedy described the medication as an answer to prayer, "Merck's gift to the World Health Organization is more than a medical breakthrough—it is truly a triumph of the human spirit."[38] Like Malala, Kopp and Vagelos led through awareness. Practicing this characteristic of servant-leadership isn't easy, however.

In a study of leadership ethics, Harvard management professor Barbara Kellerman analyzed hundreds of leaders. In her book, *Bad Leadership*, she described seven distinct forms of unethical leadership styles, ranging from incompetent, rigid, intemperate, callous, corrupt, insular, to outright evil. Each type can be subsumed under two categories—ineffective or unethical. She identified "insular leadership," which is related to awareness, as a type of unethical leadership.[39]

Insular leadership happens when a "leader and at least some followers minimize or disregard the health and welfare of 'the other'—that is, those outside the group or organization for which they are directly responsible."[40] Insular leaders take little to no interest in the world outside of their bubble. Like the ostrich with its head in the sand, they remain blissfully unaware. According to Kellerman,

---

38. "Merck Offers Free Distribution," para. 5.
39. Kellerman, *Bad Leadership*.
40. Kellerman, *Bad Leadership*, 168.

> Insular leaders and their followers establish boundaries between themselves and their immediate constituencies on the one side, and everyone else on the other. To a degree, of course, this is simply human nature. My group—my family, my tribe, my country, my company—competes with your group for resources, and in every other way as well. Still, in this day and age, when everyone knows what's happening to everyone else, it should be difficult to turn a blind eye to danger, not to speak of tragedy, even when it befalls people who are 'the other.'[41]

Ron Edmonson warned that leaders must watch out for ten obstacles as they seek to develop awareness.[42] They include the following:

1. Not knowing the real health of a team or organization.
2. Clueless to what people are really saying.
3. Unsure of measurable items because they are never measured or monitored.
4. Not asking questions for fear of an unwanted answer.
5. Not dreaming into the future; becoming content with status quo.
6. Preferring not to know there was a problem than that there is one.
7. Ignoring all criticism or dismissing all of it as negativity.
8. Not learning anything new; relying on the same old ways to consistently work.
9. Making every decision without input from others.
10. Assuming everyone supports and loves your leadership.

How then can leaders develop awareness? Psychologist Nathaniel Branden, author of *The Six Pillars of Self Esteem*, suggested it begins by choosing to live consciously. When we sleepwalk through life, our depth of awareness is "diffused or distracted rather than focused and disciplined."[43]

According to Branden, living consciously entails the following practices:

1. Maintaining a mind that is active, rather than passive.
2. Living in the moment, while keeping an eye on the wider context.
3. Assessing whether actions are aligned with purpose.

---

41. Kellerman, "Insular Leadership," para. 4.
42. Edmonson, "Are You a Clueless Leader?," para. 7.
43. Branden, *Art of Living Consciously*, 14.

4. Being sensitive to external and internal realities (needs, feelings, aspirations, and motives).
5. Being mindful of core values.

Branden, like Greenleaf and Kellerman, viewed awareness as an ethical obligation for leaders:

> Living consciously is a state of being mentally active rather than passive. It is the ability to look at the world through fresh eyes. It is intelligence taking joy in its own function. Living consciously is seeking to be aware of everything that bears our interests, actions, values, purposes, and goals. It is the willingness to confront facts, pleasant or unpleasant.... It is the quest to keep expanding our awareness and understanding, both of the world external to self and of the world within. It is respect for reality and respect for the distinction between the real and unreal. It is the commitment to see what we see and know what we know. It is recognition that the act of dismissing reality is the root of all evil.[44]

SERVANT-LEADERSHIP AND AWARENESS: THE WAY FORWARD

I once read a column in my local newspaper written by a young man. He titled his essay "Too Young to Lead." He was attending a community meeting focused on highlighting local and regional issues. Several influential people were at the event. As he found his seat, he noticed a well-dressed gentleman sitting next to him. He asked the man if he was speaking at the event. He responded, "Speaking is a strong term—I would say I'm mumbling some words." He then said to the young man, "You seem too young to be here!" The writer of the column recalled that he almost responded with, "I'm older than I look!" or "How old do you think I am?" Instead, he just smiled.

Reflecting on the experience, the young man felt the gentleman's reaction was "symptomatic of what is seen of my generation and what is expected of us. Attending a community gathering—one that touches on topics of education, economics, infrastructure, etc.—is just not something expected from many 20-somethings and younger. It is as if we unilaterally agreed that the decisions and policy-making are best left to older folks." The young man's insight spoke to the larger issue of leadership and awareness:

---

44. Branden, *Art of Living Consciously*, 11.

And that is where the doubt comes in, the doubt of whether I am to be a voice for my generation. But this is also where the hope and inspiration are. The hope and inspiration that stem from the belief that my generation has a fresh way of looking at the world and the time it takes to change it. It is not time to look for leaders, but to accept ourselves as leaders and give back to a society that has given so much to us.[45]

As seen in the servant-leadership of Malala, awareness is one of the greatest tools a servant-leader possesses. Nothing great can happen without it. Perhaps it will be the young people who will show us the way forward.

FINDING: AWARENESS

Awareness is predicated on engagement with oneself as well as the outside world. Servant-leaders spend serious time in self-interrogation and reflection, while also paying attention to what's happening around them. A student once asked a Zen teacher about the most important thing in life. The teacher replied, "Attention."

The student continued, "What is the second most important thing?"

"Attention," replied the teacher.

"So then, what's the third thing?" asked the student.

"You do not seem to be paying attention," roared the teacher![46]

---

45. Kastenbaum, "What, Me Lead?," para. 11.
46. Dhiman, *Holistic Leadership*, 234.

5

John Woolman: The Servant-Leader and Persuasion

THE NEWSPAPER HEADLINE WAS intriguing: "KKK Member Walks Up to Black Musician in Bar—But It's Not a Joke, and What Happens Next Will Astound You."[1] One night in 1983, Daryl Davis and his band had just finished playing their first set at the Silver Dollar Lounge in Frederick, Maryland. A man came up to Davis, put his arm around his shoulder, and said, "I really like your all's music. This is the first time I ever heard a Black man play piano like Jerry Lee Lewis!"[2] Amused, Davis reminded him that Lewis, whom he had known personally, learned to play piano from Black musicians. As the man laughed in disbelief, the two got into a friendly debate about the origins of rock 'n' roll. Enjoying the banter, he invited Davis to his table for a drink. Davis sipped on cranberry juice as they talked music history. That's when their conversation took an unexpected turn.

The man told Davis, "'This is the first time I ever sat down and had a drink with a Black man.' And I'm thinking, you know, this guy is really having a night of firsts here."[3] When Davis asked him why, "he didn't answer me. He stared at the tabletop and his buddy elbowed him in the ribs and said, 'tell him, tell him.' Now he says, 'I'm a member of the Klu Klux Klan.'"[4]

1. Savastio, "KKK Member Walks up."
2. Washington, "Silver Dollar Lounge," para. 4.
3. Washington, "Silver Dollar Lounge," para. 6.
4. Washington, "Silver Dollar Lounge," para. 6.

Now it was Davis's turn to laugh—he thought the man was joking. But the man showed Davis his Klan card. The reporter explained,

> Most people in this day and age probably would have turned and ran right out of that good ol' boy's bar, but not Davis. He stayed and talked with the Klansman for a long time. 'At first, I thought 'why the hell am I sitting with him?' but we struck up a friendship and it was music that brought us together,' he says. That friendship would lead Davis on a path almost unimaginable to most folks. Today, Davis is not only a musician, he is a person who befriends KKK members and, as a result, collects the robes and hoods of Klansmen who choose to leave the organization because of their friendship with him.[5]

From that day forward Davis made it his life's mission to befriend members of the Klan and help them examine the roots of their racial stereotypes and hate. Since 1983, over 200 Klan members have given up their robes through Davis's efforts—including grand dragons and imperial wizards. The man whom Davis met at the Silver Dollar Lounge that night turned in his Klan card as well. The article noted, "When that happens, Davis collects the robes and keeps them in his home as a reminder of the dent he has made in racism by simply sitting down and having dinner with people."[6] Davis explained how he works:

> If you have an adversary, an opponent with an opposing point of view, give that person a platform, regardless of how extreme it may be. And believe me I've heard something so extreme at these rallies it'll cut you to the bone. If you agree with them, great—no problem. If you don't agree with them, that's fine, too. You challenge them, but you don't challenge them rudely or violently. You do it politely and intelligently and when you do things that way, chances are they will reciprocate and give you a platform.[7]

While music is Daryl Davis's profession, persuasion has become his obsession.[8]

In this chapter we explore the servant-leadership characteristic of persuasion. Hundreds of years before Daryl Davis, Quaker abolitionist John Woolman (1720–1772) utilized persuasion to lead a campaign against slavery. Almost singlehandedly, Woolman persuaded the Quakers (or, Society

---

5. Savastio, "KKK Member Walks up," para. 3.
6. Brown, "How One Man Convinced," para. 2.
7. Washington, "Silver Dollar Lounge," para. 14.
8. Washington, "Silver Dollar Lounge." See also Ornstein, *Accidental Courtesy*.

of Friends) to abandon the profitable and socially accepted practice and exchange it for an ethos of freedom and justice. As a servant-leader, Woolman exemplified the characteristic of persuasion like few others in history.

According to servant-leadership scholar Larry Spears,

> Another characteristic of servant-leaders is reliance on persuasion, rather than on one's positional authority, in making decisions within an organization. The servant-leader seeks to convince others, rather than coerce compliance. This particular element offers one of the clearest distinctions between the traditional authoritarian model and that of servant-leadership. The servant-leader is effective at building consensus within groups. This emphasis on persuasion over coercion finds its roots in the beliefs of the Religious Society of Friends (Quakers)—the denominational body to which Robert Greenleaf belonged.[9]

Woolman's outsized impact upon the Society of Friends lies at the center of the American Quaker experience.[10] His masterful use of persuasion created sweeping changes that reverberated far beyond his lifetime and faith community. His bold leadership on the issue influenced thought leaders, abolitionists, social reformers, writers, college presidents, and possibly even President Lincoln.[11] As noted by one historian,

> Woolman belonged to a contingent of ministers within the Society of Friends who advocated thoroughgoing moral and economic reform. Over the course of two decades beginning in the 1750s, he and his associates convinced the Philadelphia Yearly Meeting to oppose slaveholding ever more vigorously and to embrace other reforms. They were not typical Quakers for their era, but they managed to effect change within their religious society by mobilizing a variety of persuasive techniques. They wrote essays and didactic journals. They took control of their Meetings' disciplinary committees and began visiting wayward Friends to correct them or in extreme cases to disown them. They also dramatized their moral positions through self-consciously exemplary behavior.[12]

Greenleaf presented Woolman as an example of how servant-leaders can employ persuasion. Besides the historical value of studying Woolman's

9. Greenleaf, *Servant-Leader Within*, 17–18.

10. Terrell, Jr., "John Woolman," 16.

11. Terrell, Jr., "John Woolman." See also Gummere, "John Woolman Memorial Association."

12. Plank, "Sailing with John Woolman," 48.

leadership, it should be noted that many of the problems he faced in his day, such as racism, inequality, and exploitation, exist in ours as well. Thus, Woolman's leadership offers valuable lessons for our generation. His life remains a powerful study in the exercise of persuasion to bring about enduring change.[13]

THE MAKING OF A QUIET RADICAL

Described by Frederick Tolles as the "quietest radical in history," Woolman's path to leadership was modest and unassuming.[14] Much of it is told in the journals and essays he left behind, including *The Journal of John Woolman*, a spiritual autobiography that centuries later still holds a rightful place as a classic of the colonial era. The work has remained in print since 1774.[15]

Woolman was born on October 19, 1720, in Burlington County, New Jersey, located about ten miles from Philadelphia. His family managed a farm near the Rancocas River. Central to life in the Woolman household was a robust Quaker faith tradition (known at the time as the "Friends of Truth" or simply "Friends"). Led by his father Samuel, family prayer and worship were regular practices in their home. Samuel also possessed a large library on subjects ranging from theology to law and navigation.[16] Accordingly, Woolman immersed himself in the study of religious, philosophical, and legal texts from a young age. These influences helped shape the core values on which he would later stand.

At that time, New Jersey was one of the centers of the slave trade in colonial America. Today, it is remarkable to consider that there was a time when there were more people on the planet who were enslaved rather than free. According to historian Adam Hochschild,

> At the end of the eighteenth century, well over three quarters of people alive were in bondage of one kind or another. . . . The age was a high point in the [slave] trade in which close to eighty thousand chained and shackled Africans were loaded onto slave ships and transported to the New World each year. In parts of the Americas, slaves far outnumbered free persons . . . The era

---

13. Levernier, "John Woolman."

14. Woolman, *Journal of John Woolman and a Plea for the Poor*, vii.

15. Woolman, *Journal of John Woolman*. See also, Plank, "Sailing with John Woolman."

16. Plank, "Sailing with John Woolman."

was one when, as the historian Seymour Drescher puts it, 'freedom, not slavery, was the peculiar institution.'"[17]

As a young man, Woolman was deeply troubled by the Quakers' participation in slavery. Having witnessed the terrors experienced by the enslaved, he found it difficult to reconcile the practice with Quaker doctrines, such as the guidance of the Holy Spirit and the Inner Light. Despite admonitions from George Fox and other influential Quakers, there remained a reluctance to examine the issue within the community, especially as it contributed to the group's economic prosperity.[18] There even remained a "prevalent conviction that Christianity endorsed slavery."[19]

Woolman struggled with this gap between faith and deed. He wrote in his journal, "to say we love God as unseen, and at the same time exercise cruelty toward the least creature moving by His life, was a contradiction in itself."[20] One Woolman scholar described the power of his insight:

> Such a conclusion, uncommon in the young, was doubtless the result of Woolman's knowledge that a portion of the cruelty which existed about him was embodied in the enslaving of humans and that a part of the blame for this evil originated with the religious sect to which he belonged. Slavery had become vicious before Woolman's time and the Quakers were among the religious groups whose passive attitude toward the system had encouraged its growth.[21]

With his formal education completed, Woolman took a job as a bookkeeper for a storeowner in Mount Holly, New Jersey. While Woolman found an aptitude for the work, he felt disillusioned by the idea of pursuing profit and material gain by any means.[22] He decided to look for work that was more aligned with his values, particularly after experiencing two memorable events. In one incident, his boss had enslaved a number of people from Scotland. When one man became deathly ill, Woolman was left to watch him die. The man spent his final hours feeling angry and bitter, mourning his lot in life. The encounter shook Woolman to the core.[23] In 1742, another

---

17. Hochschild, *Bury the Chains*, 2.
18. Houston, "John Woolman's Efforts," 128.
19. Houston, "John Woolman's Efforts," 126.
20. Woolman, *Journal of John Woolman*, 58.
21. Lask, "John Woolman," 33.
22. Terrell, Jr., "Public Order," 16–30.
23. Plank, "Sailing with John Woolman."

incident also proved influential. Woolman's boss asked him to prepare a Bill of Sale for an enslaved woman. He described his awkwardness thusly:

> The thing was sudden; and though I felt uneasy at the thoughts of writing an instrument of slavery for one of my fellow-creatures, yet I remembered that I was hired by the year, that it was my master who directed me to do it, and that it was an elderly man, a member of our Society, who bought her; so through weakness I gave way, and wrote it; but at the executing of it I was so afflicted in my mind, that I said before my master and the Friend that I believed slave-keeping to be a practice inconsistent with the Christian religion. This in some degree abated my uneasiness; yet, as often as I reflected seriously upon it, I thought I should have been clearer if I had desired to be excused from it, as a thing against my conscience; for such it was. Sometime after this a young man of our Society spoke to me to write a conveyance of a slave to him . . . I told him I was not easy to write it; for though many of our meeting and in other places kept slaves, I still believed the practice was not right, and desired to be excused from the writing. I spoke to him in goodwill; and he told me that keeping slaves was not altogether agreeable to his mind; but that the slave being a gift made to his wife, he had accepted her.[24]

Despite Woolman's attempt to rationalize his actions, he felt extremely guilty. Lask, a Woolman scholar, shed light on Woolman's personal development at this juncture of his life. He described how Woolman was forced to confront the dissonance he was experiencing:

> The point of the incident, however, is not that Woolman actually did take an active part in the business transaction, for he was to do this again in a last attempt to square his religion with its public conduct. It was rather that it placed the question of the moral rightness of slavery on Woolman's mind and helped him to come to a decision to actively crusade against the evil. The incident caused him to weigh carefully the persuasive arguments of his previous training and his respect for his sect against his own inner revolt at performing the duty which was asked of him. Here was the issue before him and the decision which he made after he had written the bill of sale was the beginning of the powerful motive which carried him on journeys throughout the surrounding states to speak out against the slave system."[25]

24. Woolman, *Journal of John Woolman*, 33.
25. Lask, "John Woolman," 33.

Again, Lask is helpful in describing Woolman's struggle:

> Woolman did not immediately oppose the slave system when he began to make his own way in life. Like all young men of his time he was absorbed in learning a trade which would yield him a livelihood. However, during his early employment experiences and his apprenticeship as a tailor, his attention was constantly forced to the question of slavery. During these years there were recurring incidents of torture and punishment for Negroes. Stories of these acts must have reached the ears of a young man who was becoming increasingly concerned about the Christian welfare of his fellowman. He could not reconcile these stories with his own convictions regarding the deeds which were pleasing in the sight of God.[26]

Looking for a way to resolve this tension, Woolman asked his boss, a tailor by profession, to teach him the trade so that he could start a small business. After two years as an apprentice, Woolman opened his own shop. Besides providing tailoring services, he also ran a small grocery store.

Around this same time, Woolman experienced an inner call to vocational ministry. He noted that tailoring afforded him a flexible lifestyle as an itinerant minister. As the Friends employed no paid staff, Woolman worked as a tailor to support himself. In 1746, Woolman and his friend Isaac Andrews embarked on an ambitious missionary journey through Pennsylvania, Maryland, Virginia, and the Carolinas. The trip took nearly three months and covered over 1,500 miles. During the journey, Woolman directly witnessed chattel slavery and observed how the enslaved endured physical, mental, and emotional bondage, while straddling between life and death. The experience proved transformative in at least two ways.

First, as he visited the homes, plantations, and congregations of fellow Friends, he discovered that most of them engaged in slavery. Woolman's conscience was pricked and he initiated a dialogue about the impact of slavery, hoping to gently persuade them to rethink their participation in the practice. Woolman believed that enslavement dishonored the God they professed to serve. Woolman explained his strategy:

> Two things were remarkable to me in this journey: first, in regard to my entertainment. When I ate, drank, and lodged free-cost with people who lived in ease on the hard labour of their slaves, I felt uneasy; and as my mind was inward to the Lord, I found this uneasiness return upon me, at times, through the whole visit. Where the masters bore a good share of the burden,

26. Lask, "John Woolman," 32.

and lived frugally, so that their servants were well provided for, and their labour moderate, I felt more easy; but where they lived in a costly way, and laid heavy burdens on their slaves, my exercise was often great, and I frequently had conversation with them in private concerning it.[27]

As Woolman continued his trip, a pattern soon emerged:

> [T]he private conversations which he held with slave owners were to graduate into public discussions and petitions in behalf of the enslaved; the arguments which he met were to furnish him with a better understanding of the socio-economic nature of the slave system and to provide him with strong arguments against the inevitable defenses which slaveholders were to present to him.[28]

Secondly, Woolman gained insight into how deeply slavery was embedded in the colonial economy. He grasped the difficulty enslavers faced in disentangling themselves from the system; even those who felt conflicted about their participation. More than ever, Woolman was convinced that slavery was rooted in the unfettered and unanchored pursuit of material gain, fueled by self-interest and an all-consuming desire for more. After reaching home, he reflected:

> . . . this trade of importing slaves from their native country being much encouraged amongst them, and the white people and their children so generally living without much labour, was frequently the subject of my serious thoughts. I saw in these southern provinces so many vices and corruptions, increased by this trade and this way of life, that it appeared to me as a dark gloominess hanging over the land; and though now many willingly run into it, yet in future the consequence will be grievous to posterity. I express it as it hath appeared to me, not once nor twice, but as a matter fixed on my mind.[29]

Historian Edward Baptist, in his book *The Half Has Never Been Told: Slavery and the Making of American Capitalism*, made a similar argument.[30] Through an extensive study of the narratives of the enslaved, plantation records, slavery-era newspapers, and a number of other primary sources,

---

27. Woolman, *Journal of John Woolman*, 36.
28. Lask, "John Woolman," 34–35.
29. Lask, "John Woolman," 36–37.
30. Baptist, *Half Has Never Been Told*.

he concluded that slavery was first and foremost an economic enterprise.[31] Baptist examined just how far the tentacles of enslavement extended. He asserted that industrial and economic prosperity in the centuries following the introduction of the country's original sin was literally built on the backs of an enslaved people. Woolman considered an amoralistic and unmoored pursuit of wealth to be antithetical to the foundations of Quakerism:

> Indeed, for all his obvious skills at business, Woolman spoke with the values of "competency" and the moral economy and against the emergent capitalist ethos. If Woolman saw slavery as a particular evil, and if he believed that certain forms of wages could be just, he did not view slavery as a system separate from emergent capitalism. Instead, he saw it as the excessive but not unpredictable result of that organized pursuit of wealth.[32]

Troubled by this contradiction, Woolman dedicated his life to eradicating slavery among the Quakers. His experiences converged with a "deep religious feeling to form a substantial basis for his later attacks on slavery and the slave system."[33]

THE APOSTLE OF FREEDOM

After his transformative experiences in the South, Woolman felt compelled to express his convictions in a more visible manner. The Center for Ethical Leadership defines ethical leadership as "knowing your core values and having the courage to live them in all parts of your life in service of the common good."[34] Woolman courageously dedicated himself to "purge his profession of its ideological paradoxes."[35] He employed two primary tactics in this effort, both centered on persuasion.

First, because he was a minister, Woolman composed letters that provided guidance to the Quaker community on matters of faith and practice. Similar to New Testament epistles written during the first century, these letters circulated among Friends and even beyond their community. Woolman used this platform to encourage the Society of Friends to cast off slavery and return to the core values of their faith. He composed his first letter with the support of his father Samuel, who opposed the practice. Secondly, over a

---

31. Foner, "Brutal Process."
32. Meranze, "Materializing Conscience," 72.
33. Lask, "John Woolman," 32.
34. Center for Ethical Leadership, "Concepts and Philosophies," para. 6.
35. Lask, "John Woolman," 31.

period of twenty-nine years, Woolman personally traveled to Quaker settlements throughout Pennsylvania, New Jersey, Maryland, Delaware, North Carolina, Virginia, New York, and Virginia. He spread his gospel of freedom to anyone who would listen.[36] He visited Native American communities and even made a voyage to England to minister to Quaker communities on the Continent. He also planned a trip to visit plantations in the West Indies, intending to make reparations for profits he had gained from selling sugar, rum, and molasses in his shop.[37]

During his travels, Woolman continued his practice of engaging in one-on-one dialogues. His conversations were intentional and strategic, as he challenged enslavers to reflect on the nature of the act, its impact on the enslaved, and its effect on their own lives. These dialogues planted seeds of change at an individual level. As noted by one Woolman scholar,

> And as he pushed for social change, he usually worked outside the main channels of the social and political structure, preferring instead to promote his ideas either on the institutional level with the Society of Friends, or in one-on-one encounters as he traveled in the Friends ministry.[38]

As Woolman put these persuasion-based strategies into action, little did he realize how his leadership would prove remarkably fruitful in changing the status quo.[39]

In the summer of 1749, Woolman married Sarah Ellis. They had two children, only one of whom survived beyond infancy. His father Samuel passed away one year later. He described how his father helped him cultivate an ethic of compassion and empathy as he "often endeavoured to imprint in our minds the true principles of virtue, and particularly to cherish in us a spirit of tenderness, not only towards poor people, but also towards all creatures of which we had the command."[40]

In 1753, Woolman was presented with another opportunity to stand up for his values. An enslaver who had fallen gravely ill approached Woolman about drafting his last will and testament. He wanted to ensure that those he had enslaved would be transferred to his children. Despite the fact that the job would pay well, and an innate desire to avoid conflict, Woolman declined the offer:

---

36. Stewart, "John Woolman's 'Kindness Beyond Expression,'" 263.
37. Plank, "Sailing with John Woolman," 52, 71.
38. Terrell, Jr., "John Woolman," 24.
39. Houston, "John Woolman's Efforts," 126.
40. Woolman, *Journal of John Woolman*, 40.

> I told the man that I believed the practice of continuing slavery to this people was not right, and that I had a scruple in my mind against doing writings of that kind; that though many in our Society kept them as slaves, still I was not easy to be concerned in it, and desired to be excused from going to write the will. I spake to him in the fear of the Lord, and he made no reply to what I said, but went away; he also had some concerns in the practice, and I thought he was displeased with me. In this case I had fresh confirmation that acting contrary to present outward interest, from a motive of divine love and in regard to truth and righteousness, and thereby incurring the resentments of people, opens the way to a treasure better than silver, and to a friendship exceeding the friendship of men.[41]

Though Woolman's refusal to fulfill a fellow Quaker's last request placed him at risk for social ostracism, he considered his personal integrity more valuable than any material or social benefit he might have gained. He described the conflict in his journal from the perspective of a business owner:

> Tradesmen and retailers of goods, who depend on their business for a living, are naturally inclined to keep the good-will of their customers; nor is it a pleasant thing for young men to be under any necessity to question the judgment or honesty of elderly men, and more especially of such as have a fair reputation. Deep-rooted customs, though wrong, are not easily altered; but it is the duty of all to be firm in that which they certainly know is right for them.

The decision emboldened Woolman to act courageously in other matters. During another incident, an elderly and well-respected Friend asked Woolman to draft his will. As he gathered information, Woolman discovered that the man had enslaved several people, including young children. Woolman told the man,

> I then said, 'I cannot write thy will without breaking my own peace,' and respectfully gave him my reasons for it. He signified that he had a choice that I should have written it, but as I could not, consistently with my conscience, he did not desire it, and so he got it written by some other person.[42]

---

41. Woolman, *Journal of John Woolman*, 41.
42. Woolman, *Journal of John Woolman*, 44.

A few years later, the man approached Woolman again, hoping that he had a change of heart. Woolman took the opportunity to engage in a persuasive dialogue. This time, the results were transformative, "We had much friendly talk on the subject, and then deferred it. A few days after he came again and directed their freedom, and I then wrote his will."[43]

In another instance, Woolman was asked to compose the will of a Quaker suffering from a life-threatening injury. As the process unfolded, Woolman discovered the man had enslaved a person whom he intended to transfer to his children. Considering the man was near death, Woolman wrote his will—with one exception. He explained,

> I considered the pain and distress he was in, and knew not how it would end, so I wrote his will, save only that part concerning his slave, and carrying it to his bedside, read it to him. I then told him in a friendly way that I could not write any instruments by which my fellow-creatures were made slaves, without bringing trouble on my own mind. I let him know that I charged nothing for what I had done, and desired to be excused from doing the other part in the way he proposed. We then had a serious conference on the subject; at length, he agreeing to set her free, I finished his will.[44]

Woolman held many similar discussions within the Society of Friends. During these conversations, he employed persuasion, rather than coercion or confrontation. When he was met with excuses and rationalizations, he skillfully answered each objection. For example, when one man tried to argue that slavery provided a "better life" for the enslaved, Woolman responded that if compassion was the underlying motive for enslavement, Friends should act with a "spirit of tenderness [treating them] as strangers brought out of affliction" rather than enslaving them.[45] When he was confronted by a member of a local militia who described the enslaved as lazy, Woolman challenged the man to consider how such a notion squared with the privileges he enjoyed, which included the unfettered ability to start his own business. The enslaved, however, were condemned to a lifetime of bondage and exploitation with no hope of freedom.

Woolman's aim through these discussions was to arouse a sense of awareness and empathy. One historian described how Woolman set aside time to study the nature of the slave trade in order to learn about the "process of capture, shipment, and sale. He then drove home the point that a

---

43. Woolman, *Journal of John Woolman*, 44.
44. Woolman, *Journal* of *John Woolman*, 44.
45. Houston, "John Woolman's Efforts," 131.

person who enslaved others was guilty of contributing to that very system."[46] Between 1754 and 1758, Woolman traveled widely throughout the colonies hoping to persuade the Society of Friends to reflect on their participation in the cruel practice:

> During these years Woolman made many journeys to communities of Friends and everywhere he introduced the story of the slave, of human equality, and of the dangers which neglect and delay in eliminating the system held for the sect. Everywhere he argued and pleaded and cajoled and implored, in public and in private, in general debate and in conversational disputation. He considered and answered social arguments, economic arguments, religious arguments, arguments which belittled the Negro and arguments which sought to extenuate the complicity and guilt of the Friends.... Woolman did not seek at one stroke to bring to an end the system which he had come to hate. It is to his credit that he did not allow his preoccupation with the abolition of the slaves to blind him to the necessity for bringing slaveholders to a voluntary recognition that the system was wrong. He sought to open the minds of his hearers to the fact that the spirit in which the slave traffic was stopped was equal in importance to the stoppage itself.[47]

Woolman backed up his words with powerful actions. For example, members of Quaker congregations provided free room and board to itinerant ministers during their travels. During his journeys through Pennsylvania, Maryland, Virginia, and North Carolina, however, Woolman refused to stay in the homes of any Friend who practiced the trade. He explained that he did not want to bring more work upon the enslaved by his presence.[48] Woolman requested that any funds that would have gone toward meeting his expenses be distributed to the enslaved within a household so they could use the money as they saw fit. Woolman even carried coins to ensure his request was fulfilled.[49] He was firm in his resolve that,

> if he in any way benefited from the oppression of others, then he was guilty of condoning that oppression. For this reason, he refused to use products gained from slave labor or to benefit

---

46. Moulton, "John Woolman," 86.
47. Lask, "John Woolman," 36–37.
48. Meranze, "Materializing Conscience," 72.
49. Plank, "Sailing with John Woolman," 58.

from the services rendered by slaves unless he was allowed to offer suitable recompense.[50]

Though the decision was inconvenient, Woolman's actions provided a platform to engage in a dialogue around the effects of slavery:

> Soon after I entered this province, a deep and painful exercise came upon me, which I often had some feeling of since my mind was drawn toward these parts, and with which I had acquainted my brother before we agreed to join as companions. As the people in this and the Southern Provinces live much on the labour of slaves, many of whom are used hardly, my concern was that I might attend with singleness of heart to the voice of the true Shepherd, and be so supported as to remain unmoved at the faces of men. As it is common for Friends on such a visit to have entertainment free of cost, a difficulty arose in my mind with respect to saving my money by kindness received from what appeared to me to be the gain of oppression. Receiving a gift, considered as a gift, brings the receiver under obligations to the benefactor, and has a natural tendency to draw the obliged into a party with the giver.[51]

Woolman explained, "Conduct is more convincing than language, and where people, by their actions, manifest that the slave-trade is not so disagreeable to their principles but that it may be encouraged, there is not a sound uniting with some Friends who visit them."[52] Similarly, when planning his trip to the West Indies, Woolman insisted on paying above the standard fare: "He reasoned that the price of travel to the West Indies was artificially low—because of the oppression upon which it was based—and that consequently the only morally acceptable way to travel was not to benefit from this debasement."[53]

Soon, Woolman's private conversations evolved into public discussions on behalf of the enslaved, often in the form of his powerful letters.[54] Woolman's first letter, considered one his most influential, was distributed throughout the Quaker community in 1754; it was written in the wake of his first trip through the South. Titled *Some Considerations on the Keeping of Negroes Recommended to the Professors of Christianity of Every Denomination*, the letter focused on the brotherhood of humanity and the

50. Terrell, Jr., "John Woolman," 25.
51. Woolman, *Journal of John Woolman*, 52.
52. Woolman, *Journal of John Woolman*, 52.
53. Meranze, "Materializing Conscience," 71–72.
54. Lask, "John Woolman," 34.

centrality of the Golden Rule to faith and practice. Woolman wrote, "All men by nature are equally entitled to the equity of the Golden Rule, and under indispensable obligations to it."[55] The letter "brings together his two great themes of economic justice and slavery, demonstrating that the two are in fact a single issue: slavery, like other social evils, finds its beginnings in the economic choices of individuals."[56] Woolman specifically highlighted Friends' participation in the slave trade, asking them to consider whether it was incompatible with their religious principles. Accordingly, "Woolman felt keenly the injustice of his own religious group in its apparent sanction of slavery and he conceived his first duty as winning his group to the side of right.[57]

Over a number of years, Woolman patiently laid the groundwork for the "legitimate consideration of the question of slavery by the [Quaker] Yearly Meeting of 1758, which marked the real beginning of a sectarian movement against the slave trade."[58] Eminent abolitionist John Greenleaf Whittier described the gathering as "one of the most important convocations in the history of the Christian church"[59] Woolman engaged in silent prayer throughout the meeting. His leadership had such a pervasive influence that a petition was forwarded without him having to say a word:

> But when, towards the close of the meeting, the subject of slavery was brought up, he took such an active part in the discussion that he dominated that part of the meeting. His remarks were simple but impressive. The effect was so immediate that many slaveholders expressed a desire to pass a rule to treat as offenders Friends who in the future bought slaves.[60]

This remarkable turn of events was followed by the creation of a committee whose members would personally visit Friends throughout the colonies in order engage in a dialogue around the slave trade. Woolman was asked to be a member. His blueprint of persuasion would be the template to launch a "community-to-community and person-to-person mission to advocate the abolition of slavery within the church"[61] This effort was the first major push towards the abolition of slavery within the Society of Friends.[62]

55. Houston, "John Woolman's Efforts," 130.
56. Jolliff, "Economy of the Inward Life," 105.
57. Lask, "John Woolman," 35.
58. Lask, "John Woolman," 37.
59. Houston, "John Woolman's Efforts," 134.
60. Woodson, *Journal of Negro History*, 134.
61. Lask, "John Woolman," 37.
62. Houston, "John Woolman's Efforts," 134.

A number of logistical and psychological barriers had to be overcome if this audacious goal was to be accomplished. First, the group realized that it would take a number of years to visit any significant number of Quaker slaveholders. Secondly, the economic benefits derived from the system of slavery could not be ignored. "[I]t was by no means easy to persuade slaveholders to give up a possession which meant so much to them in power and wealth."[63] Finally, given the nature of change, self-interest would prove to be a powerful factor. Each of these concerns would need to be addressed if the denomination as a whole were to reject slavery.

While any type of change initiative can be challenging, culture change is notoriously difficult. Successful change agents, however, anticipate opposition. They take time to understand the reasons behind resistance and empathize with the concerns of the parties involved, which is not the same as agreeing. Common reasons for resisting change include self-interest, fear of loss, a lack of understanding, trust deficits, concerns about an uncertain future, and conflicting perspectives and goals.[64] Nevertheless, Woolman remained hopeful. He described his efforts in his journal:

> In the beginning of the twelfth month, I joined in company with my friends John Sykes and Daniel Stanton, in visiting such as had slaves. Some whose hearts were rightly exercised about them appeared to be glad of our visit, but in some places our way was more difficult. I often saw the necessity of keeping down to that root from whence our concern proceeded and have cause in reverent thankfulness humbly to bow down before the Lord, who was near to me, and preserved my mind in calmness under some sharp conflicts, and begat a spirit of sympathy and tenderness in me towards some who were grievously entangled by the spirit of this world.[65]

During the Yearly Meeting of 1759, Woolman was rewarded for his efforts when "it was recommended to Friends to labour against buying and keeping slaves."[66]

In order to maintain momentum, Woolman published the second half of his pamphlet in 1762. He issued another clarion call for freedom, equality, and justice. The Society of Friends offered to print and distribute the communiqué free of charge. Woolman turned down their offer and published it at his own expense, citing two reasons. First, some of the money for

63. Houston, "John Woolman's Efforts," 135.
64. Daft, *Management*, 367–368.
65. Woolman, *Journal of John Woolman*, 70.
66. Woolman, *Journal of John Woolman*, 71.

the pamphlet would have come from those engaged in the very practice he opposed. Secondly, he embraced the principle that an "exchange economy is more effective for spreading the truth than a gift economy."[67] He wanted the letter to be read by those genuinely invested in the issue:

> "[such] are not likely to be satisfied with such books being spread among a people, especially at their own expense, many of whose slaves are taught to read, and, such receiving them as a gift, often conceal them. But as they who make a purchase generally buy that which they have a mind for, I believe it best to sell them expecting by that means they would more generally be read with attention.[68]

And so, the second part of Woolman's essay was published and he continued to plant the seeds of change.

WOOLMAN'S VISION FOR CHANGE

Woolman's work as a change agent was grounded in a spiritual and ethical worldview. Three foundational notions formed the core of his convictions, including the transcendence of God, fraternal equality, and the transformation of society.[69] Taken together, these principles shaped his understanding and motivated his actions.

Woolman believed that God intended for all people to live in harmony and equality.[70] According to one historian, while most social theorists of his day derived their arguments for social reform based on a philosophy of human nature, Woolman began by "considering the nature of God, assuming that if there is, in fact, a perfect social order, it would be an obvious extension of God's holy plan for mankind."[71] Woolman sought to align humanity with the unchanged plan of a transcendent God before whom all people stood equally loved. Notably, he extended this idea beyond his own race and region: "What was true for one person was true for another, for everyone's citizenship was ultimately in the kingdom of God whose unqualified love was the possession of no one group."[72] Central to

---

67. Meranze, "Materializing Conscience," 76.
68. Houston, "John Woolman's Efforts," 136.
69. Christian, "Inwardness and Outward Concerns."
70. Christian, "Inwardness and Outward Concerns," 92.
71. Terrell, Jr., "John Woolman," 23.
72. Terrell, Jr., "John Woolman," 18–19.

his worldview was the belief that oppression, in any form, was inconsistent with God's character. For Woolman,

> Fraternity [was] incompatible with domination or submission. It seemed to Woolman a contradiction to say that men are brothers and at the same time tolerate either slavery or, as put it, "more refined" forms of oppression. Human brotherhood was more than a "spiritual" principle according to which inequities are transcended and need not be transformed. Fraternity and equality belong together.[73]

Woolman also believed that in order for faith to be meaningful, it must be radically practical, "For Woolman, the inner religious experience was not an end in itself, but rather was the beginning of pure wisdom from which one learned how to proceed in daily affairs as he interacted with other men and social institutions."[74] Woolman did not take a potluck-type approach to his faith, where he embraced certain truths he agreed with and left others aside. "Woolman's theology provided the foundation for his unique interpretation of the social, or public, order in such a way that separating his social from his religious views is usually not possible."[75] Woolman strived to put feet to his faith. For example, when he learned that sugar and molasses were products of slave labor, he refused to use or sell those products in his store.

Woolman was convinced that he could participate in the transformation of the world.[76] According to one scholar, when Woolman's small business became more profitable than anticipated, he sold it so he could live a more unencumbered life. He rearranged his economic life by taking on more work as a tailor, drafting wills, leases, deeds, and other contracts, and working as a surveyor. He even raised pigs, planted an orchard, and refused to wear any dyed clothing—all in an effort to distance himself from anything related to maritime businesses which relied on slave labor. He intended to make sure his "subsistence was on a more righteous footing."[77] His actions were an expansion of an earlier decision he had taken as a business owner when he

> abandoned the rum trade as part of a broad renunciation of unnecessary commerce, but given the timing of his decision and

---

73. Christian, "Inwardness and Outward Concerns," 100.
74. Terrell, Jr., "John Woolman," 21.
75. Terrell, Jr., "John Woolman," 17.
76. Christian, "Inwardness and Outward Concerns," 94.
77. Plank, "Sailing with John Woolman," 59. See also Davis, "Connatural Ground of John Woolman's Triangle," 137.

the trajectory of his life as a writer and a traveling Quaker minister, sugar, molasses and rum carried special significance. They were, and were increasingly recognized as being, 'fruits of the labor of slaves.' Since the seventeenth century various Quaker Meetings and individuals had argued that enslavement was a form of theft, and that those who benefited from the slave trade were in effect receiving stolen goods and guilty of larceny.[78]

Though Woolman was on track to become exceedingly wealthy, he chose to "claim an alternative identity."[79] He believed that a loving Creator had ensured the natural sustenance of the world and that transforming those resources into "usable goods required exactly the amount of labor that would be in each person's best interest, and that if all people used exactly what they needed and no more, everyone could live comfortably."[80] Woolman believed that any imbalance was due to an "elevation of self and personal concerns above the needs and concerns of others."[81] For Woolman, wealth was not an end in itself, but rather "our progress in this land was to prepare a people for more fruitful returns."[82]

A number of historians have noted that empathy was one of Woolman's strongest character traits.[83] For example, though he was not particularly physically strong, he often chose to walk rather than ride a horse in order to better identify with the sufferings of the less privileged.[84] During his travels, he slept on forest floors and in fields: "Discounting his own death led to empathy across color lines."[85] One historian noted that,

> [d]eep sensitivity to individual and social needs was Woolman's most salient characteristic. He had remarkable empathy—the capacity to participate in the feelings and ideas of another individual. He welcomed, and sometimes deliberately sought, experiences which would increase the range and depth of his empathy with those who suffered. When he journeyed through wilderness to visit the Indians, he encountered dangers of war, innumerable hardships, including treacherous swamps,

78. Plank, "Sailing with John Woolman," 55.
79. Stewart, "John Woolman's 'Kindness Beyond Expression,'" 253.
80. Jolliff, "Economy of the Inward Life," 97.
81. Terrell, Jr., "John Woolman," 26.
82. Christian, "Inwardness and Outward Concerns," 98.
83. Stewart, "John Woolman's 'Kindness Beyond Expression,'" 268.
84. Plank, "Flame of Life," 571. See also Stewart, "John Woolman's 'Kindness Beyond Expression,'" 262; Christian, "Inwardness and Outward Concerns," 89; Moulton, "John Woolman," 84; Houston, "John Woolman's Efforts" 129.
85. Stewart, "John Woolman's 'Kindness Beyond Expression,'" 264.

extremely rugged terrain, and rattlesnakes. For this he was 'Thankful to God, who thus led about and instructed me, that I might have a quick and lively feeling of the afflictions of my fellow creatures whose situation in life is difficult.' When Woolman visited slaveholders and Quaker meetings in the South, he often traveled in the hot sun on horseback in order to understand better the condition of oppressed slaves.[86]

Woolman saw the consequences of the slave trade with clarity and believed it dehumanized both enslaved and enslaver:

> Oppression is bad for the oppressor as well as for the oppressed, and Woolman observed its results on both. Those who live on the labor of others grow sluggish or seek false pleasures. But 'Man is born to labour, and experience abundantly showeth that it is for our Good.' What is more important, when one man treats another 'otherwise than a free man' the springs of his own humanity are obstructed.[87]

Woolman asserted, "Thus it is observable that the effects of oppression, both on the oppressed and on the oppressors, are evil. He who dominates another is thereby dehumanized."[88] He noted how it also sent a message to future generations that oppression was justified and the "consequence would be grievous to posterity."[89] These foundational convictions inspired Woolman to pursue a path of persuasion and dialogue. He believed that "if through reason or rhetorical question, he could enable someone else to empathize with those of less fortunate circumstance, that person would then treat others in a more concerned fashion."[90]

In 1772, Woolman traveled to England to share his message of freedom with Friends on the British Isles. Upon disembarking from the ship, he headed straight to the Yearly Meeting. Even though he presented to the local congregation his certificate from Friends in America, his "peculiar dress and manner excited attention and apprehension."[91] After spending most of the meeting listening, Woolman shared his message of freedom. He also requested assistance in securing work during his visit so as not to burden anyone with his living expenses. After he finished his sermon, "All doubt was removed; there was a general expression of unity and sympathy, and

---

86. Moulton, "John Woolman," 83–84.
87. Christian, "Inwardness and Outward Concerns," 101.
88. Christian, "Inwardness and Outward Concerns," 102.
89. Woolman, *Journal of John Woolman*, 37.
90. Terrell, Jr., "John Woolman," 22, 102.
91. Houston, "John Woolman's Efforts," 137.

John Woolman, owned by his brethren, passed on to his work."[92] He spoke at a number of gatherings in and around London during his trip. During a trip to York, Woolman was struck with smallpox and passed away.[93] On his deathbed he was "willing to take medicine only 'if it did not come through defiled channels or oppressive hands.' He wanted to be sure the ingredients were not the products of slave labor or other unjust conditions."[94]

THE ENDURING IMPACT OF JOHN WOOLMAN

It has been said that Woolman's only sermon was the Golden Rule, "Do unto others as you would have them do unto you."[95] Through dialogue, personal integrity, and faithfulness to the Inward Light, Woolman served as the conscience of his community and persuaded "the American Quaker to wrestle with the problem of social responsibility in a soul-searching way."[96] Woolman's impact was so influential that during the 1776 Quarterly Meeting in Philadelphia, four years after his death, the denomination formally agreed to "deny the right of membership to such as persisted in holding their fellowmen as property" and declared slaveholding an offense against Christianity.[97]

In 1790, a Quaker delegation from Philadelphia, which included Benjamin Franklin, sent a petition to Congress requesting an end to enslavement and the trafficking of the enslaved. The group petitioned to "devise means for removing the Inconsistency from the Character of the American People and to promote mercy and justice toward this distressed Race."[98] Through the influence of Woolman's servant-leadership, the Quakers would "peacefully, gradually, and voluntarily" eradicate enslavement within their denomination.[99]

Woolman's legacy extended far beyond The Society of Friends. Quaker scholar Philips Moulton, in a wide-ranging study of Woolman's life, described how he directly impacted the anti-slavery movement as a whole. Woolman influenced leaders such as Samuel Taylor Coleridge, George

---

92. Houston, "John Woolman's Efforts," 137.
93. Houston, "John Woolman's Efforts," 137.
94. Moulton, "John Woolman," 89.
95. Houston, "John Woolman's Efforts," 136.
96. Christian, "Inwardness and Outward Concerns," 97.
97. Davis, "Connatural Ground of John Woolman's Triangle," 135. See also, Houston, "John Woolman's Efforts."
98. "Benjamin Franklin's Anti-Slavery Petitions," para. 2.
99. See Nielsen, "Quaker Foundations," 132.

Willoughby, William Lloyd Garrison, John Greenleaf Whittier, Henry Thoreau, and Theodore Dreiser, shaping the thought and practice of abolitionists and social reformers alike. Ralph Waldo Emerson, during a speech on abolition, credited Woolman for inspiring the movement.[100] Woolman's writings were also read throughout England, France, and Russia. Particularly relevant to the other servant-leaders described in this book is Woolman's chain of influence:

> [T]oday, one senses a link between Woolman's ideas and the famed underground movement, the Emancipation Proclamation, the civil rights movement, including the doctrine of nonviolence as well as the recent riots in major American Cities.[101]

Moulton eloquently described the enduring impact of Woolman's life thusly:

> The insights of Woolman are especially needed in the late twentieth century, to point up moral realities which are too often obscured. What, in essence, does he say to us? To a callous age he exemplifies sensitivity and sympathy. To the one inclined to subordinate his conscience to superior officer or employer, he urges personal responsibility to one's conscience, to society, and to God. To the person who sees only immediate results, he reveals the ramifications and interconnections of our separate acts. To those intent only upon sensory satisfactions, he advocates simple living and the claim of one's neighbor. To the sophisticate who shifts his course to suit the situation he provides an instance of humility and integrity. To the fanatic he provides an antidote of balance and perspective. To an age of relativism, beset by anxiety and saturated with violence, he writes of moral law, truth, harmony, love, and ultimate security.[102]

THE SERVANT-LEADER AS PERSUADER: WHAT MIGHT HAVE BEEN AND WHAT COULD BE

As a member of the Religious Society of Friends, the leadership of John Woolman profoundly impacted Robert Greenleaf. He noted, "His method was unique. He didn't raise a big storm about it or start a protest movement.

---

100. Moulton, "Influence of the Writings of John Woolman," 11.
101. Davis, "Connatural Ground of John Woolman's Triangle," 135.
102. Moulton, "Influence of the Writings of John Woolman," 13.

His method was one of gentle but clear and persistent persuasion."[103] Greenleaf summarized Woolman's change strategy thusly:

> The approach was not to censure the slaveholders in a way that drew their animosity. Rather, the burden of his approach was to raise questions: What does the owning of slaves do to you as a moral person? What kind of an institution are you binding over to your children? Man by man, inch by inch, by persistently returning and revisiting and pressing his gentle arguments over a period of thirty year, the scourge of slavery was eliminated from this Society, the first religious group in America formally to denounce and forbid slavery among its members.[104]

In view of Woolman's servant-leadership, Greenleaf posed a profound question:

> One wonders what would have been the result if there had been fifty John Woolmans, or even five, traveling the length and breadth of the Colonies in the eighteenth-century *persuading* people one by one with gentle non-judgmental argument that a wrong should be righted by individual voluntary action. Perhaps we would not have had the war with six hundred thousand casualties and the impoverishment of the South, and with the resultant vexing social problem that is at fever heat one hundred years later with no end in sight.... A few John Woolmans, just a *few*, might have made the difference. Leadership by persuasion has the virtue of change by convincement rather than coercion. Its advantages are obvious.[105]

Greenleaf also used Woolman's example to explain the advantage of persuasion over coercion and manipulation. Coercion sends the message, "Do as I say, think as I do, speak as I wish—or else!" while a leader who manipulates guides people "into beliefs or actions that they do not fully understand and that may or may not be good for them."[106] A fundamental difference between the two approaches is the notion of control. Leaders want to be "in control"—controlling information, decisions, jobs, and people. Being "out of control" feels disconcerting and disorienting. The danger, however, is that we end up confusing control with leadership.

---

103. Greenleaf, *Servant Leadership: A Journey*, 29.
104. Greenleaf, *Servant Leadership: A Journey*, 29–30.
105. Greenleaf, *Servant Leadership: A Journey*, 30 (emphasis original).
106. Greenleaf, *On Becoming a Servant Leader*, 130.

Ultimately, leadership is not about control, but influence. Persuasion is about "arriving at a feeling of rightness about belief or action through one's own intuitive sense."[107] It provides followers with a chance to take an intuitive leap "untrampled by coercive or manipulative stratagems of any kind."[108] Persuasive leadership helps a person "make decisions that enhance themselves and others."[109] Through this approach, followers are "guided along in the decision-making process without losing their autonomy."[110] Greenleaf described persuasion as

> the critical skill of servant leadership. Such a leader is one who ventures and takes the risks of going out ahead to show the way and whom others follow, voluntarily, because they are persuaded that the leader's path is the right one—for them, probably better than they could devise for themselves.[111]

Servant-leaders seek to convince and build consensus, "Poor leaders coerce others. Great leaders persuade, through a way of being that involves humility, grace, common sense, and good direction. Persuasion engages others in dialogue that leads to the greater good of humanity."[112]

It is important to understand, especially in our quick-fix culture, that persuasion rarely means walking the path of least resistance. The servant-leader is prepared for the long haul as she understands that enduring change requires that people are willingly convinced, rather than forced by fiat. According to Greenleaf, persuasion is a "difficult, time-consuming process. It demands one of the most exacting of human skills."[113] He described it as a "slow, deliberate, painstaking process."[114] He was convinced, however, that persuasion provided the most "reasonable and realistic tool for institutional and social change."[115] Persuasion offers hope in addressing the challenges of our age:

> John Woolman exerted leadership in an age that must have looked as dark to him as ours does to us today. We may easily write off his effort as a suggestion for today on the assumption

---

107. Greenleaf, *On Becoming a Servant Leader*, 129.
108. Greenleaf, *On Becoming a Servant Leader*, 129.
109. Paul et al., "Advising as Servant Leadership," 54.
110. Paul et al., "Advising as Servant Leadership," 54.
111. Greenleaf, *Power of Servant-Leadership*, 44.
112. Ferch, *Forgiveness and Power*, xi.
113. Greenleaf, *On Becoming a Servant Leader*, 129.
114. Greenleaf, *On Becoming a Servant Leader*, 139.
115. Greenleaf, *On Becoming a Servant Leader*, 103.

that the Quakers were ethically conditioned for this approach. All persons are so conditioned, to some extent—enough to gamble on.[116]

Greenleaf also highlighted Woolman's personal integrity as vital to his success. Woolman took great pains to distance himself from any potential material, financial, or social benefit he might have derived from slavery. He did so in order to maintain a clear conscience and an unimpeachable testimony before those he was attempting to persuade. Greenleaf explained, "The persuader, in my view, approaches the relationship with clean hands, just as the man of peace does not bear arms when confronting one who is armed."[117] The power of Woolman's message was backed up by his example. He set aside the comforts of wealth and power in order to pursue his inner call. While one might have rejected Woolman's message, it was impossible to deny the life that backed up his message.

PUTTING PERSUASION INTO ACTION

Greenleaf offered specific guidelines for servant-leaders who are "dedicated to the exclusive use of persuasion as a means for social change."[118] First, they "create and maintain a clear space" between themselves and anyone who would use coercion in any form, knowingly or unknowingly, and regardless of degree. Secondly, servant-leaders never reject the people they are attempting to persuade. Instead, they engage "person-by-person, first to restrain their coercive tendencies, and then, if possible, to move them across the gap that separates those who use coercion in any form from those who only use persuasion."[119] Thirdly, servant-leaders engage in a practice of reflection and introspection so they can recognize the "intricate web of institutions in which most of us are enmeshed and in which coercion is rampant."[120] Finally, servant-leaders "learn to respect the integrity and autonomy of those whom one would persuade. Approach the relationship with the attitude of acceptance that oneself, the persuader, may change."[121]

116. Greenleaf, *Servant Leadership: A Journey*, 31.
117. Greenleaf, *On Becoming a Servant Leader*, 139.
118. Greenleaf, *On Becoming a Servant Leader*, 143.
119. Greenleaf, *On Becoming a Servant Leader*, 143.
120. Greenleaf, *On Becoming a Servant Leader*, 143.
121. Greenleaf, *On Becoming a Servant Leader*, 143.

Greenleaf developed a specific model of persuasion based directly on Woolman's practice. He called it "friendly disentangling."[122] During his tenure at AT&T as a trainer, manager, and executive in charge of talent management, Greenleaf taught and applied this method. He used it, for example, to strengthen the organization's diversity efforts. Nielsen, in an insightful exposition of the Quaker foundations of Greenleaf's servant-leadership, described his model:[123]

1. Frame to oneself a "we" fellowship relationship with others and look for the source of current problematic behavior within the biases of an embedded tradition rather than solely in the behaviors and governing values of individuals.
2. Approach those involved in a friendly manner.
3. Ask for help in disentangling a problematic behavior from potential biases within "our" embedded tradition system.
4. Work with those who are agreeable to experiment with alternative behaviors and/or governing values that do not rest on the troublesome biases of the tradition system.

Nielsen described Greenleaf's approach as a "triple-loop-action-learning" framework that scrutinizes 1) the legitimacy of behaviors, 2) core values driving those behaviors, and 3) the "embedded tradition systems" where those behaviors rest. He explained that

> the social tradition is both criticized and treated as partner in action-learning. The tradition system is respected but also considered to have potential negative biases that can be reformed and transformed, just as individuals and their governing values can be reformed and transformed.[124]

One can see how Greenleaf integrated Woolman's approach in his model. In the fourth step, for example, Woolman worked to free a number of enslaved men and women and provide them with sharecropping opportunities. The productivity of the emancipated was significantly higher than those who were enslaved.[125] In each step, a leader's attitude and approach

---

122. See Nielsen, "Quaker Foundations," 127. Nielsen cited four foundational principles: (1) G(o)od in everyone in our "prior we" relationship, (2) tradition system entanglements as causes of problems rather than solely individual responsibility, (3) friendly and cheerful affect, and (4) continuing experimental action-learning.
123. See Nielsen, "Quaker Foundations," 127.
124. See Nielsen, "Quaker Foundations," 128.
125. See Nielsen, "Quaker Foundations," 134.

makes all the difference.[126] Notably, the other characteristics of servant-leadership, such as listening, empathy, awareness, and the others, are also evident in Greenleaf's method.

Greenleaf was confident that if our current generation of leaders put persuasion into practice, they hold the potential to make a real difference in the world. "[O]ne able and dedicated persuader, standing alone, can be powerful."[127] A reporter once asked Mahatma Gandhi, "What is your message to humanity?" He responded, "My life is my message." The same could be said of John Woolman.[128]

FINDING: PERSUASION

Servant-leaders pursue persuasion over pressure. They choose consensus over coercion. Persuasion requires respecting the autonomy and agency of others as they encounter change. Perhaps they need more information. Maybe they need their concerns acknowledged and an assurance of support. Enduring change rarely happens through logic alone. Present a higher vision of what's possible and then engage the wings of head and heart. And above all, be ready to listen.

---

126. Greenleaf, *On Becoming a Servant Leader*, 134.
127. Greenleaf, *On Becoming a Servant Leader*, 148.
128. Reddy, *Mahatma Gandhi Letters to Americans*, 5.

6

Mahatma Gandhi: The Servant-Leader and Conceptualization

SOME OF THE WORLD'S greatest discoveries have been preceded by unexpected bursts of insight. For example, Isaac Newton's law of gravity, Albert Einstein's theory of general relativity, Alexander Fleming's discovery of penicillin, Paul McCartney's song "Yesterday," and even Spencer Silver's invention of the Post-it Note are said to have been the result of "Eureka!" moments. According to Kounios and Beeman, "Sudden comprehension that solves a problem, reinterprets a situation, explains a joke, or resolves an ambiguous percept is called an insight (i.e., the "Aha! moment")."[1] The "Eureka!" phrase originates from a story about the ancient Greek mathematician Archimedes who, while taking a bath one evening, discovered the law of buoyancy. The insight proved so powerful that he leapt out of his tub and ran naked down the street shouting *"Eureka!"* or, "I have found it!"[2]

For Mahatma Gandhi his "Eureka!" moment appeared aboard a train hissing and huffing its way across South Africa. The passage from Durban to Pretoria proved to be the genesis of his historic role as leader of the Indian independence movement.

In this chapter we explore conceptualization, the sixth characteristic of servant-leadership, through the leadership of Mahatma Gandhi. Larry Spears defined conceptualization in the following way:

1. Kounios and Beeman, "Aha! Moment," 210.
2. Leslie, "Eureka Moment," 1219.

> Servant-leaders seek to nurture their abilities to dream great dreams. The ability to look at a problem or an organization from a conceptualizing perspective means that one must think beyond day-to-day realities. For many leaders, this is a characteristic that requires discipline and practice. The traditional leader is consumed by the need to achieve short-term operational goals. The leader who wishes also to be a servant-leader must stretch his or her thinking to encompass broader-based conceptual thinking. . . . Servant-leaders are called to seek a delicate balance between conceptual thinking and a day-to-day operational approach.[3]

Conceptual thinking allows servant-leaders to see the forest for the trees. It provides the view they need to chart a course, bridging the present and the future. According to Greenleaf, "Conceptualizers are intensely practical. They are also effective persuaders and relations builders."[4] In this chapter, we examine three ways that Gandhi demonstrated conceptual thinking as a servant-leader. We begin by exploring how Gandhi conceptualized the problem of leading the Indian independence movement. We then consider how he conceptualized his leadership response against the powerful British Empire. Finally, we examine how he transformed conceptualization into action in order to lead the freedom struggle. Now, let us get back to the train ride where the seeds of Gandhi's servant-leadership were first planted.

THROW GANDHI FROM THE TRAIN

South Africa, June 7, 1893. Mohandas Karamchand Gandhi, a 24-year-old, newly minted attorney, was traveling aboard a locomotive making its way toward the Transvaal. He was preparing to serve as legal counsel for Abdulla Sheth, an Indian merchant who was in the middle of a protracted legal battle. Gandhi, who had been looking to leave India for greener pastures, accepted Sheth's offer without hesitation. After a few days in Durban, he booked a first-class train ticket to Pretoria. This was apartheid-era South Africa. The law split the population into four racial categories: White, Black, Indian, and Coloured. By this classification, Gandhi belonged in the back half of the train. A passenger, upon noticing Gandhi in the cabin, alerted officials who ordered him to move. He protested:

> 'But I have a first-class ticket!'

---

3. See Spears, "Introduction: Understanding the Growing Impact of Servant-Leadership," 18.

4. Greenleaf, *Servant Leadership: A Journey*, 66–67.

'That doesn't matter. I tell you, you must go to the van compartment.'

Gandhi replied, 'And I tell you, I was permitted to travel in this compartment at Durban, and I insist on going on in it.'

'No, you won't,' said the official. 'You must leave this compartment, or else I shall have to call a police constable to push you out.'

'Yes, you may. I refuse to get out voluntarily.'[5]

A constable arrived and threw Gandhi off the train. He recalled the humiliating incident, "I refused to go to the other compartment and the train steamed away."[6] It was winter in South Africa. Gandhi sat in the bitter cold of the Maritzburg train station, pondering his options:

> I began to think of my duty. Should I fight for my rights or go back to India, or should I go on to Pretoria without minding the insults, and return to India after finishing the case? It would be cowardice to run back to India without fulfilling my obligation. The hardship to which I was subjected was superficial—only a symptom of the deep disease of colour prejudice. I should try, if possible, to root out the disease and suffer hardships in the process. Redress for wrongs I should seek only to the extent that would be necessary for the removal of the colour prejudice. So I decided to take the next available train to Pretoria.[7]

While Gandhi waited to hear from the railway manager and Abdullah Sheth, several Indian workers shared similar stories and counseled him, "You cannot strike your head against a stone wall. But Gandhi intended to test its hardness."[8] The incident, in the unlikeliest of places, proved to be a defining moment in Gandhi's life. Indeed, it became a soul-awakening event. "Gandhi always spoke of the ensuing ordeal as the most creative passage in his whole life . . . that bitter night at Maritzburg the germ of social protest was born in Gandhi."[9] In the wake of his first act of civil disobedience, "the small, unassuming man would grow into a giant force for civil rights."[10]

As Gandhi resumed his journey, he continued to book first-class tickets whenever he arrived at a transfer station. He carefully studied the regulations and saw no legal basis for authorities to refuse his request. Whenever

---

5. Gandhi, *Autobiography*, 37.
6. Gandhi, *Autobiography*, 37.
7. Gandhi, *Autobiography*, 37.
8. Fischer, *Mahatma Gandhi*, 49.
9. Fischer, *Mahatma Gandhi*, 56.
10. "Mahatma Gandhi," para. 13.

passengers and guards attempted to prevent his seating, he simply refused to move. He would contact the stationmaster and convey his legal right to travel first-class. The authorities soon relented in the face of the young attorney's resolve. A few days later, Gandhi disembarked in Pretoria in the same manner in which he started his journey—in a first-class coach;

> So the Inner Temple Barrister reached his destination in qualified triumph. Gandhi had been frightened, but adamant—several times over. His Truth, his relentless Absolute, had taken control. He had had that experience which is occasionally given to mortals, and which Luther put in words: 'Here, I stand: so help me God, I can do no other.'[11]

Transformed by this experience, Gandhi organized a series of meetings within a week of his arrival to Pretoria. Hindus and Muslims met to strategize on how to fight the unjust laws that had become part-and-parcel of South African life. In 1894, he formed the Natal Indian Congress, an organization united against the discriminatory laws of their adopted homeland.[12] In one of their early victories, the railways agreed to ease travel conditions for Pretorian Indians.

Gandhi's early experiences in South Africa proved instructive; it was there that he formulated his philosophy of nonviolent resistance. By organizing marches, protests, and strikes, he tested his method of challenging the racist laws affecting Africans and Indians alike. Gandhi's fledgling strategy proved effective, even in the face of threats, arrests, and physical injuries. In 1914, South Africa passed the Indians' Relief Bill legalizing Indian marriages and withdrew the head tax. It was a major victory. Gandhi returned to India in hopes of applying his blueprint to the Indian freedom struggle.

Gandhi's message and methods had an enduring impact on South Africa. During his South Africa campaign, General J. C. Smuts, colonial secretary of Transvaal and a fellow attorney, served as Gandhi's counterpart in his negotiations with the government. Though positionally they were in an adversarial relationship, the two men maintained respect for one another. Before he left South Africa, Gandhi sent Smuts a pair of sandals he had made in prison. Years later, Smuts wrote, "I have worn these for many a summer, even though I may feel that I am not worthy to stand in the shoes of so great a man."[13]

11. Ashe, *Gandhi*, 51.
12. Erickson, *Gandhi's Truth*.
13. Gandhi, *Essential Gandhi*, 98.

INDIA UNDER BRITISH RULE

The British arrived in India in the mid-1600s, wooed by her natural resources and inestimable economic potential. Through economic hegemony and sheer military dominance, they established a sturdy foothold across the subcontinent. India's raw materials soon flowed throughout the British Empire via a number of unequal treaties and unfair trade practices.[14] The British also exploited the region's sociocultural diversity by fanning regional rivalries and sparking communal hostilities, executing a clever divide-and-rule strategy. By 1858, Queen Victoria assumed formal control of the subcontinent and declared India as the jewel in the crown of the British Empire. The era of British rule lasted until 1947.

Colonialism bared its ugly underbelly in several ways, including burdensome taxation, violent suppression of protests (labeled as "mutinies" or "rebellions"), and engineered famines that killed millions of people. At the beginning of the eighteenth century, India's stake in the global economy was 23 percent—as large as all of Europe combined. By the end of the British Raj, it had fallen to less than 4 percent.[15] The long-term impact of colonial rule took its toll. The 1919 Jallianwala Bagh massacre, where British soldiers fired on a group of unarmed protesters, was one of the worst atrocities committed during this era as over 400 men and women were killed during this single incident. India was at a crossroads. Prominent voices were calling for an uprising to end British occupation by any means necessary. Gandhi, understanding what was at stake, conceptualized a different path to victory. Rather than pursue violence, he sought to free India through the pillars of truth, nonviolence, and self-suffering.

GANDHI'S SERVANT-LEADERSHIP: CONCEPTUALIZING THE PROBLEM

As we study the characteristic of conceptualization in Gandhi's servant-leadership, we begin by examining how he conceptualized the freedom struggle. Gandhi's success can largely be attributed to how he framed the complex issues he faced, which in turn influenced his actions. The story of the two shoe salesmen illustrates this point.

A successful footwear entrepreneur had set his sights on global expansion. One day he asked his best salesman to visit an island to see whether it was a suitable location for his first overseas store. The salesman boarded a

---

14. Rahman et al., "British Art of Colonialism in India."
15. Tharoor, *Inglorious Empire*, 24.

plane, arrived at the locale, and headed to his hotel room. After freshening up, he hit the streets to get a sense of the place. About an hour later he called his boss and requested a plane ticket home. The boss wondered, "But why? You just got there!"

The salesman replied, "Boss, no one here wears shoes!"

Though disappointed, the savvy entrepreneur was not about to give up so easily. He sent another salesman to the same island. As soon as the second salesman arrived, he called headquarters, "Boss, send me all the product you've got!"

The boss wondered, "But why? You just got there!"

The salesman replied, "Boss, no one here wears shoes!"

In the story, both men faced the same situation, but their responses were completely different. How each salesman conceptualized the problem made the difference. In the field of negotiation, this dynamic is called framing. A frame forms the psychological backdrop against which a negotiation is managed. Gandhi applied this principle as he thoughtfully framed the freedom struggle.

In a typical negotiation, there are two main strategies one can follow. In a positional approach, the issue being negotiated is framed as a contest of wills. Here, there is only one winner and loser; the negotiation becomes a zero-sum, winner-take-all competition. In this strategy, one party takes a position, or makes an offer, and the other party responds in kind. If both agree, they have a deal. If not, one side takes a new position, as does the other. Thus, a back-and-forth process ensues, wherein each party digs in their heels in order to emerge as the last person standing.

We see this dynamic in daily life through scenarios as varied as choosing a restaurant, facing a custody battle, negotiating a salary, collective bargaining, and even international conflicts such as border disputes or nuclear inspections. Each party plants a flag and then proceeds to make a series of concessions, all the while hoping to arrive at a satisfactory answer. While this approach might work in a low-stakes negotiation, when it comes to more serious issues, outcomes rarely satisfy the long-term interests of either party. Looking back, time is wasted, gains (e.g., money) are left on the table, and feelings are hurt. The "three E's" of ego, emotion, and escalation conspire to produce unwise, inefficient, or relationship-damaging outcomes.[16]

In their classic book, *Getting to Yes: Negotiating Agreement without Giving in*, negotiation gurus Roger Fisher and William Ury of the Harvard Negotiation Project presented a different approach they called "principled negotiation." A major difference between the two strategies is how issues

---

16. Fisher et al., *Getting to Yes*, xx.

are framed. Rather than approach a negotiation as a contest of wills, Fisher and Ury recommend a four-pronged strategy: 1) Separate the people from the problem; 2) Focus on interests, rather than positions; 3) Generate a variety of possibilities; and 4) Insist that results be based on a fair standard.[17] Here, the parties work together as problem-solvers, rather than face-off as adversaries. Instead of attacking one another, they are hard on the problem. Rather than doubling down on their positions, they explore interests (i.e., the "why" behind the "what"). Finally, parties appeal to objective criteria, or a legitimate standard, in order to determine a fair outcome. At the heart of principled negotiation is framing the issue, which parallels the characteristic of conceptualization.

Communication professor Rex Mitchell used an analogy to explain the framing effect:

> Just like an artist or photographer, when we select a frame for a subject, we choose which aspects or portion of the subject we will focus on and which we will exclude. When we choose to highlight some aspect of our subject over others, we make that aspect more noticeable, more meaningful, and more memorable to others. Our framing adds emphasis or approaches the subject in unique ways. For this reason, frames determine which issues or problems people notice, how they understand and remember issues, and how they evaluate and act upon them. Frames exert their power, not only through what they emphasize, but also through what they omit. Effective framers know the perspective of their audience and take seriously the question, "For whom am I trying to manage meaning?"[18]

Framing enabled Gandhi to successfully lead the freedom movement. Rather than making the bloody overthrow of the British Empire the issue, as some of his countrymen did, he conceptualized independence as a struggle for justice and truth. As a result, the battle for freedom was to be fought using spiritual weapons (*satyagraha* or "soul-force") rather than physical violence. As noted by Varkey, "Gandhi's contribution was unique in that it offered a solution to conflicts without the use of physical force."[19]

Through the use conceptualization, servant-leaders connect their actions to a transcendent purpose.[20] According to Greenleaf, "Servant-leaders

17. Fisher et al., *Getting to Yes*, 10–11.
18. Mitchell, "'Framing' in Communications and Conflict," para. 10.
19. Varkey, "Myth and Meaning," 171.
20. See Spears, "Introduction: Understanding the Growing Impact of Servant-Leadership," 18.

seek to nurture their abilities to dream great dreams. The ability to look at a problem through conceptualization means that one thinks beyond day-to-day realities."[21] Gandhi's dream for India was *swaraj* (self-rule) and *sarvodaya* (uplift for all).[22] He sought to realize this dream by implementing three bedrock principles: *satya* (truth), *ahimsa* (nonviolence), and *tapasya* (self-suffering).[23] While an in-depth study of each concept is beyond the scope of this chapter, I will provide a brief overview of each principle as it relates to Gandhi's servant-leadership.

The word *satya*, or truth, comes from the Sanskrit word *sat* meaning "being" or "existence." Gandhi stated, "My religion is based on truth and non-violence. Truth is my God. Non-violence is the means of realising Him."[24] In Gandhi's view, a devotion to the truth was the sole reason for existence. He even titled his autobiography *My Experiments with Truth*. Gandhi considered truth to be "moral, unified, unchanging, and transcendental . . . the path of truth leads to justice."[25] Consequently, a just cause becomes a relentless pursuit of the truth.[26] Gandhi's conceptualization of truth was not just a philosophical or metaphysical concept, however. It included a moral and practical dimension. Gandhi insisted that his followers be truthful in speech, thought, and action:

> [M]ental adherence to truth is not enough, because it has to be translated into action. The idea of truth in mind must be translated into action by making actions follow truth. For Gandhi, thought, action, and speech make one unity since one is involved in the other. Therefore what is true in thought must be true in action and speech. Truth-thinking is as fundamental as truth-acting and truth-speaking.[27]

Gandhi's second conceptual pillar was *ahimsa*, which is "composed of a negative prefix 'a' and a noun 'himsa' which means 'injury.'"[28] In practice, it meant shunning all forms of violence, while simultaneously loving all beings. To Gandhi, nonviolence was more than refraining from physical hostility; it mandated a "positive love for all humanity."[29] The word *ahimsa* encompasses

21. Greenleaf, *Power of Servant-Leadership*, 6.
22. Bondurant, *Conquest of Violence*, 8.
23. Nair, *Higher Standard of Leadership*.
24. Gandhi, *Collected Works*, 61–62. See also Gandhi, *From Yeravda Mandir*, ch. 1.
25. Akella, "Satyagraha," 504.
26. Gandhi et al., *Mind of Mahatma Gandhi*, 218.
27. Pradhan, "Making Sense," 36.
28. Varkey, "Myth and Meaning," 173–74.
29. Nair, *Higher Standard of Leadership*, 20.

the notions of compassion, tolerance, benevolence, and love. Nagler, in a study of the word's etymology, described it this way: "As far as possible [we] resist wrongs without resisting people; that is, without wishing them harm or doing anything to compromise their long-term well-being and fulfillment."[30] According to Gandhi, "Love for the victim demanded struggle, while love for the opponent ruled out doing harm."[31] Gandhi was clear: "All my actions have their source in my inalienable love of humankind."[32]

Gandhi's conceptualization of *ahimsa* was influenced by Jesus' encouragement to love one's enemies. The notion of *ahimsa* also inspired another servant-leader described in this book, Dr. Martin Luther King Jr.:

> The love, as described in Gandhi's and King's non-violent philosophy, is not necessarily an affectionate or sentimental feeling, but rather goodwill and empathy towards the oppressor. This type of love, which Gandhi describes as *ahimsa*, stimulates compassion and humanity for the opponent while simultaneously harbouring resistance and passion for social justice. Activism inspired by love separates the oppressor, as a person, from oppression; it sees the oppressor equally as a victim of systems of domination.[33]

The practical outworking of *ahimsa* meant directing energy toward challenging the oppression, rather than the oppressor:

> The main goal of Gandhi and King's non-violent philosophy is to challenge systems of oppression and not necessarily those who work within the systems. . . . Gandhi and King wanted to think of a reaction to colonization and oppression that will really disturb the colonial relation, but not the colonizer and oppressor. . . . Non-violence comes from a desire not just to seek a result, but also to do it in a way that it does not reproduce violence on others.[34]

Gandhi rejected violence because he believed it "dehumanizes both the perpetrator and its victims. . . . By emulating the violent behaviour of the oppressor, she or he is becoming like the oppressor. This is why non-violent activism does not seek retaliation or any means to destroy one's opponent."[35] According to Gandhi, "The only way to conquer violence is through

---

30. Dhiman, *Gandhi and Leadership*, 120.
31. Shepard, *Mahatma Gandhi and His Myths*, 36.
32. Shepard, *Mahatma Gandhi and His Myths*, 36.
33 Adjei, "Non-Violent Philosophy," 94–95.
34 Adjei, "Non-Violent Philosophy," 91.
35 Adjei, "Non-Violent Philosophy," 95.

non-violence, pure and undefiled."[36] The litmus test was "action based on the refusal to do harm."[37] Gandhi asserted that "truth is the end; non-violence is the means. But the end and the means are irrevocably bound to each other."[38] Truth and nonviolence are thus intertwined.[39] Together, *satya* and *ahimsa* provided an "alternative paradigm of power."[40]

Gandhi's third conceptual pillar was *tapasya*, or self-suffering. While I explore the concept in more detail in the following section, a brief overview is provided here:

> Non-violence requires the victim to undergo suffering. And the mere fact that the victim willingly and consciously endures suffering does not mean s/he is submitting to the will and might of the opponent. Instead, it means "pitting one's whole soul against the will of the tyrant" (Chander, 1945: 352). Self-suffering in satyagraha is directed toward the moral persuasion of the opponent. Self-suffering means voluntary injury to the self to persuade the opponent to become empathetic to the sufferer's situation and concerns.[41]

Gandhi anchored his servant-leadership in the conceptual pillars of truth, nonviolence, and self-suffering, remaining devoted to these principles regardless of the actions or atrocities perpetrated by the other side.

GANDHI'S SERVANT-LEADERSHIP: CONCEPTUALIZING THE RESPONSE

The Gandhian strategy was not a random collection of tactics, but a cohesive framework infused with the relentless pursuit of truth through nonviolent action.[42] Gandhi described the outworking of these foundational principles as *satyagraha*. The word combines truth (*satya*) and resolve (*agraha*), which literally means to grasp or hold fast to the truth. *Satyagraha*, often translated as "soul-force," remains one of Gandhi's greatest contributions to the world. According to Gandhi,

---

36. See Vazhapilly, "Relevance of Gandhian Praxis," 100.
37. Bondurant, *Conquest of Violence*, 25.
38. Adjei, "Non-Violent Philosophy," 84.
39. Bondurant, *Conquest of Violence*, 24.
40. See Vazhapilly, "Relevance of Gandhian Praxis," 103.
41. Akella, "Satyagraha," 505.
42. Atack, *Nonviolence in Political Theory*, 22.

Mahatma Gandhi: The Servant-Leader and Conceptualization

> Truth (*satya*) implies love, and firmness (*agraha*) brings about and therefore serves as a synonym for force. I thus began to call the Indian movement '*satyagraha*' that is to say, the force is born of Truth and Love or non-violence and gave up the use of the phrase 'passive resistance' in connection with it.[43]

At its core,

> Satyagraha means literally 'clinging to truth.' . . . The true Satyagrahi is, accordingly, a man of God. Such an individual in this world finds himself up against evil, which he cannot but resist. He comes across injustice, cruelty, exploitation and oppression. These he has to oppose with all the resources at his command. . . .Truth can be attained only loving service of all, i.e., by non-violence. The weapon of the Satyagrahi is therefore non-violence.[44]

A *satyagrahi* is a person who stands against injustice and denounces all forms of violence—even if such means are available and no matter how badly he or she has been hurt. For the *satyagrahi* "there is not the remotest idea of injuring the opponent. *Satyagraha* postulates the conquest of the adversary by suffering in one's own person."[45] In his biography of Gandhi, Fischer expounded on the concept:

> This became Gandhi's target: to be strong not with the strength of the brute but with the strength of the spark of God. *Satyagraha*, Gandhi said, is 'the vindication of truth not by infliction of suffering on the opponent but on oneself. That requires self-control. The weapons of the Satyagrahi are within him. Satyagraha is peaceful. If words fail to convince the adversary perhaps purity, humility and honesty will. The opponent must be 'weaned from error by patience and sympathy,' weaned, not crushed; converted, not annihilated. *Satyagraha* is the exact opposite of the policy of an-eye-for-an-eye-for-an-eye-for-an-eye, which ends in making everybody blind. You cannot inject new ideas into a man's head by chopping it off; neither will you infuse a new spirit into his heart by piercing it with a dagger. Acts of violence create bitterness in the survivors and brutality in the destroyers; *Satyagraha* aims to exalt both sides.[46]

---

43. Johnson, *Gandhi's Experiments with Truth*, 71.
44. Gandhi and Kumarappa, *Non-Violent Resistance*, iii.
45. Fischer, *Gandhi*, 78.
46. Fischer, *Mahatma Gandhi*, 77.

According to Shepard,

> Satyagraha—Gandhi's nonviolent action—was *not* a way for one group to seize what it wanted from another. It was *not* a weapon of class struggle, or of any other kind of division. Satyagraha was instead an instrument of *unity*. It was a way to remove injustice and restore social harmony, to the benefit of *both sides*. Satyagraha, strange as it seems, was for the opponent's sake as well. When Satyagraha worked, *both sides won*.[47]

Gandhi believed *satyagraha* could be used by anyone who embraced truth and love:

> Non-violence is a power which can be wielded equally by all—children, young men and women or grown-up people, provided they have a living faith in the God of Love and have therefore equal love for all mankind. When non-violence is accepted as the law of life, it must pervade the whole being and not be applied to isolated acts.[48]

Iain Atack, a peace studies and nonviolent political theory scholar, described the power of Gandhi's method thusly:

> Another significant point for *satyagraha* as a nonviolent political action is that it is available to every human being because it is based on a moral commitment to the pursuit of truth, rather than specific knowledge as such (or access to material weapons). It is not an elite-based method of political action, nor does it depend upon hierarchical forms of political organization, because it is derived from a commitment to the pursuit of truth on the part of each individual: 'The striving does not require any quality unattainable by the lowliest among us.' *Satyagraha* is available to all individuals or social groups in the form of nonviolent political action and civil resistance.[49]

A popular misconception related to Gandhi's methods was that he promoted passive resistance. On the contrary, Gandhi never advocated remaining silent, timid, or weak in the face of injustice. According to Shepard, Gandhi's *satyagraha* was actually an offensive strategy: "There was nothing passive about Gandhi."[50] His response was "not the passive resistance of the weak. The non-violence of a *satyagrahi* is unflinching. It is the non-violence

---

47. Shepard, *Mahatma Gandhi and His Myths*, 35–36 (emphasis original).
48. Bose, *Selections*, 186–87.
49. Atack, *Nonviolence in Political Theory*, 22–23.
50. Fischer, *Gandhi*, 93.

of the brave."[51] Gandhi was clear: "Non-violence is not a weapon of the weak, but it is the supreme virtue of the brave."[52] Gandhi described how he conceptualized the struggle:

> It is quite proper to resist and attack a system, but to resist and attack its author is tantamount to resisting and attacking oneself. For we are all tarred with the same brush, and are children of one and the same Creator, and as such the divine powers within us are infinite. To slight a single human being is to slight those divine powers, and thus to harm not only that being but with him the whole world.[53]

Related to the principle of *tapasya*, or self-suffering, Gandhi believed that a *satyagrahi* must be ready to face imprisonment and even death in the pursuit of truth: "[T]he nonviolent activist, while willing to die, was never willing to kill."[54] In pursuing this path with such steadfastness, Gandhi forced the oppressor to face the truth he wanted to suppress—ignoring the issue was not an option. As noted by Mayton,

> Gandhi viewed self-suffering as a viable maneuver to confront the violence that is often leveled at those who work to remove social injustices. The willingness to endure suffering instead of retaliating for a violent act with a violent act breaks the cycle of violence. While those fighting social injustices might suffer more than those who work to maintain the status quo, Gandhi believed that in the long run the world as a whole will witness less total violence.[55]

According to Ramchiary,

> The aim of *satyagraha* is not to embarrass the wrongdoer. Its intention is to bring about, what Gandhi calls, a 'change of heart.' In fact, *satyagraha* is based on the pre-supposition that there are no 'enemies' or 'opponent,' but that there are only wrongdoers. *Satyagraha* also demands extreme patience on the part of the *Satyagrahi*. A wrongdoer cannot see his wrong at once, he will take time to win over his anger and hatred. The *Satyagrahi*

---

51. Gandhi and Kumarappa, *Non-Violent Resistance*, iii.
52. Dhiman, *Gandhi and Leadership*, 131.
53. Gandhi, *Autobiography*, 310.
54. Shepard, *Mahatma Gandhi and His Myths*, 10.
55. See Mayton, "Gandhi as Peacebuilder," 4.

must wait patiently for the good sense of the wrongdoer to be aroused.⁵⁶

Gandhi asserted, "With *satya* combined with *ahimsa*, you can bring the world to your feet. Satyagraha in its essence is nothing but the introduction of truth and gentleness in the political, i.e., the national, life."⁵⁷ With this understanding of how Gandhi conceptualized the problem of injustice, as well as his response, we now consider how Gandhi turned these principles into action as he led the freedom struggle.

GANDHI'S SERVANT-LEADERSHIP: CONCEPTUALIZATION IN ACTION

According to Gandhian scholar Bondurant, *satyagraha* remains "the most potent legacy [Gandhi] left to India."⁵⁸ While time and space do not permit a full recounting of all of Gandhi's campaigns, a few notable events can provide a sense of how he employed *satyagraha* in South Africa and India through the methods of noncooperation, demonstrations, marches, and hunger strikes.

---

56. Ramchiary, "Gandhian Concept," 68.
57. Gandhi et al., *Mind of Mahatma Gandhi*, 218.
58. Bondurant, *Conquest of Violence*, 4.

A Sample List of Satyagrahas[59]		
Place	Year	Purpose
Johannesburg (South Africa)	1906	To protest against the unfair Asiatic Registration Bill of 1906.
Johannesburg (South Africa)	1908	To protest against the discriminatory law requiring Asians to apply for registration by burning 2,000 official certificates of domicile at a public meeting and courting jail.
Transvaal area (South Africa)	1913	March from New Castle to Transvaal to protest against the imposition of a £3 tax and the passing of the Immigration Bill adversely affecting the status of married Indian women.
Viramgam (India)	1914	To seek removal of customs hardships inflicted on third-class railway passengers.
Champaran (India)	1917	To remove the hardships of indigo workers in Champaran exploited by European planters.
Ahmedabad (India)	1918	To end the deadlock between the mill owners and laborers who were overworked and underpaid.
Kheda (India)	1918	To demand relief for famine-stricken peasants of Kheda regarding the revenue dues to be paid to the government.
India	1919	The first mass *satyagraha* against the unjust Rowlatt Bill, curbing the freedom of the press.
India	1920	Nonviolent noncooperation movement to attain *swaraj* and to implement Gandhi's seven-point program including Hindu-Muslim unity and removal of untouchability by surrendering titles and honorary posts awarded by the government, boycotting government schools, colleges, law courts, and legislatures, by starting national schools, and by using Khadi.
Borsad	1923–1924	To protest against unfair increments in the land revenues imposed on the people by settlement-revision officers.

59. Mani Bhavan, "Years of Satyagrahas," See also Bondurant, *Conquest of Violence.*

Vykom Temple Road	Spring 1924-Autumn 1925	To demand the entry of "untouchables" on public roads passing the temple.
Dandi/All India	March 12, 1930	To protest against the unjust Salt law by undertaking a march from Ahmedabad to Dandi, and to demand self-rule by boycotting of foreign cloth, picketing liquor shops, and taking a pledge for fighting for *swaraj*.
India	December 31, 1931	Civil disobedience to achieve self-rule by breaking laws and ordinances and continuing the earlier program of boycotting and picketing.
Rajkot (India)	1939	To protest against the breach of the charter of liberty of the people by the local ruler instigated by the British Resident in Rajkot.
All India	October 1940	To protest against India's participation in World War II and to support freedom of propagating nonviolence as a substitute for war.
All India	August 9, 1942	Quit India movement for complete freedom for India and to demand immediate abdication of the British rule with a determination to "Do or Die."

Gandhi implemented *satyagraha* through a gradual approach. First, he attempted to persuade the oppressor through reason. If that failed, he dramatized the issue in order to convince the oppressor through the witness of suffering. In doing so, he hoped to enlighten the other party's unprejudiced judgment so that rational argument could be employed. If this proved ineffective, the *satyagrahi* turned to nonviolent coercion and civil disobedience.[60] The process would then begin again. While the specific techniques used in a *satyagraha* campaign depended on the needs of a particular situation, Gandhi provided nine stages by which they should proceed.

---

60. Bondurant, *Conquest of Violence*, 10.

STEPS IN A SATYAGRAHA CAMPAIGN[61]

1. *Negotiation and arbitration*: Make every effort to resolve the conflict through established channels.
2. *Preparation of the group for direct action*: Group members examine motives, exercise self-discipline, and engage in purifactory fasting.
3. *Agitation*: Engage in an active propaganda campaign with demonstrations, mass gatherings, marches, and slogan-shouting.
4. *Issuing an ultimatum*: A final, strong appeal, with the next steps to be taken clearly explained; present a constructive solution with a wide scope of agreement and allow the opponent to save face.
5. *Economic boycott and forms of strike*: Use of picketing, demonstrations, educating the public, sit-ins (*dharna*), nonviolent labor strikes.
6. *Noncooperation*: Depending on the issue, engage in nonpayment of taxes, boycott schools and other public institutions, or even voluntary exile.
7. *Civil disobedience*: Carefully select the laws to be disobeyed—they should be central to the issue or symbolic.
8. *Usurping of the functions of government*: Assertive *satyagraha*.
9. *Parallel government*: Parallel functions are based on Step 8 and do so in a way where the support of the public can be obtained.

In 1930, Gandhi wrote the following in the magazine *Young India* and provided instructions for *satyagrahis*.

RULES FOR AN INDIVIDUAL[62]

1. A satyagrahi, i.e., a civil resister, will harbour no anger.
2. He will suffer the anger of the opponent.
3. In so doing he will put up with assaults from the opponent, never retaliate; but he will not submit, out of fear of punishment or the like, to any order given in anger.
4. When any person in authority seeks to arrest a civil resister, he will voluntarily submit to the arrest, and he will not resist the attachment

---

61. Bondurant, *Conquest of Violence*, 40.
62. Misra, "Mahatma Gandhi's Rules for Satyagrahas."

or removal of his own property, if any, when it is sought to be confiscated by authorities.

5. If a civil resister has any property in his possession as a trustee, he will refuse to surrender it, even though in defending it he might lose his life. He will, however, never retaliate.

6. Non-retaliation excludes swearing and cursing.

7. Therefore a civil resister will never insult his opponent, and therefore also not take part in many of the newly coined cries which are contrary to the spirit of *ahimsa*.

8. A civil resister will not salute the Union Jack, nor will he insult it or officials, be they English or Indian.

9. In the course of the struggle, if anyone insults an official or commits an assault upon him, a civil resister will protect such official or officials from the insult or attack, even at the risk of his life.

In practice, this meant that Gandhi and his followers would first "politely" break a law; the authorities would then conduct an arrest. Anticipating this response, he accepted the consequences with joy, which surprised his oppressors. Upon seeing his reaction, the public would sympathize with Gandhi and seek to learn more about his cause, for they saw a man willing to go to prison for his struggle and even "die with a smile on his lips and with no trace of hatred in his heart."[63] Stirred by Gandhi's example, the public would then pressure authorities to consider his demands. This process would occur in a series of cycles until authorities would be forced to the negotiation table. Shepard summarized Gandhi's train of thought:

> [W]hen you see my depth of concern, and how 'civil' I am in going about this, you're bound to change your mind about me, to abandon your rigid, unjust position, and to let me help you see the truth of my cause.[64]

As we consider the impact of Gandhi's leadership, it's interesting to note the effect his method had on the British. According to Vazhapilly, Gandhi believed that both the colonizer and the colonized needed liberation.[65] Thus, Gandhi's campaign was conducted in spirit of inclusivity. "[H]e invited the British for soul searching. For Gandhi, the British were an adversary

---

63. Gandhi and Kumarappa, *Non-Violent Resistance*, iii.
64. Shepard, *Mahatma Gandhi and His Myths*, 21.
65. Vazhapilly, "Relevance of Gandhian Praxis," 103.

who should leave Indian shores; but he did not consider them as enemies."[66] Shepard observed that "maybe the most amazing thing about Gandhi's nonviolent revolution is, not that the British left, but that they left as friends, and that Britain and India became partners in the British Commonwealth."[67] Through his conceptualization of the problem and his leadership response, Gandhi helped lead India to freedom. On August 15, 1947, at the stroke of midnight, his goal of *swaraj*, or self-rule, was realized, as India became a free nation. *Sarvodaya*, uplift for all, remains a work in progress. On January 30, 1948, Gandhi gave his life for the cause of freedom when he met an untimely death at the hands of an assassin. His legacy of servant-leadership lives on around the globe.

THE CONCEPTUAL TALENT OF THE SERVANT-LEADER

Conceptual thinking is a foundational characteristic of servant-leadership. Through conceptualization, Gandhi developed a realistic view of the issue, formulated a thoughtful response, and then acted with courage. The hearts and minds of both the oppressed and the oppressor were liberated through the process. Kouzes and Posner, in their seminal book, *The Leadership Challenge*, described conceptualization as a hallmark of leadership. They compared it to the creation of a literary or musical theme:

> It's the broad message that you want to convey, it's the primary melody that you want people to remember. . . . Every leader needs a theme, something on which they can structure the rest of his or her performance. What's *your* central message? What's *your* theme?"[68]

As noted by the authors, leaders develop conceptual thinking by reflecting on the past, forecasting the future, attending to the present, and then responding with passion. This was evident in Gandhi's life as he reflected on his early experiences of discrimination and prejudice, framed a long-term view of the problem based in *satya*, *ahimsa*, and *tapasya*, conceptualized a principled response through *satyagraha*, and activated his vision through campaigns of nonviolent resistance. Neither imprisonment nor physical violence, not even the prospect of death, could stop him.

---

66. Vazhapilly, "Relevance of Gandhian Praxis," 101.
67. Shepard, *Mahatma Gandhi and His Myths*, 33.
68. Kouzes and Posner, *Leadership Challenge*, 106–7 (emphasis original).

According to Greenleaf, "Conceptualizers are intensely practical. They are also effective persuaders and relations builders."[69] Conceptual thinking allows servant-leaders to hold the tension between the present and the future and then build a bridge connecting the two. Conceptual talent empowers servant-leaders to go out ahead and show the way. Operational talent enables them to manage day-to-day issues on the ground. This balance requires sound judgment, emotional intelligence, ethical integrity, and an ability to manage relationships.[70] In practicing conceptualization, Gandhi took a stand against injustice based on the principles of truth, love, and self-suffering, ultimately leading his people to freedom.

Out of conceptualization emerges foresight—a characteristic of servant-leadership we consider in the following chapter. Mike Figliuolo, author and managing director at thoughtLEADERS, LLC, a leadership development firm, described it as a powerful and essential element of leadership,

> Many leaders become complacent about looking into the future. They believe they know what lies ahead for their organization. They stop focusing on the future because it seems clear what is in store for them, and they believe that the best use of their energy is to drive current operations. These leaders would do well to heed the sage words of Paul Saffo: "Never mistake a clear view for a short distance." Great leaders consistently look beyond clarity into the uncomfortable ambiguity ahead. They embrace their responsibility to find new ideas that prepare their organization to win in uncertain future environments. Failure to look beyond those short distances will lead you to miss the opportunities and crises that inevitably await.[71]

FINDING: CONCEPTUALIZATION

Servant-leaders dream great dreams. Through conceptualization they create a pathway for possibility. Robert Greenleaf said, "Not much happens without a dream. And for something great to happen, there must be a great dream. Behind every great achievement is a dreamer of great dreams. Much more than a dreamer is required to bring it to reality; but the dream must be there first."[72] What is your great dream?

69. Greenleaf, *Servant Leadership: A Journey*, 66–67.
70. Greenleaf, *On Becoming a Servant Leader*.
71. Figliuolo, *One Piece of Paper*, 111–12.
72. Greenleaf, *Servant as Leader*, 16.

7

Eleanor Roosevelt: The Servant-Leader and Foresight

In their bestselling book, *Built to Last*, management professors Jim Collins and Jerry Porras explored why some organizations experience a measure of longevity far beyond their competitors. Chronologically, these companies endured for at least fifty years—a remarkable feat when the average lifespan of an S&P 500 company is around fifteen years.[1] To lay the conceptual background for their findings, the authors offered an interesting thought experiment.

Visualize yourself living about 600 years ago. One day, you meet someone with an incredible ability. This person can tell you the exact time and date just by looking at the sun or stars. "Today is April 23, 1401, 2:36 a.m. and 12 seconds." Now, imagine what the reaction to such talent would be! Collins and Porras suggested astonishment, and maybe even reverence. Now, suppose this person then developed a device that could measure time itself—they called it a "clock." This innovation, far surpassing the first feat, would literally change the world.

Collins and Porras's illustration framed the thesis for their findings. They contended that organizations that are built to last are based on the principle of clock-building, rather than time-telling.[2] The difference between the two approaches is significant. A charismatic leader typically manages

---

1. Hill et al., "How Winning Organizations Last 100 Years."
2. Collins and Porras, *Built to Last*, 22–23.

organizations strong in time-telling or the company excels at launching a series of best-selling products. Contrary to popular thinking, however, neither of these characteristics guarantees long-term success. Instead, what organizations need is a blueprint that can stand the test of time. So, how does this happen? According to Collins and Porras, the answer is not found in some secret method, or even a particular set of practices. Rather, foresight—the seventh characteristic of servant-leadership—is the key. Collins and Porras pointed to the founding of the United States as an example of foresight in action:

> The critical question at the Constitutional Convention in 1787 was not, "Who should be president? Who should lead us? Who is the wisest among us? Who would be the best king?" No, the founders of the country concentrated on such questions as "What *processes* can we create that will give us good presidents long after we're dead and gone? What type of enduring country to do we want to build? On what principles? How should it operate? What guidelines and mechanisms should we construct that will give us the kind of country we envision?" . . . they were organizational visionaries. . . . They focused on building a country. They rejected the good-king model. They took an architectural approach. They were clock-builders![3]

According to Larry Spears,

> Closely related to conceptualization, the ability to foresee the likely outcome of a situation is hard to define, but easier to identify. One knows foresight when one experiences it. Foresight is a characteristic that enables the servant leader to understand the lessons from the past, the realities of the present, and the likely consequence of a decision for the future. It is also deeply rooted within the intuitive mind.[4]

IBM Leadership Fellow Michael Keegan described foresight as the ability to envision, shape, and safeguard the future. Leaders with foresight make thoughtful decisions about the future while in the present. Keegan argued that foresight is a mindset, illustrated by the US Coast Guard motto, "*Semper Paratus*" or, "always ready."[5] Greenleaf referred to foresight as the *lead* in leadership. A servant-leader who possesses foresight "cares more, prepares better, and foresees more clearly than others."[6]

---

3. Collins and Porras, *Built to Last*, 42 (emphasis original).

4. See Spears, "Introduction: Understanding the Growing Impact of Servant-Leadership," 18.

5. Keegan, "Strategic Foresight and Leadership," para. 7.

6. Greenleaf, *On Becoming a Servant Leader*, 170.

Clock-builders are able to see around the corner and over the horizon. They reflect on the past, acknowledge the exigencies of the present, and anticipate the future. Indian author and social activist Arundhati Roy described the challenge of developing foresight: "Our inability to live entirely in the present (like most animals do), combined with our inability to live very far into the future, makes us strange in-between creatures, neither beast nor prophet."[7]

In this chapter we explore foresight through the life and leadership of Eleanor Roosevelt. Roosevelt was a clock-builder who left a legacy that was built to last. It is not my intention to present a biography of her life, but rather a concise study of how her early life experiences, marriage to Franklin Delano Roosevelt (FDR), and experiences as First Lady allowed her to develop, deepen, and then deploy foresight. The three elements described in Spears's definition of foresight—lessons from the past, realities of the present, and the likely consequence of a decision for the future—provide the lenses through which I explore her servant-leadership.

DEVELOPING FORESIGHT: LESSONS FROM THE PAST

Foresight grows as a leader reflects on the joyful as well as painful influences of the past. In his bestselling book, *True North: Discover Your Authentic Leadership*, Harvard professor and CEO Bill George asserted that leaders would do well to explore their life story in order to develop the characteristic of foresight.[8] According to George, our personal experiences give shape to our unique contributions as a leader. Reflecting on the lessons from of Eleanor Roosevelt's past, particularly her family dynamics, helped her develop foresight and influenced her path to servant-leadership.

Anna Eleanor Roosevelt (hereafter referred to as Roosevelt), the eldest of four siblings, was born on October 11, 1884, in New York. Her mother, Anna Livingston Hall, was a physically attractive and cultured woman who hailed from a wealthy and influential family. Her father, Elliot Roosevelt, came from an aristocratic New York family, though he spent most of his teenage years in the Texas countryside, hunting, scouting, and enjoying sport. Elliot's brother was Theodore Roosevelt, the American statesman and twenty-sixth President of the United States.

Roosevelt's parents shared a commitment to social service and community responsibility—volunteerism and philanthropy were family values. Thus, Anna actively engaged in community-based efforts and supported

7. Roy, *Field Notes on Democracy*, 2.
8. George, *Discover Your True North*.

local causes. As early as six years old, Roosevelt helped serve Thanksgiving dinners to underprivileged children in New York City. Every year, she helped decorate Christmas trees for children's hospitals throughout the city, including Hell's Kitchen, one of New York's poorest neighborhoods. Roosevelt empathized with children struggling with physical infirmities. She recalled, "Some of them lay patiently for months in strange and curious positions. I was particularly interested in them because I had a curvature myself and wore for some time a steel brace, which was vastly uncomfortable and prevented my bending over.[9] Later in life, this blend of social privilege and social responsibility enabled Roosevelt to move skillfully in high society, while remaining grounded enough to empathize with the struggles of the less fortunate.

Roosevelt and her father enjoyed a close relationship. Because of his love for the outdoors, he emphasized the importance of physical activity. Roosevelt held fond memories of family vacations with her father. During one memorable trip to Venice, Elliot swept her up from a gondola and serenaded her. Sadly, he struggled with health issues most of his adult life, exacerbated by an abuse of narcotics and alcohol. His addiction became severe enough to strain his marriage to Anna and warrant an extended stay in a sanitarium.

Roosevelt's relationship with her mother was quite different and can be described as emotionally distant. Though they spent time together in activities such as reading books and poetry, Anna appeared to favor her other children. She believed that Eleanor lacked certain qualities she valued, such as physical attractiveness and elegance. Roosevelt recalled, "She tried to bring me up well so that my manners would compensate for my looks, but her efforts only made me more keenly conscious of my shortcomings."[10] Anna even nicknamed her "Granny"; it was a label that pierced Roosevelt's soul:

> I can see the look in her eyes and hear the tone of her voice as she said, 'Come in Granny.' If a visitor was there, she might turn and say, 'Granny is such a funny child, so old-fashioned that we call her 'Granny.' I wanted to sink through the floor in shame.[11]

The family moved to France when Anna was expecting their third child. Roosevelt had just turned six and was enrolled in a French Catholic convent school. Her mother's parting remark was particularly raw, "You

---

9. Roosevelt, *Autobiography*, 13.
10. Roosevelt, *Autobiography*, 6.
11. Roosevelt, *Autobiography*, 9.

have no looks, so see to it that you have manners."[12] The language barrier at the convent, and dissimilarity in faith tradition, invoked a deep sense of loneliness in the young girl. The authoritarian environment only compounded her sense of alienation. One day, Roosevelt was expelled from the institution when she was caught lying about swallowing a penny. She noticed that one of her classmates had swallowed a coin and received a great deal of attention—something that Roosevelt was desperately seeking. The news infuriated Anna. Roosevelt shuffled between her mother and her grandmother's home until the family moved back to New York.

When Roosevelt was eight years old, her mother died of diphtheria. The news devastated her father—not only did Elliot lose his wife, but the children as well. Before her death, Anna had appointed her mother Mary Ludlow Hall as the children's guardian. The children were sent to live in Tivoli, New York. Life in the Hudson River Valley was much different than Roosevelt's privileged upbringing in the city. Her grandmother's house lacked electricity and the children were assigned chores. Roosevelt described the environment as strict and exacting. "Looking back I see that I was always afraid of something: of the dark, of displeasing people, of failure. Anything I accomplished had to be done across a barrier of fear."[13] Dismayed at how far behind Roosevelt had fallen in her studies, her grandmother hired private tutors so she could catch up on grammar, literature, and world languages such as French, Italian, German, and Spanish. She also learned to sew, play piano, and took ballet lessons in the city once a week as her grandmother felt her height made her particularly suitable for dance. The house also contained a large library, which helped satisfy Roosevelt's intellectual curiosity.

Before Roosevelt's tenth birthday, two personal tragedies struck in rapid succession. Her four-year-old brother, Ellie, died suddenly from scarlet fever. A year later, her beloved father, Elliot, passed away after falling from a window during an alcohol withdrawal seizure. As was customary in those days, her grandmother did not permit the children to attend the funeral, which only made Roosevelt's grief even worse. She wept for days, as her best friend was no more.

A turning point in her life arrived when Roosevelt's grandmother enrolled her in Allenswood Academy, a private school for girls outside London. She referred to this time as the "second period of my life."[14] At Allenswood she came under the tutelage of Marie Souvestré, the school's headmistress. Souvestré's influence proved transformational. She tutored Roosevelt in

12. Smith, *Eleanor*, 25.
13. Roosevelt, *Autobiography*, 12.
14. Roosevelt, *Autobiography*, 20.

languages, political science, philosophy, workers' rights, and etiquette. She also took her young charge on trips across Europe, visiting not only the usual tourist sites, but working-class neighborhoods as well. Roosevelt was put in charge of booking the travel arrangements and creating their itinerary, which inspired a spirit of self-reliance and self-confidence: "This was the first time in my life that my fears left me. If I lived up to the rules and told the truth, there was nothing to fear."[15]

After graduation, Roosevelt and her unmarried aunt moved to New York for their social debut. While they attended the usual get-togethers, luncheons, and other events, what really inspired Roosevelt was meeting artists, musicians, and anyone interested in volunteerism and social causes. In that spirit, Roosevelt and a group of like-minded society women formed the New York Junior League, a charity devoted to social service. "There was no clubhouse; we were just a group of girls anxious to do something helpful in the city in which we lived."[16] The women opened community centers across the city to serve immigrant populations, particularly children. Roosevelt volunteered at Rivington Street Settlement House on the Lower East Side, teaching piano, calisthenics, and fancy dance.

Roosevelt also joined the National Consumers League, whose mission was to ensure fair and safe labor practices. She served as a volunteer investigator, exposing unsafe working conditions in the garment district. It was around this time that Roosevelt became reacquainted with Franklin Delano Roosevelt (FDR), her fifth cousin, once removed. After an extended courtship, they married on St. Patrick's Day, March 17, 1905. President Theodore Roosevelt ("Uncle Ted") gave away the bride. Married life would soon open up a new chapter in Roosevelt's life.

Looking back, we can see that Roosevelt's early life experiences laid the groundwork for a life of service. As a child, she experienced what Greenleaf described as "the natural feeling that one wants to serve, to serve first."[17] Her sense of empathy was particularly deep. "Very early I became conscious of the fact that there were people around me who suffered in one way or another. . . . I was not in ignorance that there were sharp contrasts, even though our lives were blessed with plenty."[18] As noted earlier in the chapter, Bill George highlighted the role of early-life experiences in shaping one's leadership. Each of the leaders in his book struggled with the "dueling narrative" of the past, much like Roosevelt. Former Starbucks CEO Howard

---

15. Roosevelt, *Autobiography*, 24.
16. Roosevelt, *Autobiography*, 40.
17. Greenleaf, *Servant as Leader*, 13.
18. Roosevelt, *Autobiography*, 12–13.

Schultz, whose childhood struggles particularly impacted his leadership, shared how "the reservoir of all my life experiences shaped me as a person and a leader."[19]

Eleanor's Roosevelt's journey to servant-leadership began during childhood. Painful experiences such as rejection by her mother, the tragic loss of her father, and the emotionally distant environment of her home reminded her of the importance of care and compassion. George noted the impact of life experiences on the development of foresight. "All of them, like the other leaders interviewed, found the inspiration to lead in their own life stories. By understanding the formative experiences of their early lives, they have been able to reframe their understanding of their life stories and shape their leadership around fulfilling their passions and following their True North."[20]

In her memoir, *Tomorrow Is Now*, Roosevelt described the impact of her childhood experiences and how she leveraged them to lead with foresight:

> In the past I have written of the era in which I grew up and of the experiences which shaped my life, from a lonely childhood in a caste-bound society with narrow traditions . . . I have come to see that nothing of what has happened to me, or to anyone, has value unless it is a preparation for what lies ahead. We face the future, fortified only with the lessons we have learned from the past. It is today that we must create the world of the future. Spinoza, I think, pointed out that we ourselves can make experience valuable when, by imagination and reason, we turn it into foresight. It is that foresight we must acquire. In a very real sense, *tomorrow is now*.[21]

DEEPENING FORESIGHT: THE REALITIES OF THE PRESENT

As Roosevelt settled into married life, FDR attended law school. Roosevelt's mother-in-law soon took a more prominent role in the couple's life. For example, when she felt the couple's living quarters were too small, she built two houses—one for the newlyweds and one for herself right next door. She freely offered advice on how the couple should rear their children. Roosevelt

---

19. George, *Discover Your True North*, 15.
20. George, *Discover Your True North*, 24.
21. Roosevelt, *Tomorrow Is Now*, xv–xvi (emphasis original).

struggled to establish a life apart from the influence of her mother-in-law. She believed it was likely due to a fear of rejection from her childhood. "I left everything to my mother-in-law, requiring her help on almost every subject, and never thought of asking for anything that I thought would not meet with her approval."[22] As she attempted to find her place as a wife and young mother, Roosevelt experienced frequent bouts of anxiety and depression.

After graduating from Columbia Law School, FDR worked as an attorney on Wall Street. Though quite successful, he was drawn to public service and decided to run for New York State Senate. While Roosevelt observed her husband's political campaign with interest, she felt unsure about her role in the process. "I was having a baby, and for a time at least, that was my only mission in life."[23] FDR was elected to the state senate in 1910 and again in 1912. The Roosevelts moved to an official residence in Albany. The couple had six children, but one child passed away before his first birthday. During this time of transition, Roosevelt observed the power of the political system to influence change, particularly through FDR's support of the suffrage movement.

As a senator's wife, Roosevelt's private and public life began to merge. She described the experience as a "dual existence."[24] Her obligations impacted the time she had set aside for social work, her first love. The other senators' wives encouraged her to channel her volunteerism in the direction of philanthropy and nonprofit board work "because I had been told I had no right to go into the slums or into hospitals, for fear of bringing diseases home to my children."[25] Though she followed their advice for a time, she always preferred a hands-on approach to service.

President Woodrow Wilson selected FDR as his Assistant Secretary of the Navy, a capacity in which he served from 1913–1920. As World War I commenced, Roosevelt volunteered at the Red Cross canteen and visited wounded soldiers at St. Elizabeth's Hospital in Washington, DC. She was appalled by the conditions in the wards and observed soldiers experiencing posttraumatic stress. Roosevelt contacted the Secretary of the Interior, and through her influence, the Secretary obtained a congressional increase in hospital funding. Roosevelt also lobbied the Red Cross to set up recreation rooms for recovering troops and helped establish the nation's first occupational therapy unit for soldiers. She recalled how these efforts deepened her foresight:

---

22. Roosevelt, *Autobiography*, 61.
23. Roosevelt, *Autobiography*, 63.
24. Roosevelt, *Autobiography*, 66.
25. Roosevelt, *Autobiography*, 68.

> Out of these contacts with human beings during the war I became a more tolerant person, far less sure of my own beliefs and methods of action but more determined to try for certain ultimate objectives. I had gained some assurance about my ability to run things and the knowledge that there is joy in accomplishing a good job. I knew more about the human heart.[26]

At the end of the war, Roosevelt turned her attention toward domestic issues, particularly the suffrage movement. She recalled a conversation with a senator's wife who encouraged her to take a public stand against ratification. When the amendment passed, Roosevelt learned a valuable lesson,

> Before she could succeed, the amendment was ratified, and soon after I undertook work, which proved to me the value of a vote. I became a more ardent citizen and feminist than anyone about me in the intermediate years would have dreamed possible. I had learned that if you wanted to institute any kind of reform you could get far more attention if you had a vote than if you lacked one.[27]

In 1920, presidential hopeful James Cox selected FDR as his Vice-President. Roosevelt joined FDR for his campaign trips and learned more about the social problems facing communities across the nation. Though Cox's bid failed, the couple gained exposure to larger issues facing the country, as well as the potential of the American people to solve those problems.[28] When they returned to New York, Roosevelt was invited to join the League of Women Voters and create reports to guide national legislation. Roosevelt recalled feeling "humble and inadequate" for the task and questioned her ability to manage large amounts of data and compose technical reports.[29] She finally agreed to the request when the League offered to provide an attorney to help her analyze voting records and debate transcripts. While she continued to sit on a few nonprofit boards, Roosevelt felt called to serve in a personal capacity. "I had developed an aversion to serving on boards and having no contact with the actual personal work."[30]

In 1921, when FDR was thirty-nine years old, he was diagnosed with polio and paralyzed from the waist down. Despite the intense difficulties the couple faced by this turn of events, they refused to allow it to hinder their

---

26. Roosevelt, *Autobiography*, 93.
27. Roosevelt, *Autobiography*, 103.
28. Roosevelt, *Autobiography*, 110.
29. Roosevelt, *Autobiography*, 112.
30. Roosevelt, *Autobiography*, 113.

personal life or passion for service. Roosevelt was central in helping FDR regain basic mobility, learn to walk using crutches, drive a car, and reengage in his hobbies and interests. She recalled,

> Franklin's illness proved to be a blessing in disguise, for it gave him strength and courage he had not had before. He had to think out the fundamentals of living and learn the greatest of all lessons—infinite patience and never ending persistence."[31]

FDR stayed active by serving on nonprofit boards and assisting with the Democratic presidential campaign. Roosevelt was asked to serve as a party delegate to promote women's issues. In this capacity, she lectured across New York state, addressing concerns such as infant mortality, health, employment, and housing. Roosevelt also volunteered in a number of organizations, including the League of Women Voters, the Women's Trade Union League, the World Peace Movement, and served as the finance committee chair for the New York State Democratic Party.

Roosevelt encouraged FDR to return to the political arena, despite his physical struggles. She believed his talent as an administrator and passion for social, environmental, and labor issues could make a real difference. Roosevelt's support renewed FDR's self-confidence. He ran for New York governor and won. During his tenure, Roosevelt accompanied FDR on visits to state hospitals, nursing homes, and prisons. When he was unable to tour a facility due to mobility issues, Roosevelt conducted the inspections in his stead. She also helped reform the Public Employment Service by documenting employee concerns such as overcrowding, staffing, food service, and medical care in state institutions, once again deepening her foresight:

> I learned to look into the cooking pots on the stove to find out if the contents corresponded to the menu. I learned to notice whether the beds were too close together. . . . I learned to watch the patients' attitude toward the staff, and before the end of our years in Albany I had become a fairly expert reporter on state institutions.[32]

In the mid-1920s, Roosevelt helped establish Val-Kill Industries, a furniture-making initiative providing young farm workers a job in the city during their seasonal down time. She also launched the Todhunter School for Girls, teaching history and government several times per week. Meanwhile, FDR's governorship helped him better understand the larger issues facing the country. His objective, as Roosevelt described it, never wavered.

---

31. Roosevelt, *Autobiography*, 142.
32. Roosevelt, *Autobiography*, 155.

He was determined "to help make life better for the average man, woman, and child."[33] FDR was inspired to run for the presidency, and in 1933, became the thirty-second President of the United States. Eleanor Roosevelt was forty-eight years old when she became First Lady.

During this period of Roosevelt's life she actively pursued her passion for service. As a mother, teacher, and social reformer, she was a servant-leader to her family, community, and nation. In the process of serving, she developed a level of foresight that would prove vital in the next phase of her life. Greenleaf described foresight as a "better than average guess about *what* is going to happen *when* in the future. It begins with a state of mind about *now*."[34] By entering into and engaging the problems of others, and integrating thinking from the past and present, Roosevelt gained foresight for the future.[35] As we'll see in the next section, Roosevelt would impact the nation and the world in her historic role as First Lady. It would become the pinnacle of her foresight as a clock-builder.

DEPLOYING FORESIGHT: MEANINGS TO THE FUTURE

FDR is the only United States President to have served four terms, with a little over twelve years in office (1933–1945). Roosevelt became the longest-serving First Lady in United States history. The couple helped guide the country through two of its most difficult periods—the Great Depression and World War II. As FDR took office, Roosevelt transitioned from the traditionally ceremonial role of First Lady to an even more passionate servant-leader. Her legacy of social reform and servant-leadership can be directly traced to her depth of foresight. When asked about her motivation for service, Roosevelt often quoted American poet Walt Whitman, "Not for the past alone—for meanings to the future."[36] In this section we explore her servant-leadership and influence in four vital areas: 1) The New Deal, 2) women in the media, 3) civil rights, and 4) human rights.

Impact on the New Deal

When FDR began his first term, the United States was in the throes of the Great Depression. Economists note that between 1929 and 1933, the

---

33. Roosevelt, *Autobiography*, 159.
34. Greenleaf, *Servant Leadership: A Journey*, 24 (emphasis original).
35. See Showkeir and Showkeir, "Clarifying Intention," 163.
36. Roosevelt, *Tomorrow Is Now*, 25.

quantity of goods and services produced in the United States fell by one-third, unemployment impacted twenty-five percent of the labor force, and some 7,000 banks had failed.[37] Between 1929 and 1932, the stock market lost $72 billion—a shocking statistic considering gross domestic product (GDP) in 1932 was $59.4 billion. The human costs were even more exacting.

The national suicide rate rose from 12.1 percent in 1920 to 18.9 percent in 1928. Homelessness and food shortages were common.[38] Ben Bernanke, former Chairman of the Federal Reserve, described this period of American history as an "incredibly dramatic episode—an era of stock market crashes, bread lines, bank runs, and wild currency speculation, with the storm clouds of war gathering ominously in the background all the while."[39]

To navigate the crisis, FDR advanced a series of *ad hoc* legislative proposals. The New Deal evolved into a massive economic, political, and social program that would help guide the country out of the Great Depression. The regulation of the private sector through newly established federal agencies, accompanied by progressive social reforms, would become its backbone. The New Deal included the creation of the Social Security Act (1935), the National Labor Relations Act (1935), which led to the formation of the National Labor Relations Board and the G. I. Bill of Rights (1944). For the first time in years, many Americans felt a sense of optimism and hope.[40]

The achievements of The New Deal were not FDR's alone, however. Eleanor Roosevelt helped shape its legacy through her foresight. Due to her influence, the role of women in American public life expanded as never before. Women were appointed to several high-profile positions in the FDR administration and key roles in the Democratic Party. According to historian Frances Seeber, though she never ran for elected office, Roosevelt exerted the greatest impact on women's issues in the 1930s.[41] Seeber attributed much of the country's progress on these issues to Roosevelt's "pervasive role in patronage" and the strong social and political network she established on behalf of women.[42] Roosevelt encouraged women to participate in social justice efforts, join workers' unions, establish consumer groups, and share their views in books, newspapers, and magazine articles. As head of the Democratic Party's National Women's Campaign, she was instrumental in encouraging the party to bring independent, underrepresented, and women voters into its fold.

37. Wheelock, "Great Depression."
38. Wood and Jordan, *Party Polarization in America*, 90.
39. Bernanke, *Essays on the Great Depression* vii.
40. See Pederson, "Franklin Delano Roosevelt," 409–26.
41. Seeber, "Eleanor Roosevelt and Women in the New Deal," 707.
42. Seeber, "Eleanor Roosevelt and Women in the New Deal," 709.

Roosevelt, along with her colleague Molly Dewson, the Chair of the Women's Division of the Democratic National Committee, recruited over 100 highly skilled women to high-profile positions within the Administration. Frances Perkins, as Secretary of Labor, became the first woman appointed to a presidential cabinet position. Perkins was responsible for historic New Deal social welfare programs such as the Social Security Act, the Fair Labor Standards Act, the Wagner Act, unemployment insurance, and a number of child labor laws. She served during FDR's entire 12-year tenure. Ellen Sullivan Woodward, considered the most important non-Cabinet woman appointee of the administration, headed the Works Progress Administration (WPA). By 1936, 460,000 women were employed by the WPA.[43] According to Seeber, Roosevelt inspired women to lead in the nation's capital and across the country:

> Without doubt, there would have been some women executives in the federal government in the thirties no matter who was president, and it is quite possible that a network of communication and cooperation could have existed among these top women administrators as well, but Eleanor Roosevelt's position as First Lady made the 1930's unique for women. Even after 1945 when she left Washington, Mrs. Roosevelt was sorely missed and frequently consulted by women in government and in the press. (Her papers for the post-presidential years amply attest to this fact.) Eleanor Roosevelt had opened up opportunities for these women and the affection and friendship that united them in a network in the 1930's stayed with most of them for the rest of their lives. The friends and colleagues of Eleanor Roosevelt in New Deal Washington were not a part of a great women's movement but through their personal and professional interaction or networking they had laid the groundwork for future women and demonstrated to all what women could do.[44]

Impact on the Role of Women in the Media

As First Lady, Roosevelt penned a six-day-per-week, syndicated newspaper column titled "My Day," alongside numerous magazine articles and radio scripts. She authored several books in which she shared her inspiring life story. She was open about her struggles and vision for change. As First Lady, Roosevelt received thousands of letters from people sharing their concerns

---

43. See History, "America," 471–72.
44. Seeber, "Eleanor Roosevelt and Women in the New Deal," 715.

and needs. Rather than respond with a form letter, she strived to personally write to as many people as possible, either by hand or dictation, "After I had fulfilled my obligations to my guests . . . I signed the mail and read such letters as I had not seen before . . . This often keeps me busy far into the night."[45]

Roosevelt significantly expanded the role of female journalists as well. The social conventions of the day prevented women reporters from covering the White House and they were typically assigned lifestyle stories (e.g., entertainment and fashion). Roosevelt singlehandedly changed this practice by holding weekly press conferences exclusively for female reporters. In fact, she held 348 such press conferences.[46] Newspapers that employed only male reporters suddenly found themselves without access. As a result, they scrambled to hire women reporters in order to cover the First Lady's popular press conferences on issues such as the economy, foreign affairs, and the war effort.[47] Over forty news outlets sought credentialing for Roosevelt's weekly conferences. Besides helping women gain access to the White House, Roosevelt's press conferences fulfilled her stated goal of keeping female reporters employed during the Great Depression:

> I soon discovered that the women reporters in Washington were living precariously. People were losing their jobs on every hand, and unless the women reporters could find something new to write about, the chances were that some of them would hold their jobs for a very short time.[48]

When the Washington Press Corps refused to allow its female members to attend the annual Gridiron dinner, Roosevelt arranged an exclusive women-only "Gridiron Widows" banquet. As a result of Roosevelt's leadership on the issue, female correspondents became a permanent part of the White House Press Corps, which had the concurrent effect of raising their profile as professional journalists.[49] The presence of female reporters at the White House, something we take for granted today, can be directly attributed to the foresight and leadership of Eleanor Roosevelt.

---

45. Roosevelt, *Autobiography*, 170.
46. "Eleanor Roosevelt."
47. Caroli, "Eleanor Roosevelt."
48. Roosevelt, *Autobiography*, 171.
49. Caroli, "Eleanor Roosevelt."

Impact on Civil Rights

Roosevelt also made a lasting impact in the area of civil rights. Issues of race and discrimination weighed heavily on the First Lady. Roosevelt scholar and historian Allida Black described her as "The First Lady of American Civil Rights."[50] She asserted, "No First Lady is more closely associated with the issue of civil rights for African Americans than Eleanor Roosevelt."[51] Roosevelt's advocacy in this area was evident on several fronts. She served on the national board of directors of the NAACP, Howard University's Board of Trustees, and the National Urban League. Through her influence, she helped those institutions extend their voice and visibility. During her first week in the White House, she hired an entirely Black domestic staff. In 1933, she visited Black coal miners in West Virginia to highlight their living conditions. Though her efforts were portrayed as race-baiting by the media, she remained undeterred in her pursuit of equality.

In 1935, Roosevelt was instrumental in the selection of Mary McLeod Bethune, a Black educator, to the National Advisory Committee of the National Youth Administration (NYA). A year later, she launched the "Negro Affairs" branch of the NYA with Bethune as director.[52] In 1936, she infuriated Southern segregationists when she was pictured being escorted by a member of Howard University's honor guard. In 1938, during the Southern Conference for Human Welfare in Birmingham, Alabama, she positioned her chair between the segregated sections—sending a powerful message to a country struggling with legalized discrimination and racial violence. In 1939, when the Daughters of the American Revolution refused to rent Constitution Hall to acclaimed Black opera singer Marian Anderson, Roosevelt promptly resigned from the organization. She publicly stood with Anderson and organized a free concert on the steps of the Lincoln Memorial.[53] Two months later, Roosevelt invited Anderson to the White House to sing for the King and Queen of England.[54]

Roosevelt exerted tremendous pressure on FDR to address economic and political inequities faced by Blacks. In the 1930s, especially during the Great Depression, lynching and mob violence were on the rise. Roosevelt supported an anti-lynching bill sponsored by the NAACP, and worked with its president, Walter White, to campaign for federal legislation. White had

---

50. Black, "Championing a Champion," 730.
51. Black, "Championing a Champion," 719.
52. "Eleanor Roosevelt."
53. Black, "Championing a Champion," 719.
54. "Eleanor Roosevelt."

been fighting for this law since 1922.⁵⁵ Presidential scholars suggest that FDR hesitated on the issue because he needed the support of certain powerful senators to pass New Deal legislation.⁵⁶

When White tried to meet with FDR through official channels, White House staff rebuffed his efforts in order to keep the issue far from the President. Roosevelt took matters in her own hands by quietly arranging a private meeting between the two men. One afternoon, as FDR was returning from a leisurely outing along the Potomac River, he saw White waiting in his office:

> As the President explained his predicament, giving one reason after another why he couldn't support the bill, White countered with detailed arguments. Finally, exasperated, FDR said, 'Somebody's been priming you. Was it my wife?' He looked accusingly at Mrs. Roosevelt. He explained to White, 'If I come out for the anti-lynching bill now, they will block every bill I ask Congress to pass the keep America from collapsing. I just can't take the risk.'⁵⁷

Roosevelt's overt support of the anti-lynching bill drew even more political and public opposition. FBI Director J. Edgar Hoover is reported to have said that Roosevelt was trying to get the legislation passed because she had "black blood."⁵⁸ The Monteagle Ku Klux Klan offered a $25,000 bounty for any member who would kidnap the seventy-four-year-old First Lady.⁵⁹ Undeterred, she continued to publicly and privately press the issue. Ultimately, FDR failed to back the bill. Biographers recalled Roosevelt's struggle, as she stood alone on the issue:

> Eleanor fought the deep racist element in the New Deal as originally conceived and fought it in every other form that she encountered it. Her pain and bewilderment at her husband's inaction, especially where the anti-lynching bill was concerned—she would have to come back empty-handed to leaders of the black movement with whom she had become close friends—is wrenching.⁶⁰

In 1945, after watching *Strange Fruit*, a Broadway play on the issue, Roosevelt penned a newspaper column. She wrote,

---

55. Sparrow, "Eleanor Roosevelt's Battle."
56. Sparrow, "Eleanor Roosevelt's Battle."
57. Sparrow, "Eleanor Roosevelt's Battle," para. 11.
58. Sparrow, "Eleanor Roosevelt's Battle," para. 14.
59. Cooper, *Eleanor Roosevelt*.
60. Lessard, "First Lady," 48.

> We need to understand these circumstances in the North as well as in the South. There are mental and spiritual lynchings as well as physical ones, and few of us in this nation can claim immunity from responsibility for some of the frustrations and injustices which face not only our colored people, but other groups, who for racial, religious or economic reasons, are at a disadvantage and face a constant struggle for justice and equality of opportunity.[61]

Roosevelt also advocated for Black farmers in the administration of the Agricultural Adjustment Act. She sought to ensure that Black administrative workers were paid the same as their White counterparts in the Federal Emergency Relief Administration. She lobbied Congress to increase federal aid to Howard University's Freedman Hospital as well. During World War II, Roosevelt was a strong supporter of the Tuskegee Airmen. In 1941, after flying with a Tuskegee pilot to dispel racial stereotypes, she encouraged FDR to launch a training program for Black pilots. Roosevelt also lobbied for Black battalions to have combat roles in the war. In 1943, Roosevelt led a public campaign to integrate a public housing project in Detroit for Black defense workers. When the Federal Works Agency failed to support the plan, she personally appealed to FDR. Two dozen Black families moved into the project escorted by state police. Two months later, a riot ensued and twenty-five Blacks and nine Whites died in the violence. Some blamed the deaths on Roosevelt.[62]

Despite the smear campaigns and personal attacks, Roosevelt continued to lobby for civil rights. Allida Black spoke directly to Roosevelt's foresight and explained how it laid the groundwork for lasting change: "Indeed, Mrs. Roosevelt rocked the boat and rocked it hard. It is quite certain that her courageous efforts on behalf of African Americans served to hasten the end of the segregated and unjust society she abhorred."[63] Historian Fran Burke summed up Roosevelt's leadership on the issue thusly:

> Civil rights illustrates the unique partnership of Franklin and Eleanor in which she took the risk and he, unable and unwilling to disturb his stable, *status-quo* constituency, gained credibility through her visible, outspoken support of racial equality.... While Franklin preserved votes for recovery programs, Eleanor acted."[64]

---

61. Roosevelt, "My Day," para. 5.
62. Black, "First Lady of Civil Rights."
63. Black, "First Lady of Civil Rights," 141.
64. Burke, "Eleanor Roosevelt," 370 (emphasis original).

Impact on Human Rights

As a clock-builder, Roosevelt also left an enduring impact on human rights, demonstrating foresight at a time when the country and the world were just starting to awaken to the notion of individual rights and freedoms. According to the United Nations:

> Human rights are rights inherent to all human beings, regardless of race, sex, nationality, ethnicity, language, religion, or any other status. Human rights include the right to life and liberty, freedom from slavery and torture, freedom of opinion and expression, the right to work and education, and many more.[65]

During World War II, Roosevelt advocated for European refugees who had fled the Nazis, as well as those devastated by the Spanish Civil War. She received letters from around the world requesting assistance to help relocate families displaced by the war. Roosevelt also visited American troops stationed in the Pacific and Europe, boosting the morale of soldiers by her presence. Her international tours kept FDR informed about realities on the ground, while helping sharpen her own insight on global issues. This knowledge proved valuable when, in December 1945, President Harry Truman asked Roosevelt to serve as a member of the first United States delegation to the newly formed United Nations—she was only woman among the five delegates.

Roosevelt felt unqualified for the appointment, but with the encouragement of friends and colleagues, she accepted the charge "with fear and trembling."[66] So began what she described as "one of the most wonderful and worthwhile experiences of my life."[67] Roosevelt was assigned to Committee Three, a group of delegates working on the Social Humanitarian and Culture Committee. As her work commenced, she understood why Truman had asked her to serve:

> As I learned more about my work, I realized why I had been put Committee Three which dealt with humanitarian, educational, and cultural questions. . . . I began to realize the committee might be much more important than had been expected. And in time, this proved to be true.[68]

---

65. United Nation, "What Are Human Rights?," para. 1.
66. Roosevelt, *Autobiography*, 299.
67. Roosevelt, *Autobiography*, 299.
68. Roosevelt, *Autobiography*, 302–3.

The committee also developed policy around refugees displaced by war, an issue Roosevelt had worked on.

As Roosevelt settled into her role, she used the tact and diplomacy she developed over a lifetime to build working relationships with the UN's global delegates. She noticed that members accomplished more during informal meetings than official committee sessions. In that spirit, she invited delegates to teas, luncheons, and evening dinners so they could talk on a personal level, and in the process, break down social barriers. "I found that often a few people of different nationalities meeting on a semi-social basis, could talk together about a common problem with better results than when they were meeting officially as a committee."[69]

After her successful tenure, President Truman asked Roosevelt to serve as a delegate to the UN General Assembly. In 1953, she was concurrently appointed as the United States representative on the Human Rights Commission. Roosevelt considered this her most important position during her years of service at the United Nations. As elected chair of the commission, she led the group to create the groundbreaking "Universal Declaration of Human Rights." Roosevelt encouraged the commission to "name and define all the human rights, not only the traditionally recognized political and civil rights, but also the more recently recognized social, economic, and cultural rights."[70] She even recommended a legally binding treaty to back the nonbinding declaration by the signatory countries.

While the committee reached consensus around civil and political rights, the issues of economic and social rights proved far more challenging. Much of this was due to the socioeconomic variance among member nations. The United States and other Western countries pushed for more rights in areas such as primary and secondary child instruction and higher education. Some developing countries pushed back, arguing that guaranteeing anything beyond a primary education would strain their economies. Despite this difference of opinion, through Roosevelt's leadership as chair of the commission, the group came together, sometimes working eighteen-hour days, to draft the "Universal Declaration of Human Rights."

On December 10, 1948, the United Nations General Assembly formally accepted the historic document. Roosevelt received a standing ovation. She considered her work on the Human Rights Commission and the Declaration of Human Rights to be a meaningful step toward realizing her vision of a more peaceful world.[71] The trailblazing document continues to

---

69. Roosevelt, *Autobiography*, 305.
70. Roosevelt, *Autobiography*, 314.
71. Roosevelt, *Autobiography*, 322.

be used today as a standard by which countries can gauge how they treat their most precious resource—their people.

After the death of FDR, Roosevelt served for another seventeen years, leaving an unmatched legacy of servant-leadership powered by foresight. She ably executed the basic tasks of a servant-leader, utilizing foresight as she 1) anticipated the unforeseeable; 2) used the art of discernment; 3) practiced foresight; and 4) developed a creative, measurable plan.[72] The world continues to benefit from her leadership in the areas described in this chapter and beyond.

On November 7, 1962, Eleanor Roosevelt passed away in New York City at seventy-eight years of age. She was laid to rest next to FDR on the Roosevelt estate in Hyde Park. President Kennedy, President Truman, and General Dwight D. Eisenhower attended her funeral. President Truman described her as the "First Lady of the World."[73] At a memorial service held at the UN General Assembly, American statesman Adlai Stevenson mourned the loss of Roosevelt and her leadership: "I had lost more than a friend—I had lost an inspiration: for she would rather light candles than curse the darkness and her glow had warmed the world."[74]

ELEANOR ROOSEVELT: FORESIGHT IN ACTION

According to servant-leadership scholar Larry Spears, "Foresight remains a largely unexplored area in leadership studies, but one most deserving of careful attention."[75] Greenleaf considered foresight to be the central ethic of leadership.[76] In Eleanor Roosevelt we see a flesh-and-blood example of foresight in action. In this chapter we explored how Roosevelt developed foresight amidst a painful childhood and adolescence. She was empathetic toward those on the margins and reframed her experiences of rejection, loneliness, fear, and abandonment as preparation for the future. Roosevelt's partnership with FDR, along with her role as mother, teacher, and governor's wife, also expanded her foresight. As First Lady, her foresight enabled her to lead the country through some of its darkest days. Her foresight made her the conscience of a nation as a clock-builder who stood on the right side of history.

72. See Young, "Foresight," 246.
73. United for Human Rights, "Champions of Human Rights," para. 5.
74. "Adlai Stevenson," para. 2.
75. See Spears, "Introduction: Understanding the Growing Impact of Servant-Leadership," 18.
76. Frick, *Robert K. Greenleaf*.

INSEAD professor Ian Woodward asserted that in order to be successful, leaders must fly at three altitudes: 50,000 feet, fifty feet, and five feet. At 50,000 feet, the leader sees the big picture, which is necessary for large-scale transformation. At fifty feet, the leader remains close to the ground, executing short-term goals. The five-foot view is characterized by self-awareness. According to Woodward,

> Effective leaders develop the capacity to "fly" their thinking at all three altitudes, not getting trapped at any one of them. They travel up and down easily, making the connections between all the altitudes. Using this analogy can focus people in a simple, yet profound way, to generate crucial leadership insights.[77]

Eleanor Roosevelt soared at all three levels, generating foresight that guided her servant-leadership. Leadership professor Shann Ferch described foresight as a liberating vision:

> The ability to see, with clarity and acuity, what needs to be seen before undesired elements of small or great impact come to pass.... Greenleaf posits it as the servant-leader's responsibility to purposefully develop these in order to help people, organizations, and nations avoid undue entrapment in poor thinking, mental enslavement, lack of wisdom, or lack of autonomy.[78]

The fruit of foresight is a great dream. Robert Greenleaf said, "Nothing much happens without a dream. For something really great to happen, it takes a really great dream."[79] As seen in the example of Roosevelt, foresight enables the servant-leader to take action in the present based on a vision of the future. Servant-leaders with foresight dwell in possibility as clock-builders. The foresight of Eleanor Roosevelt reminds us that what we experience today is the result of how we behaved yesterday—and what we do today, creates our tomorrow.

FINDING: FORESIGHT

Harvard Business School professor Rosabeth Moss Kanter recommended "kaleidoscope thinking" as a way to develop foresight. According to Kanter, a kaleidoscope is the "symbol of ever-changing patterns and endless new possibilities, powered by human imagination" and the "ultimate weapon to

---

77. Woodward, "Three Altitudes of Leadership," para. 4.
78. Ferch, *Forgiveness and Power*, xi.
79. Greenleaf, *Servant Leadership: A Journey*, 16.

help leaders meet the challenges of the twenty-first century."[80] Kaleidoscope thinkers cultivate foresight by changing their usual patterns and doing things outside the norm. Visit other parts of your organization to exchange ideas, travel to meet new people and see new places, engage in discussions with critics and challengers, and read outside your field. Shift what's possible by pursuing new combinations and immersing yourself in the new and unfamiliar.

---

80. Lagace, "Tigers to Kaleidoscopes," para. 25.

8

Wangari Maathai: The Servant-Leader and Stewardship

A RAGING FIRE WAS racing across the forest floor; the angry flames lapped up everything in their path. The animals, overwhelmed and helpless, watched as the inferno consumed their home—all except for a tiny hummingbird. The little bird said, "I'm going to do something about this!" She flew to the nearest stream, gathered a single drop of water in her beak, and dropped it onto the fire. The other animals, such as the elephant with his large trunk and the cheetah with her fast legs, watched as she flew back and forth, up and down, as fast as she could between the stream and the fire. They said to her, "What are you doing? You are too little, and the fire is too big. Your wings are too small. Your beak is so tiny—you can only gather a small drop of water each time." As they kept trying to discourage the little bird, she turned to them and said, "I am doing the best I can."

Wangari Maathai, servant-leader and Nobel Prize laureate, often told this story to her audience. The forest represented the planet. The flames symbolized deforestation, erosion, and food insecurity. Maathai explained,

> And that to me is what all of us should do. We should always be like a hummingbird. I may be insignificant, but I certainly don't want to be like the animals watching as the planet goes down the drain. I will be a hummingbird; I will do the best I can.[1]

---

1. Maathai, "Be a Hummingbird," para. 1.

During a 1977 World Environment Day event, Maathai planted seven small seedlings; it became the first step in reversing decades of irresponsible land management practices in her native Kenya. Her tree-planting strategy quickly expanded to over a thousand seedlings, which grew into long rows of protected trees known as green belts. Maathai's hummingbird-like effort blossomed into the Green Belt Movement. To date, the organization has planted over 51 million trees in farms, schools, churches, and riverbanks throughout Kenya.[2] What first started as a drop has inspired thousands around the world to do their part in protecting our planet's natural resources.

In this chapter we explore the servant-leadership characteristic of *stewardship* through the life of Wangari Maathai. Larry Spears described it this way:

> Peter Block (1993)—author of *Stewardship and The Empowered Manager*—has defined stewardship as 'holding something in trust for another' (p. xx). Robert Greenleaf's view of all institutions was one in which CEO's, staffs, and trustees all played significant roles in holding their institutions in trust for the greater good of society. Servant-leadership, like stewardship, assumes first and foremost a commitment to serving the needs of others. It also emphasizes the use of openness and persuasion, rather than control.[3]

As noted by Block, a steward is someone who holds something in trust for another. At its essence, stewardship is about caretaking. A caretaker looks after something or someone on behalf of the owner. There is an important difference between an owner and a caretaker. The owner of a property, business, or item maintains an "exclusive right to hold, use, benefit from, enjoy, convey, transfer, and otherwise dispose of an asset or property."[4] Caretakers, however, manage and maintain an asset that belongs to someone else. Maathai understood this distinction. She viewed leadership as an act of stewardship. She served to preserve and protect Kenya's natural resources on behalf of a future generation. Like the hummingbird, she faced much opposition along the way, yet she persevered, undaunted by discouraging words and actions that tried to stop her from taking flight and doing the best she could.

Over a lifetime of leadership, Maathai earned a number of distinctions. She was the first woman in Central and East Africa to earn a Doctor of Philosophy degree. Between 1973 and 1981, she served as Chair of

---

2. http://www.greenbeltmovement.org/who-we-are.
3. Spears, "Tracing the Growing Impact," 5.
4. Schmid, *Construction Estimating*, 228.

the Department of Veterinary Anatomy and Professor at the University of Nairobi, becoming the first woman to attain those positions in that part of the world. She was also awarded the Goldman Environment Award, the Africa Prize for Leadership, and the Netherlands' Golden Ark Award. In 2001, *Time Magazine* named her one of the top environmental leaders of the century.[5] In 1990, she received an Honorary Doctor of Laws degree from Williams College.[6]

In 2002, Maathai won a seat in Kenya's parliament and was named Deputy Minister for Environment, Natural Resources and Wildlife. In 2004, she became the first woman from Africa to win the Nobel Peace Prize. The committee lauded her contribution to "sustainable development, democracy, and peace."[7] Two years later, she co-founded the Nobel Women's Initiative with five other Nobel laureates, aspiring to promote peace and equality around the world. In her Nobel Lecture she shared these inspiring words:

> Today, we are faced with a challenge that calls for a shift in our thinking so that humanity stops threatening its life support system. We are called to assist the world, to heal our wounds; and in the process, heal our own. Indeed, to embrace the whole creation in all its diversity, beauty, and wonder. This will happen if we see the need to revive our sense of belonging to a larger family of life, with which we have shared our evolutionary process. In the course of history, there comes a time when humanity is called to shift to a new level of consciousness, to reach a higher moral ground. A time when we have to shed our fear and give hope to each other. That time is now.[8]

Today, issues such as climate change, environmental stewardship, and sustainability draw increasing attention. Many scientists believe that the rapid consumption of the earth's natural resources, along with development-driven deforestation, have combined to reduce forest cover, accelerate the loss of biodiversity, and create food shortages. In this chapter we explore how Maathai addressed these problems through stewardship—serving her people and the planet just like the hummingbird that did the best she could.

---

5. Vick, "2001."
6. Yale News, "International Environmental Leaders."
7. "Nobel Peace Prize 2004," para. 1.
8. "Wangari Maathai—Nobel Lecture," para. 26.

THE BIRTH OF THE HUMMINGBIRD

Maathai was born on April 1, 1940, in Nyeri, a rural district in central Kenya. She was the first girl among six children. Her family were Kikuyu, a Bantu-speaking people group who traditionally lived near the base of Mount Kenya. They considered the mountain sacred, and its beauty and biodiversity remained a source of inspiration for Maathai throughout her life. During her childhood, Nyeri was lush, green, and productive, watered by the annual monsoon rains. The fertile soil produced an abundance of crops and hunger was rare.

Life as the Kikuyu knew it changed with the arrival of the British and other colonists. The vibrant ecocultural landscape was slowly reshaped. Landmarks, traditions, and geographical boundaries were altered. The local population was displaced as more settlers arrived and divided the land. Maathai and her family relocated to a plantation owned by a British farmer. They cultivated non-native crops such as wheat and maize. Because of her rural upbringing, Maathai grew to love and appreciate the land. She considered herself "as much a child of my native soil as I am of my father."[9] Looking back on her upbringing, she recalled:

> These experiences of childhood are what mold us and make us who we are. How you translate the life you see, feel, smell, and touch as you grow up—the water you drink, the air you breathe, and the food you eat—are what you become. When what you remember disappears, you miss it and search for it, and so it was with me.[10]

Maathai's brother recognized her academic potential and persuaded her parents to send her to school.[11] She joined her cousin at St. Cecilia's Intermediate Primary School in Nyeri Hill, a boarding school run by the Consolata Missionary Sisters. The school was academically rigorous and Maathai made the most of the opportunity by excelling in her studies. It was also at St. Cecilia's where Maathai converted to Catholicism.

The school provided a refuge during the Mau Mau rebellion, an uprising against British rule. As the movement intensified, Maathai's mother was forced to relocate to another village. Maathai was briefly detained while on a trip to visit her family. Though the rebellion paved the way for Kenya's independence, the violence exacted a toll on the minds and hearts of the people for years.

9. Maathai, *Unbowed*, 4.
10. Maathai, *Unbowed*, 52.
11. Pal, "Wangari Maathai," 35.

Maathai did well enough at St. Cecilia's to earn admission to Loreto Girl's High School in Limuru, a town just outside Nairobi. Loreto was the only Catholic high school for African women in the country. Through the influence of her mentor, Mother Teresia, Maathai discovered a passion for the natural sciences. As graduation neared, Maathai found her career choices limited. Most occupations, other than teaching and nursing, were reserved for men. Maathai wasn't interested in either—she wanted to pursue higher education.

As Maathai considered her options, Kenya was moving toward independence. With the British leaving their administrative posts, the nation needed an educated work force to fill key government positions. To aid in this effort, Senators John F. Kennedy and Andrew Young set up a scholarship program to help African students pursue higher studies in America. Known as the "Kennedy Airlift," the initiative assisted over 600 young people who would return to serve their nation after completing an advanced degree. Maathai graduated at the top of her high school class. She was awarded a scholarship to Mount St. Scholastica College in Atchison, Kansas. After a successful four years, she earned another scholarship, this time to pursue a master's degree in biology at the University of Pittsburgh. Her studies in embryology, microanatomy, and microscopy prepared her for a professorship in Kenya. Maathai reflected on her time in the United States: "I was taking back to Kenya five-and-half years of higher education, as well as a belief that I should work hard, help the poor, and watch out for the weak and vulnerable."[12]

Makerere University's Department of Veterinary Anatomy invited Maathai to join their research and teaching team. The department head, a professor from Germany, encouraged Maathai to pursue her doctorate, which she worked on while lecturing at the University of Nairobi. Around this time, she met her husband, Mwangi Maathai. As the couple started a family, Mwangi made plans to run for a seat in Kenya's Parliament. The campaign proved difficult for Maathai. She felt pressured to uphold the traditional gender role of a politician's wife, and soon, cracks began to form in the couple's relationship.

In 1971, Maathai earned her doctorate. She would be the first woman in Central and Eastern Africa to achieve this distinction. Around this time, Maathai engaged in her first stint in activism. She and a colleague launched a campaign to contest a university policy that provided full-time benefits exclusively to male professors. After a great deal of resistance, the university changed the policy. A short time later, Maathai was promoted to Department

---

12. Maathai, *Unbowed*, 95.

Chair of Veterinary Anatomy at the University of Nairobi—another first for women in Africa.

THE HUMMINGBIRD TAKES FLIGHT

During her tenure at the university, Maathai joined a number of civic organizations related to environmental and health issues, including the Environment Liaison Centre (ELC), a nongovernmental organization (NGO) that partnered with the United Nations Environment Programme. The opportunity elevated her exposure to environmental problems facing Africa. The combination of research and community service would prove instrumental in shaping her focus on environmental stewardship. Maathai's role on the board coincided with her postdoctoral research on East Coast Fever, a parasitic disease sickening cattle.

While conducting fieldwork in rural communities outside Nairobi, Maathai made a series of discoveries that led to the founding of the Green Belt Movement. First, she noticed that during heavy rains, silt would cover the flooded roads. Landslides were common and soil erosion seemed to pose a greater threat than East Coast Fever. As a result, fresh drinking water became increasingly scarce. She also observed that the people and cattle in these areas appeared malnourished and attributed this to a lack of proper nutrients in the grass and soil.

While visiting family in Nyeri, Maathai observed commercial tree, tea, and coffee plantations displacing indigenous forests—further contributing to forest degradation and silt-filled rivers. In her ancestral village, a beloved fig tree had been cut down to build a tea plantation. Maathai noted, "By then I understood the connection between the tree and water, so it did not surprise me that when the fig tree was cut down, the stream where I had played with tadpoles dried up."[13] As entire forests were felled, topsoil washed away and rivers dried up.

As a volunteer with the National Council of Women of Kenya, an NGO focused on providing clean water and affordable education to students, Maathai learned that children in central Kenya suffered from higher rates of disease due to malnutrition. Maathai was shocked, as the area had been one of the most fertile regions in the country during her childhood. As she looked deeper into the issue, the causal chain became clear. Farmers had turned to raising cash crops, such as coffee and tea, which reduced natural food production. Children were consuming more processed foods, such as white bread, maize, flour, white rice—a diet high in carbohydrates, but low

---

13. Maathai, *Unbowed*, 122.

in nutritional value. This, in turn, exacerbated deforestation as low-quality food required less firewood. The result was a degraded forest ecosystem and a malnourished population.

Maathai learned that this was not a problem unique to Kenya; women in rural areas around the world faced similar issues related to water, energy, and nutrition. The common thread was the environment:

> The connection between the symptoms of environmental degradation and their causes—deforestation, devegetation, unsustainable agriculture, and soil loss—were evident. Something had to be done. We could not just deal with the manifestations of the problems. We had to get to the root causes of these problems.[14]

Maathai resolved to address the problem. "Now it is one thing to understand the issues. It is quite another to do something about them. But I have always been interested in finding solutions."[15] A potential solution soon emerged:

> It just came to me: 'Why not plant trees?' The trees would provide a supply of wood that would enable women to cook nutritious foods. They would also have wood for fencing and fodder for cattle and goats. The trees would offer shade for humans and animals, protect watersheds and bind the soil, and, if they were fruit trees, provide food. They would also heal the land by bringing back birds and small animals and regenerate the vitality of the earth. This is how the Green Belt Movement began. The rest of it perhaps was sheer luck.[16]

Maathai realized that her plan might also work because trees held symbolic value to the Kenyan people:

> The act of planting trees conveys a simple message. It suggests that at the very least you can plant a tree and improve your habitat. It increases people's awareness that they can take control of their environment, which is the first step toward greater participation in society. Since the trees we have planted are visible, they are the greatest ambassadors for our movement.[17]

In the meantime, Maathai's husband Mwangi won a seat in parliament. During his campaign he pledged to pursue job creation. Maathai felt

14. Maathai, *Unbowed*, 125.
15. Maathai, *Unbowed*, 125.
16. Maathai, *Unbowed*, 125.
17. Anbarasan, "Wangari Muta Maathai," 46.

he was failing to live up to this promise and decided to take matters into her own hands by launching a small business named Envirocare. Her plan was to provide jobs for locals who would maintain the luxurious gardens of well-heeled city residents while planting trees. She soon ran into some unanticipated obstacles, however. First, affluent residents proved reluctant to trust the poor around their homes. Secondly, Maathai had no capital; she struggled to cover basic expenses such as employee transportation. To raise money, Maathai decided to sell tree seedlings, which she hoped would also raise awareness for her fledgling initiative. She purchased a lot of seedlings at an environmental trade show and stored them in her home. Mwangi was not pleased with the takeover. Maathai's plan did not go as intended, however, as she barely sold any seedlings, while the rest withered away during a water shortage. Despite these setbacks, Matthai's vision remained intact.

Two years later, the National Council of Women of Kenya (NCWK) adopted Maathai's tree-planting enterprise in an effort to help its members in rural Kenya. Maathai named the initiative "Save the Land *Harambee*." *Harambee* is a Kiswahili word meaning "let us all pull together." On World Environment Day in June 1977, the NCWK planted seven trees in Kamukunji Park on the outskirts of the city. The trees, which included the Nandi Flame, broad-leaved Cordia, African fig, and East African yellow wood, represented seven leaders from different ethnic groups. These seedlings would eventually form Maathai's first "green belt." Several of the trees provide shade in the park to this day.

On the heels of the successful event, Maathai and the NCWK sought to expand the Green Belt Movement throughout the country, but it failed to catch on as quickly as they had hoped. Maathai realized that because of cultural variations, it was difficult to establish a single tree-planting method across the country as each community had their unique ways of working the land. The Green Belt Movement also lacked grassroots leadership. "I learned that if you do not have local people who are committed to the process and willing to work with their communities, the projects will not survive."[18]

Undaunted, Maathai and the NCWK encouraged farmers, schools, and churches throughout Kenya to join the movement and contribute their expertise. Soon, local communities realized the potential in tree-planting. Within a few months, Maathai had the opposite problem—there were so many requests for seedlings that she could barely keep up and expenses were quickly rising. In response, Maathai arranged a meeting with the government's chief forest official. "We wanted to plant a tree for every person in Kenya—at the time, a total of fifteen million. We even had a slogan, 'One

---

18. Maathai, *Unbowed*, 132.

Person, One Tree.'"[19] Humored, the official told her to take as many seedlings as she wanted free of charge.

Maathai returned a few months later for more seedlings. This time, the official was not as generous, "You are taking too many seedlings from the foresters."[20] The women were proving to be more efficient than the men. Not only this, but officials did not understand why Maathai wanted to teach women in rural areas to plant trees as they considered them unqualified for the task and lacking professional training. Maathai believed they were overcomplicating the task. She encouraged her colleagues to keep using their "woman sense" and plant the seedlings as they had done their whole lives:

> What the foresters were saying didn't seem right to me. You might need a diploma to understand a tree's growth . . . but all they needed to know was how to put the seedlings in the soil and help it grow, and that didn't seem too hard. Anybody can dig a hole, put a tree in it, water it, and nurture it.[21]

The lack of seedlings, as well as logistical issues such as transportation for women outside the cities, became problematic. Maathai again adapted. This time she planted her own seedlings. Her effort took root, and soon, tree nurseries were planted in farms and public spaces around the country. Maathai encouraged the women to plant indigenous trees and meet their challenges with creativity. They responded by using broken pots to hold soil, making watering cans out of old pots with holes, and developing other innovative techniques. As an incentive, Maathai offered four US cents for each seedling planted. Through persistence and creativity, Maathai slowly nurtured the Green Belt Movement. In the process, she empowered women to share the message of stewardship with their local communities:

> As women and communities increased their efforts, we encouraged them to plant seedlings in rows of at least a thousand trees to form green 'belts' that would restore to the earth its cloth of green. This is how the name Green Belt Movement began to be used. Not only did the 'belts' hold the soil in place and provide shade and windbreaks, but they also re-created habitat and enhanced the beauty of the landscape. . . . The future of the planet concerns all of us, and all of us should do what we can do it protect it. As I told the foresters and the women, you don't need a diploma to plant a tree.[22]

19. Maathai, *Unbowed*, 134.
20. Maathai, *Unbowed*, 134.
21. Maathai, *Unbowed*, 135.
22. Maathai, *Unbowed*, 138.

HOW HUMMINGBIRDS FLY IN THE WIND

Researchers have discovered a remarkable quality about hummingbirds. Though they weigh less than a nickel, their wings oscillate to produce extra lift and stability so they can hover and feed in place.[23] These lightweight birds are avian acrobats, able to fly in gusty winds and stormy weather. Their unique ability serves as a fitting metaphor for the headwinds Maathai would face in the next phase of the Green Belt Movement.

Maathai's environmental and professional work was taking a toll on her marriage. Her achievements clashed with Mwangi's ideas about a woman's role in the home. According to Maathai, Mwangi felt that her advanced education and growing success were eclipsing his achievements. One day, Maathai came home to find that Mwangi had left without any warning. She was devastated and wondered what she could have done to preserve their marriage. The separation felt like the death of a close relative.

Mwangi made the couple's divorce a matter of public record and the proceedings soon became fodder for gossip columns and rumor mills. During the trial, Mwangi described his wife as "too educated, too strong, and too hard to control."[24] His words made headlines across the country. After their divorce was finalized, Maathai sat down for a media interview where she told the reporter that the judge presiding over the case must have been either incompetent or corrupt. Infuriated, the judge ordered her to withdraw her statement. When she refused, she was sentenced to six months in jail for contempt of court. Her three children, all under ten years old, were left without their mother.

Maathai's jail sentence became another turning point in her life. She believed that she was arrested, not for committing a criminal act, but for contesting male authority. Her punishment was intended to send a message to women across the country. She was hopeful, however, that the public would perceive her as a woman who stood strong in the face of adversity and that the couple's decision to part ways was best for everyone involved. With her income now significantly reduced, Maathai's financial situation became tenuous. She sent the children to live with Mwangi, as he had the financial means to care for them. He reared them for the next several years. When they grew older the children returned to live with Maathai and continued to stay in touch with Mwangi.

Amidst these personal struggles, the Green Belt Movement was growing. Individuals and organizations from around the world were recognizing

---

23. Sadiq, "What Happens?"
24. Maathai, *Unbowed*, 146.

the wisdom of Maathai's tree-planting strategy. As her popularity grew, Maathai was encouraged to run for the presidency of the NCWK. During the campaign, she encountered strong opposition, particularly from factions in the Moi Government: "Now I was known to the authorities and they didn't like what they saw—an educated, independent African woman aspiring to leadership."[25] Maathai refused to back down and won the election. The NCWK paid a political price for the victory, however, as the government endorsed another women's group for the next twenty years.

Undeterred, the NCWK renewed their focus on the Green Belt Movement. Finding alternative sources of funding proved difficult. Through the encouragement of friends, Maathai decided to run for Parliament. In order to focus on the campaign, she resigned from her position at the university. Her effort was short-lived, however, as the election commission deemed her ineligible to run because she had not registered to vote in the previous election. When she attempted to return to her job, she discovered that it had been filled; the university was no longer in need of her services. To make matters worse, because she had resigned, she was deemed ineligible for healthcare or a pension. While she contested the decision, she received an eviction notice from university housing.

Despite these setbacks, Maathai maintained her focus on the Green Belt Movement. The Norwegian Forestry Society offered a small stipend. The UN Voluntary Fund for Women provided a $122,700 grant to expand the work. As a result, Maathai was able to employ young people to provide technical assistance to community groups, maintain a record of seedlings the organization sold, and also pay the women who planted trees. To help sustain the movement, Maathai encouraged workers to plant nurseries closer to their homes. She also instituted a requirement that each tree must survive for at least six months in order for payment to be disbursed.

Soon, the Green Belt Movement transformed from an individual effort to one involving entire families. Maathai hired husbands and sons to work as nursery attendants. They kept records of the number and type of seeds planted, served as ambassadors to nearby villages and farms, and encouraged other farmers to join the movement. As the work flourished, the mission of the Green Belt Movement expanded in scope. Maathai felt that local communities, rather than depending on government aid, needed to take more ownership of their future. The organization's mission evolved to include the "civic and environmental education"[26] of the Kenyan people:

---

25. Maathai, *Unbowed*, 157.
26. Maathai, *Unbowed*, 174.

> Gradually, the Green Belt Movement grew from a tree-planting program into one that planted ideas as well. We held seminars with the communities in which Green Belt worked, in which I encouraged women and men to identify their problems . . . and develop personal responsibility for their quality of life.[27]

The renewed mission revitalized the organization and more people joined the effort. By the mid-1980s, over 2,000 women's groups were planting nurseries and raising trees across the country. Over 1,000 green belts and several million trees were planted. The movement established more than 600 community-based networks involving several hundred thousand people. By the early 1990s, over 30 million trees had been planted in Kenya alone. The UN partnered with Maathai to extend the Green Belt's reach across Africa and around the world.

Several years of political turmoil followed the Green Belt Movement's success. In 1989, Maathai learned that the government was planning to tear down Uhuru Park, a large green space similar to New York City's Central Park, in order to make way for a skyscraper. The park provided one of the few areas in Nairobi where families could gather outdoors. Its footprint had started to shrink due to the construction of hotels, a golf course, and a football stadium. Now, there were plans to build a sixty-story office building for a number of businesses, including the *Kenya Times*.

Maathai wrote letters to the managing director of the newspaper, the office of the President of Kenya, and several government agencies, pleading with them to halt construction. When her appeals were ignored, she turned to the media, public forums, court injunctions, and other outlets for help. She encouraged the public to reclaim their power as citizens and stand against the government's plans. Maathai became the public face of the campaign and was once again belittled as a "wayward" and misinformed woman.[28] President Moi labeled her "a mad woman" and described her as a "threat to the order and security of the country." A government minister called her an "ignorant and ill-tempered puppet of foreign masters."[29] As the fight intensified, the Green Belt Movement was evicted from their government-owned office space in the city. When landlords refused to rent her a space, she moved the headquarters to her small home.

Maathai's efforts to save the park attracted worldwide attention. In 1990, under intense public scrutiny, the government withdrew its plans for the multi-story tower. Maathai referred to the campaign as the slaying of

---

27. Maathai, *Unbowed*, 174.
28. Maathai, *Unbowed*, 196.
29. Sears, "Wangari Maathai," para. 10.

the "park monster." Her victory inspired the Kenyan public and she felt a renewed sense of confidence.[30] Through the experience, Maathai realized that environmental stewardship was inextricably linked to other civic issues such as governance and human rights:

> I realized in the 1970s that in a young democracy like ours it was very easy for leaders to become dictators. As this happened, they started using national resources as though they were their personal property. I realized that the constitution had given them powers to misuse official machinery. So, I became involved in the pro-democracy movement and pressed for constitutional reforms and political space to ensure freedom of thought and expression. We cannot live with a political system that kills creativity and produces cowardly people.[31]

Maathai paid a price for her activism as the government ostracized her, yet she continued to advocate for environmental stewardship and good governance. When she heard that President Moi was planning a government-sponsored coup in order to postpone national elections, she organized a group of activists to publicly confront him. As a result, Maathai received a number of death threats, forcing her to live in a series of safe houses. She was arrested and charged with sedition and treason—convictions that carried the death penalty. During her trial, leaders from around the world, including the United States and Europe, warned President Moi that arresting pro-democracy leaders would affect political ties. Maathai and her colleagues were subsequently freed and all charges dropped.

Maathai pressed on and continued to hold the government accountable on issues such as the arrest of political activists, human rights abuses, land-grabbing, and deforestation. Under the auspices of the Green Belt Movement, she conducted seminars, teach-ins, and other protests. In 1992, during a hunger strike, she was beaten unconscious by the police and hospitalized in critical condition.[32] Still, the scope of the movement grew to include protection of public lands against privatization and encroachment. The Department of Forests also partnered with the organization to conserve and restore water towers throughout the country.

In 2001, the Kenyan government announced plans to remove legal protections from nearly 170,000 acres of old-growth timber in the Karura Forest. The land was to be portioned out to government ministers and their supporters. Notably, in 1977, 2.9 percent of Kenya was covered by forest.

30. Maathai, *Unbowed*, 204.
31. UNESCO, "We Pay Tribute to Wangari Maathai," 15.
32. Perlez, "Violence," para. 5.

When the Green Belt Movement started in 2001, the country had less than 2 percent of forested land remaining.[33] Maathai collected signatures, raised awareness through public speeches, and led protests. At one of her rallies, a few days before International Women's Day, Maathai was again arrested. She was set free when her detention drew worldwide attention. Following her release, the Yale School of Forestry and Environmental Studies offered her a fellowship to study the environment and sustainable development. After her tenure as a McCluskey Fellow, the university awarded Maathai an honorary doctorate in humane letters.[34]

When Maathai returned to Kenya, she attempted another run for Parliament. Her campaign slogan, "Rise Up and Walk," was inspired by the story of Peter and John in the book of Acts. Her message was similar to the apostles. While she had no silver or gold to entice the voters, she assured them that "together we could lift ourselves up and address the conditions of our poverty and disempowerment and regain our sense of self-respect."[35] Maathai's campaign was so successful that she was elected with 98 percent of the vote. It was a clear mandate for change.

In 2004, Maathai received the Nobel Peace Prize for her "contribution to sustainable development, democracy and peace."[36] Maathai became the first African woman to receive the award. Upon hearing the news, Maathai walked outside and planted a tree.[37] In her acceptance speech, she described peace as a three-legged stool consisting of good governance, equity for all citizens, and sustainable management of resources. Maathai reflected on her twenty-four-year struggle as a steward of the land and its people:

> What I have learned over the years is that we must be patient, persistent, and committed. When we are planting trees sometimes people will say to me, 'I don't want to plant this tree because it will not grow fast enough.' I have to keep reminding them that the trees they are cutting today were not planted by them, but by those who came before. So they must plant the trees that will benefit communities in the future. . . . I have always believed that no matter how dark the cloud, there is always a thin, silver lining, and that is what we must look for. The silver lining will come, if not to us then to the next generation or the

---

33 Anbarasan, "Wangari Muta Maathai," 46.
34. Yale News, "International Environmental Leaders."
35. Maathai, *Unbowed*, 287.
36. "Nobel Peace Prize 2004," para. 1.
37. MacDonald, "Something Wonderful Happens."

generation after that. And maybe with that generation the lining will no longer be thin.³⁸

Maathai passed away in 2011 at seventy-one years of age. Her legacy lives on in a new generation of stewards and in the millions of trees planted around the world. Achim Steiner, the executive director of the United Nations' environmental program described Maathai as "a force of nature," likening her to Africa's beloved acacia trees, "Strong in character and able to survive sometimes the harshest of conditions."³⁹

THE STEWARDSHIP OF WANGARI MAATHAI

The life of Wangari Maathai is a lesson in servant-leadership and stewardship. While she remained grounded in the realities of the present, she acted in view of the future. She was asked in an interview how she persuaded people to plant trees, an activity some might perceive as a simplistic solution to vexing problems such as erosion, malnutrition, and disenfranchisement. Her answer was clear, "We tell them, 'If you don't take care of this land today, tomorrow you will have rocks, not soil.'"⁴⁰ As noted earlier in this chapter, a steward holds an item in trust for another. Through Maathai's leadership we see that a steward accomplishes this by keeping one eye on the present and one on the future. Servant-leaders lead today in light of tomorrow; in doing so they help create the future.

Maathai's servant-leadership also reminds us that stewardship is not only about the well-being of objects and institutions, but people as well. Maathai began by planting trees to combat environmental damage. She soon realized that she must also care for the people who inhabited the environment. Stewardship means investing in people and their potential to solve those problems. Her strategy expanded to include human concerns such as empowerment, human rights, good governance, and democratic rule. She described it this way, "Nobody would have bothered me if all I did was to encourage women to plant trees. But I started seeing the linkages between the problems we were dealing with and their root causes."⁴¹ The producers of the documentary *Taking Root: The Vision of Wangari Maathai*, said the following:

---

38. Maathai, *Unbowed*, 290.
39. Gettleman, "Wangari Maathai, Nobel Peace Prize Laureate, Dies at 71," para. 6.
40. Condé Nast, "Conversation with Wangari Maathai," para. 10.
41. Pal, "Wangari Maathai," 35.

It was not only what Wangari had accomplished that was stunning, it was also the way she had done it. She had a way of choosing the right issue at the right time and not letting anything or anybody get in her way. She had the moral courage to speak truth to power and the patience, persistence, and commitment to take action—against enormous odds. In Wangari's story, we could follow a path that linked hitherto separate realms. Her path was a blueprint of her developing understanding, and hence our understanding, of the nature of holistic change and the inextricable linkages between environmental justice, human rights, good governance, and peace. We were compelled to tell her story.[42]

Another lesson we can learn from Maathai is that stewardship begins with what we have. We may not have all the money, materials, and people we want, but we can deploy the resources we do have. Great leadership begins with small movements toward change. Sometimes we may feel that we are too small or not _____ enough to make a difference. When we think this way, we short-circuit the possibility of change.

During an environmental lecture in Los Angeles, Maathai told her audience, "[I'm] talking about simple things that can be done, such as recycling, planting trees, changing light bulbs and using public transportation. It doesn't have to start with big things; start with small things, start with ourselves."[43] Maathai began by planting seven tree seedlings alongside a handful of women that society considered illiterate and unqualified. Her efforts were misunderstood and mocked. But, like the hummingbird, she did the best she could. Maathai encouraged her followers, "Find something you can do. It doesn't have to be a big thing. It's the little things that matter."[44] Her stewardship as a servant-leader stands as a testament to cultural anthropologist Margaret Mead's well-known reminder, "Never doubt that a small group of thoughtful, committed citizens can change the world. Indeed, it is the only thing that ever has."[45]

Robert Greenleaf believed that stewardship was closely aligned with the notion of trust and the role of trustees. He described trustees simply as "persons in whom ultimate trust is placed."[46] The servant-leader, acting as a

---

42. Independent Television Service, "Taking Root Discussion Guide," 2.
43. Mitchell, "Nobel Laureate Talks," para. 5.
44. Little, "Planting Trees for Peace," 46.
45. Lutkehaus, *Margaret Mead*, 261.
46. Greenleaf, *Servant Leadership: A Journey*, 40.

steward, takes action "only in the best interests of those to come."[47] Stewards serve as trustees of the present and the future. Block expanded the idea to include the notion of creating an environment where others can join the effort.[48] Ferch described how servant-leaders rise above themselves for the greater good of society, "The servant-leader transcends himself or herself to become the steward of others, capable of raising up future generations, and confident in building community."[49]

Like Maathai, everyone who aspires to servant-leadership has a responsibility to be a caretaker, whether at home, work, or in the community. Stewardship does not arise magically, nor can we pass the buck to someone else. Rather, it begins with a conscious decision "to care and to conserve.... It requires that leaders remember that actions in one part of the world have repercussions in other parts of the world because the planet is a system, delicately balanced."[50] Like the hummingbird, each of us can do the best we can—no more and no less.

FINDING: STEWARDSHIP

In ancient Rome, after a military general returned home from a victory, the city would throw a parade. As the general marched down the streets to the chorus of applause, a minder would quietly whisper in his ear, "*Memento Mori*," or, "Remember that you must die." Someone explained, "The point of this reminder isn't to be morbid or promote fear, but to inspire, motivate and clarify."[51] Servant-leaders understand that, ultimately, they are caretakers of the resources and people they are entrusted to lead. Our time is limited. As noted by Marshall Goldsmith, "Passing the baton is the final challenge of great leadership."[52] Let us pass it well.

47. See Baldwin, "Learning Servant-Leadership," 143.
48. See Lee and Zemke, "Search for Spirit."
49. Ferch, *Forgiveness and Power*, 155.
50. See Braye, "Servant Leadership," 302.
51. "History of Memento Mori," para. 2.
52. Goldsmith, "Passing the Baton," para. 13.

9

Viktor Frankl: The Servant-Leader and Commitment to the Growth of People

THE SPIRES OF ST. Stephen's Cathedral extended above central Vienna like silent sentries. Viktor Frankl gazed pensively at the landmark as he made his way through its labyrinthine streets. As he got closer, the towers seemed to grow in size—a fitting analogy for the decision he was facing. The church was a familiar place as the sanctuary provided a quiet place for Frankl to ponder his next steps.

It was 1941, and Frankl had received a visa to emigrate to the United States. The opportunity presented a chance to further his practice as a psychiatrist, and perhaps, a professorship. Leaving Vienna would also mean escaping life—and almost certainly death—in a Nazi concentration camp. Frankl's beloved city had become a part of Hitler's Germany. The Nazis had forced thousands of Austrian Jews into "labor camps" in Poland and Eastern Europe. It was only a matter of time before Frankl and his family suffered the same fate. Many of his colleagues had already left. Frankl worried most of all about his elderly parents. He quietly prayed for a "hint from heaven."[1]

When Frankl got home, he noticed a chunk of marble laying on the coffee table. His father had picked up the fragment from a nearby synagogue demolished by the Nazis. Frankl ran his fingers over the stone and felt the outline of a Hebrew letter. It was the first letter of the Fifth Commandment: "Honor thy father and thy mother, that thy days may be long in the land

1. Redsand, *Viktor Frankl*, 6.

Viktor Frankl: The Servant-Leader and Commitment to the Growth of People

which the Lord thy God giveth thee."[2] It provided the answer he was seeking. Frankl cancelled his visa and decided to stay with his parents in Vienna. His decision and actions in the days and months that followed epitomized the ninth characteristic of servant-leadership—commitment to the growth of people. Servant-leadership scholar Larry Spears, speaking of the characteristic in the context of organizational leadership, described it this way,

> Servant leaders believe that people have an intrinsic value beyond their tangible contributions as workers. As such, the servant leader is deeply committed to the growth of each and every individual within his or her organization. The servant leader recognizes the tremendous responsibility to do everything in his or her power to nurture the personal and professional growth of employees and colleagues. In practice, this can include (but is not limited to) concrete actions such as making funds available for personal and professional development, taking a personal interest in the ideas and suggestions from everyone, encouraging worker involvement in decision-making, and actively assisting laid-off employees to find other positions.[3]

Whether leading within or outside an organization, the ninth characteristic of servant-leadership is applicable across any context. In this chapter we explore how Viktor Frankl exemplified commitment to the growth of people while imprisoned during the Holocaust. His actions serve as an example of a servant-leader who contributed to the growth of others even in the darkest of circumstances.

VIKTOR FRANKL: AN OVERVIEW

Frankl's experiences of suffering, survival, and resilience have inspired millions of people around the world ever since he described them in his book, *Man's Search for Meaning*. The bestselling memoir recounts his experiences as a prisoner during the Holocaust and lays out the psychological basis for his survival. Frankl was deported to a series of concentration camps, including Theresienstadt in Czechoslovakia and Auschwitz-Birkenau in Poland. Despite a lack of control over his situation, Frankl made a choice that ended up saving his life. He decided that no matter the circumstance, he would always maintain the ability to choose his attitude. Frankl famously declared, "Everything can be taken from a man but one thing; the last of the human

---

2. Redsand, *Viktor Frankl*, 6.
3. Spears, "Tracing the Growing Impact" 6.

freedoms—to choose one's attitude in any given set of circumstances, to choose one's own way."[4] His attitude toward unavoidable suffering was evident in his servant-leadership—even when he was imprisoned and facing certain death. This choice would become the key to his survival and resilience.

After his liberation, Frankl lectured around the world, sharing his experiences as a Holocaust survivor. He published over thirty books and founded the Third Viennese School of Psychotherapy, known as logotherapy—an approach to mental health grounded in the notion that a person's fundamental need in life is the discovery of meaning. Although Frankl faced a unique set of circumstances, his experience provides insight and inspiration into the transformative nature of servant-leadership and commitment to the growth of people.

FRANKL'S DISCOVERY OF MEANING

Viktor Frankl was born on March 26, 1905, in Vienna, Austria. Though his father Gabriel was a bookbinder by trade, he moved to Austria in hopes of entering medical school. When financial difficulties forced a change in plans, he entered government service and became the director of the Austrian Ministry of Social Service. Frankl's father was austere, religious, and a strong believer in the power of personal responsibility. His mother, Elsa, was pious and kindhearted. When Frankl took an inkblot test later in life, the psychiatrist exclaimed that he had never seen such a mix of rationality and emotion in one person. Frankl attributed this balance to his parents.

Frankl was an intellectually curious and precocious child. At age three, he determined to become a doctor. By age five he was contemplating the meaning of life and his own mortality. Upon seeing Frankl's philosophical bent, a family friend nicknamed him the "The Thinker." Frankl later stated that he was not so much a "big thinker" as a "thinker-through"[5] He also reflected on ideas such as nihilism, the limits of rationality, and the existence of God. Frankl balanced these intellectual interests with physical activity. He was particularly fond of mountain climbing, a hobby he enjoyed well into his seventies.

As a teenager, Frankl attended evening classes to study experimental and applied psychology. When he was fifteen, the local philosophical society asked him to conduct a workshop on meaning in life. His intellectual interests led him to write a letter to famed psychoanalyst Sigmund Freud,

---

4. Frankl, *Man's Search for Meaning*, 75.
5. Frankl, *Man's Search for Ultimate Meaning*, 32.

who returned the favor. In 1924, upon Freud's suggestion, Frankl published his first article in the *International Journal of Psychoanalysis*. Their correspondence was so frequent that when they met for the first time, Freud recited Frankl's address from memory. When Frankl entered medical school in 1924, he developed a rapport with Alfred Adler, another pioneering psychiatrist. A year later he published another article in the same journal, this time at Adler's urging. These timely interactions would help Frankl form the foundations for his own psychotherapy.

In 1928, as Frankl was finishing his medical studies, he organized youth counseling centers in Vienna and six other cities. It was the first year that no student suicides were reported in Vienna.[6] By the time he graduated in 1930, logotherapy had gained enough recognition that Frankl was asked to provide psychiatric consultations throughout Europe. He accepted a position at Vienna's University Clinic, specializing in neurology. In 1933, Frankl was promoted to chief of Vienna's Female Suicidals Pavilion where he treated several thousand patients each year. In 1937, Frankl opened a thriving psychiatric practice. Shortly thereafter, his life changed forever.

In March 1938, Hitler invaded Austria, unleashing the state-sponsored persecution and genocide of some 6 million Jews and other minorities.[7] Germany was recovering from its defeat in World War I. In a political and economic climate characterized by "deprivation, disillusionment, bitterness, and social unrest," Hitler and the National Socialist Party scapegoated the Jewish people for the problems of the German nation.[8] Hitler was determined to annihilate the Jewish race through the systematic slaughter of millions of men, women, and children based on his diabolical anti-Semitic worldview.

Shortly after Frankl had allowed his visa to expire, he was appointed director of neurology at Rothschild Hospital, the only hospital for Jews in Vienna. The position temporarily delayed his family's deportation to the concentration camps. During Frankl's tenure, he risked his life by diagnosing mentally ill patients with organic brain disease and fever delirium, thus circumventing Nazi orders for euthanasia. Around this time, he began writing his first book, *The Doctor and the Soul: An Introduction to Logotherapy*.

In 1941, Frankl married Tilly Grosser, a nurse at Rothschild Hospital. They were the last couple to obtain permission to marry before the Nazis dissolved the Jewish registrar's office. Jewish couples were forbidden to have children and pregnant women were deported to the concentration camps.

6. Frankl, *Man's Search for Meaning*.
7. Rubenstein and Roth, *Approaches to Auschwitz*.
8. Shantall, *Life's Meaning*, 7.

Frankl and his wife were not untouched by this diktat. He recalled, "Tilly had to sacrifice the fetus she was carrying. My book, *The Unheard Cry for Meaning*, is dedicated to this, our unborn child."[9]

In 1942, Frankl, Tilly, his parents, and brother were arrested and sent to Theresienstadt, a ghetto-labor camp. Frankl's sister, Stella, managed to flee to Australia. Theresienstadt styled itself as a special camp for "privileged Jews" because it housed a nursery, infirmary, and even a café. In reality it was a "joke hatched in hell" characterized by dreadful conditions and starvation.[10] Early in his imprisonment, Frankl demonstrated a commitment to the growth of others by serving his fellow prisoners. He provided psychotherapy, devised a program to help new arrivals adjust to camp life, and became involved in suicide prevention efforts.

Frankl's father died of starvation and pneumonia while in Theresienstadt. In October 1944, Frankl, Tilly, and his sixty-five-year-old mother were transferred to Auschwitz-Birkenau, the largest and most feared of the Nazi concentration camps. Tilly was granted a two-year transfer exemption because of her work in a munitions factory. Frankl urged her to stay at Theresienstadt, but she volunteered to take the transport with him to Auschwitz. They were separated after their arrival, never to see one another again. Upon his arrival, Josef Mengele, the infamous "Angel of Death," assigned Frankl to the gas chambers. He managed to avoid a gruesome end through some quick thinking. When Frankl noticed that some of his friends were standing in another line, he switched from the left line to the right line while Mengele had his back turned, thus saving his life.[11] Frankl's mother and brother were not as fortunate—they were murdered in the gas chambers shortly after their arrival. Tilly was moved to Bergen-Belsen where she died of sickness and starvation.[12] Frankl was transferred among Theresienstadt, Auschwitz, Kaufering III, and Turkheim before his liberation on April 27, 1945.

Frankl returned to Vienna where he learned about the death of his family. He accepted the directorship of the Vienna Neurological Polyclinic, a position he held for the next twenty-five years. During this time, he finished his bestselling book, *Man's Search for Meaning*, dictating it in only nine days. In 1947, Frankl married Eleonore Schmidt and completed his doctorate in philosophy. In 1950, he established the Austrian Medical Society for Psychotherapy.

---

9. Frankl, *Man's Search for Ultimate Meaning*, 87.
10. Pytell, "Man Who Would Be King," 201.
11. Frankl, *Man's Search for Meaning*.
12. Frankl, *Man's Search for Meaning*, 91.

Frankl spent the rest of his life lecturing around the world until his death on September 2, 1997. Over the course of his life, Frankl authored thirty-two books, which were subsequently published in thirty-two languages. *Man's Search for Meaning* has sold over 5 million copies in the US alone. Its success helped promote logotherapy, which has been applied in a variety of settings, including clinical psychology and social work. A summary of its major concepts is presented in the next section as it formed the basis for Frankl's survival and servant-leadership during his imprisonment.

LOGOTHERAPY: HEALING THROUGH MEANING

As a psychiatrist, Frankl noticed a range of reactivity among his patients who were dealing with unavoidable suffering. He observed that while some would contemplate or commit suicide, others facing the same circumstances not only survived, but thrived. Frankl was intrigued, but found the psychological theories of his day inadequate to explain the contrast. Based on his research and clinical practice, he attributed the difference to the discovery of meaning. In response, he developed logotherapy, a psychotherapeutic system that attempts to facilitate healing through the search for meaning. The term derives from the Greek word *logos*, which means "spirit" or "word."[13]

Logotherapy is based on the concept of the *will to meaning*, which Frankl identified as humanity's deepest need. Three pillars form the basis of this approach, namely, 1) freedom of the will, 2) the will to meaning, and 3) the meaning of life.[14] Logotherapy stood in contrast to the dominant psychological views of Frankl's day, particularly Freud's "will to pleasure" and Adler's "will to power." Diverging from Freud and Adler, Frankl asserted that humanity was motivated by something greater than sexual instincts or a striving for superiority. He stated, "I am convinced that in the final analysis there is no situation that does not contain within it a seed of meaning."[15] Frankl contended that an exclusively biological perspective of humanity failed to address the need for meaning. According to Frankl, "it turned out that if a neurosis could be removed, more often than not when it was removed, a vacuum was left. The patient was beautifully adjusted and functioning, but meaning was missing."[16]

Logotherapy took a different approach from introspective therapies that tended to look backward with a focus on resolving prior trauma. Instead,

13. Frankl, *Unheard Cry for Meaning*.
14. Frankl, *Man's Search for Meaning*, 104.
15. Pattakos, *Prisoners of Our Thoughts*, 19.
16. Frankl, *Unheard Cry for Meaning*, 20.

logotherapy embraced a teleological, future-oriented perspective that encouraged a person "to find out what is considered the unique and specific meaning to his existence."[17] Frankl believed that when people lack meaning they experience existential frustration.[18] To Frankl, *existential* referred to: 1) existence itself (i.e., the human mode of being), 2) the meaning of existence, and 3) the striving to find concrete meaning in personal existence (i.e., the will to meaning). While Freud postulated that neuroses emerged from a conflict between drives and instincts, Frankl attributed it to a lack of meaning. According to Frankl, "Logotherapy regards its assignment as that of assisting the patient to find meaning in his life . . . the hidden *logos* of his existence."[19]

To Frankl, mental health was not about achieving a tension-free or painless state. Rather, he viewed it as a natural byproduct of pursuing a worthwhile goal: "What [a person] needs is not the discharge of tension at any cost but the call of a potential meaning waiting to be fulfilled by him."[20] According to Frankl, every person has a responsibility, presented by life itself, to discover and fulfill a concrete and personal meaning. This begins by taking ownership for one's choices, the greatest of which is the ability to choose one's attitude when facing unavoidable suffering.

Frankl asserted that there were two types of meaning: 1) the meaning of the moment, which consists of the tasks and challenges of everyday life, and 2) super or ultimate meaning, which includes metaphysical or spiritual ideas such as God, truth, and justice.[21] While the meaning of the moment might change according to the demands of a situation, ultimate meaning "never ceases to be."[22] He believed that the tasks and problems we encounter each day provide an opportunity to search for meaning in the moment.[23] Ultimate meaning, however, is immutable, regardless of the situation—it lies independent of anyone or anything. Frankl believed a person could discover meaning through three ways: 1) by creating a work or a deed, 2) by experiencing something or encountering someone, or 3) by the attitude one takes toward suffering. Amidst the genocidal horrors of the Holocaust, Frankl chose to confront suffering courageously by choosing how he would respond.

In a therapeutic setting, a logotherapist encourages clients to move away from self-embeddedness and toward personal responsibility; the

17. Pytell, "Man Who Would Be King," 2.
18. Frankl, *Man's Search for Meaning*, 106.
19. Frankl, *Man's Search for Meaning*, 108.
20. Frankl, *Man's Search for Meaning*, 110.
21. Frankl, *Man's Search for Meaning*.
22. Frankl, *Man's Search for Meaning*, 115.
23. Guttmann, *Logotherapy for the Helping Professional*.

goal is self-transcendence through the discovery of meaning. Therapeutic techniques include paradoxical intention, which requires contemplating and even doing the very thing one fears, and de-reflection, which involves shifting emphasis from oneself and onto others. A number of professional organizations such as the American Medical Association, the American Psychiatric Association, and the American Psychological Association have formally recognized logotherapy as a scientifically based school of psychotherapy. With this background, we now examine how Frankl faced his circumstances and discovered meaning through a commitment to the growth of others.

THE SHADOW OF DEATH

The average life expectancy of prisoners during the Holocaust rarely exceeded three months due to brutal treatment, forced labor, starvation, and disease.[24] Frankl stated, "Little does [the outsider] know of the hard fight for existence which rages among the prisoners. This was an unrelenting struggle for daily bread and for life itself" alongside a "multitude of small torments."[25] In his book, *Man's Search for Meaning*, Frankl vividly described his experience at Auschwitz, the largest of the Nazi death camps. Its four crematoria gassed more than 9,000 people a day.[26] Frankl was among 1,500 prisoners sent to the extermination center at Auschwitz under the guise of a transport to a munitions factory:

> There were eighty people in each coach. All had to lie on top of their luggage, the few remnants of their personal possessions. The carriages were so full that only the top parts of the windows were free to let in the grey of dawn. Any naïve or wishful thinking about camp life was quickly shattered when the prisoners heard the train's ghastly whistle and realized where they had arrived. Everyone's heart missed a beat at that moment. Auschwitz—the very name stood for all that was horrible: gas chambers, crematoriums, massacres. Slowly, almost hesitatingly, the train moved on as if it wanted to spare its passengers the dreadful realization as long as possible: Auschwitz![27]

---

24. Shantall, *Life's Meaning*.
25. Frankl, *Man's Search for Meaning*, 17–18.
26. Shantall, *Life's Meaning*, 59.
27. Frankl, *Man's Search for Meaning*, 22.

Upon his arrival to the death camp, Frankl was "horrified."[28] As the borders of the camp became visible in the early morning light, he noticed "long stretches of several rows of barbed wire fences; watch towers; search lights; and long columns of ragged human figures, grey in the greyness of dawn, trekking along the straight desolate roads, to what destination we did not know."[29] His confusion increased as guards shouted orders he did not understand. The grounds echoed with shrieks that sounded as if they were coming "from the throat of a man who had to keep shouting like that, a man who was being murdered again and again."[30] Upon arrival, prisoners were placed in cramped conditions. Fifteen hundred people lived in a shed built for 200. Communicable diseases and vermin were unending sources of misery.

The guards stripped the prisoners of their clothing and seized their belongings. Frankl and the other inmates were driven into a mass shower with leather whips:

> While we were waiting for the shower, our nakedness was brought home to us: we really had nothing now except our bare bodies—even minus hair. All we possessed, literally, was our naked existence. What else remained for us as a material link to our former lives?[31]

Frankl exchanged his clothes for a "uniform of rags, which would have made a scarecrow elegant by comparison."[32] He was prisoner #119104."[33] The number was tattooed on his arm and sewn into his clothing. The experience was deliberately dehumanizing. A majority of prisoners experienced "a kind of inferiority complex. We all had once been or had fancied ourselves to be 'somebody.' Now we were treated like complete nonentities. Without consciously thinking about it, the average prisoner felt himself utterly degraded."[34]

Life in the camps was marked by endless uncertainty; prisoners lived under the shadow of death. Even a glance from a guard could mean immediate execution. The interminable length of the imprisonment had a particularly devastating effect:

28. Frankl, *Man's Search for Meaning*, 23.
29. Frankl, *Man's Search for Meaning*, 23.
30. Frankl, *Man's Search for Meaning*, 23.
31. Frankl, *Man's Search for Meaning*, 28.
32. Frankl, *Man's Search for Meaning*, 33.
33. Frankl, *Man's Search for Meaning*, 21.
34. Frankl, *Man's Search for Meaning*, 72.

The most depressing influence of all was that a prisoner could not know how long his term of imprisonment would be. He had been given no date for his release . . . [unable to] aim for an ultimate goal in his life. He ceased living for the future, in contrast to a man in normal life.[35]

Frankl observed how this altered sense of time affected one prisoner so acutely that "he had felt as though he were marching at his own funeral. His life had seemed to him absolutely without future. He regarded it as over and done, as if he had already died."[36]

Prisoners were loaned to construction companies who paid a fixed price for each worker. Physical abuse, for even the most minor of infractions, was a part of daily life. A guard beat Frankl because the food line in which he stood was not in perfect symmetry. While laying a railroad line, Frankl paused to catch his breath and leaned on his shovel. A guard hit him on the head with a rock. On another occasion, Frankl reached out to steady a prisoner who collapsed while carrying a heavy girder. "I jumped to his assistance without stopping to think. I was immediately hit on the back, rudely reprimanded and ordered to return to my place."[37] The violence was compounded by sickness and starvation. A typical meal consisted of a few ounces of bread and watery soup—hardly sufficient for prisoners working in freezing temperatures. The majority of prisoners suffered from edema and frostbite as they were forced to march for hours through snow-covered fields while wearing inadequate and ill-fitting clothing. At one point, Frankl nearly died from typhus.

Some of the prisoners attempted to cope by numbing themselves with alcohol. Others struggled with suicidal ideation. Frankl explained how such despair emanated from the "hopelessness of the situation, the constant danger of death looming over us daily and hourly, and the closeness of the deaths suffered by many of the others."[38] The atmosphere of violence and death produced hopelessness and apathy:

> [F]eelings were blunted. . . . Disgust, horror and pity are emotions that our spectator could not really feel any more. The sufferers, the dying and the dead, became such commonplace sights to him after a few weeks of camp life that they could not move him anymore.[39]

35. Frankl, *Man's Search for Meaning*, 79.
36. Frankl, *Man's Search for Meaning*, 79.
37. Frankl, *Man's Search for Meaning*, 37.
38. Frankl, *Man's Search for Meaning*, 31.
39. Frankl, *Man's Search for Meaning*, 34.

It was in the center of these circumstances that Frankl made a decision that he would not allow anyone take away the one thing he had left—the ability to choose his attitude. He described it as the "last of the human freedoms."[40] Not only this, but Frankl made a commitment to serve his fellow prisoners. Rather than turn inward, as many would be tempted to do, he turned outward. Paradoxically, in serving others, he managed to ensure his own survival. In the next section we explore the servant-leadership of Frankl and how he expressed commitment to the growth of others.

SERVANT-LEADERSHIP AND THE LAST OF THE HUMAN FREEDOMS

Frankl believed that every person has the ability to choose his or her response to suffering—even amidst the worst of circumstances. If a person's physical freedom is taken away, Frankl maintained that one could hold fast to one's inner freedom. This belief became the basis of his survival and his servant-leadership:

> We who lived in concentration camps can remember the men who walked through the huts comforting others, giving away their last piece of bread. They may have been few in number, but they offer sufficient proof that everything can be taken from a man but one thing: the last of the human freedoms—to choose one's attitude in any given set of circumstances, to choose one's own way. And there were always choices to make. Every day, every hour, offered the opportunity to make a decision, a decision which determined whether you would or would not submit to those powers which threatened to rob you of your very self, your inner freedom; which determined whether or not you would become the plaything of circumstance, renouncing freedom and dignity to become molded into the form of the typical inmate. ... It is this spiritual freedom which cannot be taken away—that makes life meaningful and purposeful.[41]

Frankl took on the role of a servant and made a conscious choice to attend to the needs of his fellow prisoners. Through acts of service, Frankl embodied Greenleaf's maxim that a servant-leader desires, above all, to serve first.

Frankl's commitment to the growth of others diverged from the tendency toward self-preservation. Frankl observed that each prisoner was

40. Frankl, *Man's Search for Meaning*, 74.
41. Frankl, *Man's Search for Meaning*, 74–75.

"controlled by one thought only: to keep himself alive for the family waiting for him at home, and to save his friends."[42] This was particularly evident when guards decided which prisoners would be transferred to a death camp and who would remain in the work camp:

> The majority of prisoners would with no hesitation arrange for another prisoner, another 'number,' to take his place in the transport. . . . There seemed to be a rationalization that allowed a prisoner to think that if he or she escaped a particular transport by switching with another prisoner, then he or she was only exchanging a number, rather than jeopardizing another's life. It appears that self-preservation was exaggerated among prisoners as they began to view their comrades through the same lens of dehumanization that the guards used—every prisoner was merely another number destined for death.[43]

Frankl, however, sought opportunities to inspire and encourage his fellow prisoners, even when he was personally suffering. On one particularly difficult and depressing day, a senior block warden sensed the lack of hope. He asked Frankl to speak to his fellow prisoners. Frankl recalled the incident,

> God knows I was not in the mood to give psychological explanations or to preach any sermons—to offer my comrades a kind of medical care of their souls. I was cold and hungry, irritable and tired; but I had to make the effort and use this unique opportunity. Encouragement was now more necessary than ever.[44]

Frankl continued,

> So, I began by mentioning the most trivial of comforts first. I said that even in this Europe in the sixth winter of the Second World War, our situation was not the most terrible we could think of. I said that each of us had to ask himself what irreplaceable losses he had suffered up to then. I speculated that for most of them these losses had really been few. Whoever was still alive had reason for hope. Health, family, happiness, professional abilities, fortune, position in society—all these were things that could be achieved again or restored. After all, we still had all our

---

42. Frankl, *Man's Search for Meaning*, 19.
43. Frankl, *Man's Search for Meaning*, 19.
44. Frankl, *Man's Search for Meaning*, 89.

bones intact. Whatever we had gone through could still be an asset to us in the future.[45]

Through his message of hope, Frankl renewed the prisoners' sense of meaning. He was convinced that no matter how dark the circumstances, life "never ceases to have meaning, and that this infinite meaning of life includes suffering, dying, privation and death."[46] Frankl asked his fellow prisoners to consider how their friends, wives, and God wanted them to endure their circumstances with dignity. Indeed, they were making "a sacrifice of the deepest significance."[47] While at Theresienstadt, Frankl lectured in a similar manner at least ten times.[48]

Frankl assisted a prisoner who was grieving the loss of his wife. Using a Socratic dialogue, he asked the man to consider how his wife would have felt if he had preceded her in death. The man believed his wife would have suffered greatly. Frankl told him,

> 'Your wife has been spared this suffering, and after all, it is you who are sparing her this suffering—to be sure, at the price that now you have to survive and mourn her.' At the same moment, he could see a meaning in his suffering, the meaning of a sacrifice. There was still suffering, but no longer despair, because despair is suffering without meaning.[49]

Frankl also used humor to creatively serve others. He noted,

> It is well known that humor, more than anything else in the human make-up, can afford an aloofness and an ability to rise above any situation, even if only for a few seconds. I practically trained a friend of mine who worked next to me on the building site to develop a sense of humor. I suggested to him that we would promise each other to invent at least one amusing story daily, about some incident that could happen one day after liberation.... The attempt to develop a sense of humor and to see things in a humorous light is some kind of trick learned while mastering the art of living. Yet it is possible to practice the art of living even in a concentration camp, although suffering is omnipresent.[50]

---

45. Frankl, *Man's Search for Meaning*, 89.
46. Frankl, *Man's Search for Meaning*, 91.
47. Frankl, *Man's Search for Meaning*, 91.
48. Biller et al., "Viktor Frankl."
49. Frankl, *Man's Search for Meaning*, 133.
50. Frankl, *Man's Search for Meaning*, 54–55.

Frankl served not just his fellow prisoners, but the guards as well. He described an instance where he was assigned to work on a road crew, an experience far different from his career as a physician:

> I even allowed myself to say once to a kindly foreman, 'If you could learn from me how to do a brain operation in as short a time as I am learning this road work from you, I would have great respect for you.' And he grinned.[51]

In another incident, Frankl listened as a guard shared his personal struggles. He helped him sort through his difficulties,

> He had taken a liking to me because I listened to his love stories and matrimonial troubles, which he poured out during the long marches to our work site. I had made an impression on him with my diagnosis of his character and with my psychotherapeutic advice.[52]

Frankl provided medical care to prisoners quarantined in the typhoid block and participated in suicide prevention efforts. He noted,

> The tender beginnings of a psychotherapy or psychohygiene were, when they were possible at all in the camp, either individual or collective in nature. The individual psychotherapeutic attempts were often a kind of 'life-saving procedure.' These efforts were usually concerned with the prevention of suicides. A very strict camp ruling forbade any efforts to save a man who attempted suicide. It was forbidden, for example, to cut down a man who was trying to hang himself. Therefore, it was all important to prevent these attempts from occurring.[53]

Frankl's commitment to the growth of others was tested during an incident where he and a fellow physician were offered a chance to escape. A foreign resistance fighter stood outside the gates, ready to provide clothing and documents. Under the guise of a medical consult, Frankl was smuggled out of the camp. Due to some unspecified "technical difficulties" the two men returned to camp and Frankl proceeded to complete his rounds.[54] One of his patients noticed Frankl acting a bit strange and asked him whether he was planning an escape. The question gripped Frankl so intensely that he

---

51. Frankl, *Man's Search for Meaning*, 40.
52. Frankl, *Man's Search for Meaning*, 38.
53. Frankl, *Man's Search for Meaning*, 87.
54. Frankl, *Man's Search for Meaning*, 67.

decided to never again abandon his patients, even if it meant his own death. He shared his decision with his colleague,

> As soon as I had told him with finality that I had made up my mind to stay with my patients, the unhappy feeling left me. I did not know what the following days would bring, but I had gained an inward peace that I had never experienced before. I returned to the hut, sat down on the boards at my countryman's feet and tried to comfort him; then I chatted with the others, trying to quiet them in their delirium.[55]

In another situation, Frankl was offered an opportunity to cross his name off a transport list that had been assigned to a death camp. He declined, choosing instead to "let fate take its course."[56] The next morning he made a startling discovery,

> Those who had pitied me remained in a camp where famine was to rage even more fiercely than in our new camp. They tried to save themselves, but they only sealed their own fates. Months later, after liberation, I met a friend from the old camp. He related to me how he, as camp policeman, had searched for pieces of human flesh that was missing from a pile of corpses. He confiscated it from a pot in which he found it cooking. Cannibalism had broken out. I had left just in time.[57]

The incident reminded Frankl of the story "Death in Tehran." A servant told his prince that he had just seen Death and that it had threatened him. Fearful of his fate, the servant begged the prince to lend him his fastest horse so he could flee to Tehran. The prince agreed and the servant rode off. When the prince came home, he saw Death and asked him why he had threatened his servant. Death replied, "I did not threaten him; I only showed surprise in still finding him here when I planned to meet him in Tehran tonight."[58] Frankl noted, "They had tried to save themselves, but they only sealed their own fates."[59]

At first glance, Frankl's decision to serve others appears counterintuitive. In an encounter with unavoidable suffering, the tendency is to turn inward and focus on self-preservation. Frankl's choice, however, speaks to the paradox of servant-leadership. Frankl observed that prisoners who

---

55. Frankl, *Man's Search for Meaning*, 69.
56. Frankl, *Man's Search for Meaning*, 65.
57. Frankl, *Man's Search for Meaning*, 66.
58. Frankl, *Man's Search for Meaning*, 66.
59. Frankl, *Man's Search for Meaning*, 66.

transcended self-embeddedness and served selflessly not only survived, but in the process, discovered a reason for living,

> Thus, human existence—at least as long as it has not been neurotically distorted—is always directed to something, or someone, other than itself, be it a meaning to fulfill or another human being to encounter lovingly. I have termed this constitutive characteristic of human existence as 'self-transcendence.'[60]

To Frankl, self-actualization was a byproduct of self-transcendence:

> The more [a person] forgets himself—giving himself to a cause or another person—the more *human* he is. And the more he is immersed and absorbed in something or someone other than himself the more he really becomes *himself*.[61]

Frankl explained his reasoning using two illustrations. First, he compared a candid photo with a picture where a person strikes a pose, such as an artificial smile. Frankl wondered,

> Why do most people have that stereotyped expression on their faces whenever they are photographed? This expression stems from their concern with the impression they are going to leave on the onlooker. It is 'cheese' that makes them so ugly. Forgetting themselves, the photographer, and the future onlooker would make them beautiful.[62]

Frankl's second example came from the human body. As a physician, he considered the human eye a metaphor for self-transcendence. He explained that if an eye is considered healthy, it cannot "see" itself—it can only gaze outward. When a person begins to see flashes or floaters, however, it indicates that the eye has ceased to function as intended. He observed,

> The eye, too, is self-transcendent. The moment it perceives something of itself, its function—to perceived the surrounding world visually—has deteriorated. . . . Equally, by virtue of the self-transcendent quality of human reality, the humanness of man is most tangible when he forgets himself—and overlooks himself![63]

---

60. Frankl, *Man's Search for Meaning*, 78.
61. Frankl, *Man's Search for Meaning*, 85 (*emphasis original*).
62. Frankl, *Man's Search for Meaning*, 85.
63. Frankl, *Man's Search for Meaning*, 85.

Frankl argued that Freud's *will to pleasure* hindered self-transcendence as it reduced a human being to an animal-like state. In that paradigm, the sole goal of existence becomes tension reduction and a pursuit of pleasure, which is rarely satisfied. He asserted that happiness was a byproduct of serving a higher cause or loving another person. Frankl also opposed Adler's *will to power*, as he believed that it failed to sufficiently address humanity's need for self-transcendence:

> It mainly considers man a being who is out to overcome a certain inner condition, namely, the feeling of inferiority which he tries to get rid of by developing the striving for superiority—a concept that is by and large congruent with the Nietzschean will to power.[64]

As a prisoner during the Holocaust, Frankl demonstrated that a person could rise above his or her circumstances through selfless service. According to Frankl,

> What was really needed was a fundamental change in our attitude toward life. We had to learn ourselves and, furthermore, we had to teach the despairing men, that it did not really matter what we expected from life, but rather what life expected from us. We needed to stop asking about the meaning of life, and instead to think of ourselves as those who were being questioned by life—daily and hourly. Our answer must consist, not in talk and meditation, but in right action and in right conduct. Life ultimately means taking the responsibility to find the right answer to its problems and to fulfill the tasks, which it constantly sets for each individual. Ultimately, man should not ask what the meaning of his life is, but rather must recognize that it is he who is asked. In a word, each man is questioned by life; and he can only answer to life by answering for his own life; to life he can only respond by being responsible.[65]

Frankl's servant-leadership and commitment to the growth of others provides a profound answer to a question once posed by Rabbi Hillel, "If I am not for myself, who will be for me? If I am only for myself, what am I?"[66]

---

64. Frankl, *Man's Search for Meaning*, 138.
65. Frankl, *Man's Search for Meaning*, 98.
66. Shantall, *Life's Meaning*, 35.

A RESPONSIBILITY TOWARD THE GROWTH OF PEOPLE

In the experience of Viktor Frankl, we see a servant-leader who was oriented toward the growth of others. Servant-leaders believe that every individual has inherent worth and value. From an organizational leadership perspective, such care and concern extends beyond what a person can "do" for an organization to "who they are" as an individual.[67] Such leaders are committed to the personal, professional, and spiritual growth of the whole person. Greenleaf was clear about the difference,

> The servant-leader is servant first . . . It begins with the natural feeling that one wants to serve, to serve *first*. Then conscious choice brings one to aspire to lead. That person is sharply different from one who is *leader* first.[68]

The central question for servant-leaders is, "Whose interests are being served?" Former General Electric (GE) CEO Jack Welch asserted, "Before you are a leader, success is all about growing yourself. When you become a leader, success is all about growing others."[69] Frankl's actions during the Holocaust reflect this fundamental truth of servant-leadership. Greenleaf proposed a "best test" to gauge one's effectiveness as a servant-leader: "Do those served grow as persons? Do they, while being served, become healthier, wiser, freer, more autonomous, more likely themselves to become servants?"[70] Servant-leaders measure their effectiveness by assessing their impact on their followers. In doing so, they follow a higher standard of leadership.

CEO Joe Batten illustrated the difference between a me-first and an others-first model of leading with an interesting story. He described two countries in the Middle East whose economies were based on sheep herding and mutton production. Despite the similarity, the neighboring countries managed their work in starkly different ways. In the first, shepherds followed their flocks and herded the sheep from behind. In the other, shepherds walked in front of their flocks so the sheep follow. In the country where shepherds walked behind their flock, the quality of mutton and wool was poor, resulting in significant economic losses. In the nation where shepherds walked in front of their flocks, the mutton and wool were highly

---

67. See Spears, "Introduction: Understanding the Growing Impact of Servant-Leadership," 13.
68. Greenleaf, *Servant Leadership: A Journey*, 13 (emphasis original).
69. Guest, *Built to Grow*, 46.
70. Greenleaf, *Servant Leadership: A Journey*, 13.

prized and profits high. Batten explained the difference between the two approaches.

When sheep are pushed and driven from the back, the shepherd is always in charge. As a consequence, lambs get in line, feel afraid of the guard dogs, and worry about being struck on the head by the shepherd's staff. Batten explained, "They have no opportunity to explore for better grass and water or to play with other young lambs. They simply become obedient, passive, apathetic, and unhealthy."[71] The result of such excessive dependence and control is evident in the country's quality of output. In the nation where shepherds walked in the front, however, the lambs were free to explore, play, and take risks before rejoining the flock. According to Batten,

> Instead of feeling overcontrolled and compressed, repressed, depressed, and suppressed, they feel free, empowered, enhanced, stretched, and healthy. They eat more, sleep better, and grow up large and healthy. *They are truly led.*[72]

The story is a metaphor for the power inherent within a commitment to the growth of people. Servant-leaders prioritize the interests and needs of their followers. From an organizational perspective, leading from the front means supporting employee development, listening to feedback, soliciting ideas, being open to mutual influence, involving followers in decision-making, and helping them find employment if they were ever to be laid off.[73] In short, servant-leaders build an environment where "people are encouraged and supported as they develop their unique talents and maximize their potential."[74] Ferch noted the benefit of this approach: "People, even under conditions of defensiveness, self-fortification, and denial, are well-served by the servant-leader's robust and durable commitment to the growth of others."[75]

Frankl's commitment to the growth of others was rooted in the notion of personal responsibility. He asserted, "Life ultimately means taking the responsibility to find the right answer to its problems and to fulfill the tasks which it constantly sets for each individual."[76] Frankl believed that freedom is maximized in the presence of responsibility and helps us find meaning. Frankl proposed an interesting idea. He suggested creating a Statue of

---

71. See Batten, "Servant-Leadership," 47.

72. See Batten, "Servant-Leadership," 47 (emphasis original).

73. See Spears, "Introduction: Understanding the Growing Impact of Servant-Leadership," 14.

74. See Showkeir and Showkeir, "Clarifying Intention," 163.

75. Ferch, *Forgiveness and Power*, xii.

76. Frankl, *Man's Search for Meaning*, 98.

Responsibility on the West Coast of the United States to complement the Statue of Liberty on the East Coast. For Frankl, with great freedom comes great responsibility—ultimately realized through a commitment to the growth of people.

FINDING: COMMITMENT TO THE GROWTH OF PEOPLE

Professor Cornel West once shared these powerful words, "I am who I am because somebody loved me—somebody cared for me. I wouldn't be able to utter a word if it wasn't for their love and their care, and the least I can do is manifest that to the best of my ability to the younger generation."[77] After attending one of his lectures, a young girl was asked by her mother what she had learned. Her answer was swift, "Nobody gets anywhere without being loved."[78]

77. Questlove, "Cornel West," para. 60.
78. Solomon, "On Being Maladjusted to Injustice," para. 13.

10

Martin Luther King Jr.: The Servant-Leader and Building Community

A CULTURAL ANTHROPOLOGIST HAD spent several weeks in South Africa studying conflict management practices. As her research was nearing its end, she wanted to express gratitude to the community that hosted her stay. On the last day she gathered the children together and placed a large bag filled with candy and toys under a tree. She told the young people, "Now when I say 'Go!' run as fast as you can. Whoever gets to that tree first wins the whole bag of goodies!" Excited, the children lined up and waited for the signal. But then something curious happened.

When the anthropologist said "Go!" instead of racing toward the prize, the children held hands and walked together towards the tree. Once there, they shared the treats with one another. The researcher was bewildered, "Why didn't anyone run? The person who ran the fastest could have had the entire bag!" A young girl replied, "But ma'am, how can one of us be happy if all the others are sad?" The anthropologist was stunned. She had spent weeks studying the African philosophy of *ubuntu*, but it was not until that moment that she truly understood the concept. The children were practicing *ubuntu*.

The ethic of *ubuntu* is a philosophy of community. South African Nobel Laureate Archbishop Desmond Tutu described it this way,

> Africans have a thing called *Ubuntu* . . . the essence of being human. It is part of the gift that Africans will give the world. It

embraces hospitality, caring about others, being willing to go the extra mile for the sake of others. We believe that a person is a person through another person, that my humanity is caught up, bound up and inextricable in yours. When I dehumanize you, I inexorably dehumanize myself. The solitary individual is a contradiction in terms, and, therefore, you seek to work for the common good because your humanity comes into its own in community, in belonging.[1]

Komives et al., defined community as the "binding together of diverse individuals committed to a just, common good through shared experiences in a spirit of caring and social responsibility."[2] Today, we live in a world where many feel increasingly isolated. Polarization, inequality, xenophobia, and violence have deepened socio-spatial divides. As noted by Palmer, "We may honor community with words, but the history of the twentieth century has been a determined movement away from life together."[3] I believe that a primary reason for this disunity and fragmentation is the weakening of a community ethic. Robert Greenleaf worried about the consequences of such a breakdown:

If it is seriously lacking for long, there will be no community, no civilization, and in the end, no family. The relatively short lifespan of democracies in the history of the world might be explained by a decline in the range and intensity of familial feeling, a basic erosion in the sense of responsibility on the part of persons who are perfectly capable of being responsible and whose lives would have greater significance for them if they cultivated their sense of responsibility.[4]

Servant-leadership calls us to build community and practice *ubuntu* in its truest sense. In this chapter we explore the tenth characteristic of servant-leadership—building community. Larry Spears described it in the following way:

The servant leader senses that much has been lost in recent human history as a result of the shift from local communities to large institutions as the primary shaper of human lives. This awareness causes the servant leader to seek to identify some means for building community among those who work within

---

1. Tutu, *No Future without Forgiveness*, 22.
2. See Ferch, "Servant-Leadership and the Interior of the Leader," 42.
3. Palmer, *Promise of Paradox*, 67.
4. Greenleaf, *On Becoming a Servant Leader*, 42.

a given institution. Servant-leadership suggests that true community can be created among those who work in businesses and other institutions. Greenleaf (1977/2002) said: "All that is needed to rebuild community as a viable life form for large numbers of people is for enough servant-leaders to show the way, not by mass movements, but by each servant-leader demonstrating his or her unlimited liability for a quite specific community-related group."[5]

Here we consider building community through the servant-leadership of Dr. Martin Luther King Jr. The notion of community was central to his leadership and expressed most directly through his vision of the *beloved community*. We begin by exploring the meaning of the beloved community as articulated by King. We then examine three examples of the beloved community drawn from his leadership during the civil rights movement—the Montgomery Bus Boycott (1955–56); "The Letter from Birmingham Jail" (1963); and finally, the March on Washington and his famous "I Have a Dream" speech (1963). Each provides a glimpse of the beloved community and a vision of how servant-leaders can become community builders in a fractured world.

UNDERSTANDING THE BELOVED COMMUNITY

While many people are familiar with King's leadership during the civil rights struggle, the philosophy that guided his actions often remains less examined. A closer look reveals that the beloved community was central to King's servant-leadership. The concept was his lodestar and was woven throughout his speeches, writings, and actions.[6] King scholars Smith and Zepp, in their seminal work on the intellectual sources of King's thoughts, described the beloved community as the capstone of his thinking:

> The vision of the Beloved Community was the organizing principle of all of King's thought and activity. His writings and his involvement in the civil rights movement were illustrations of and footnotes to his fundamental preoccupation with the actualization of an inclusive human community.[7]

The notion of the beloved community originated in the work of philosopher-theologian Josiah Royce. Royce described it as a "perfectly living

---

5. Spears, "Tracing the Growing Impact," 6.
6. Herstein, "Roycean Roots," 91–107.
7. Smith and Zepp, *Search for the Beloved Community*, 119.

unity of individual men joined in one chorus."[8] Inspired by Royce, King envisioned a society where people from every class, race, and faith live together as brothers and sisters, sharing equality, opportunity, fairness, and social and economic justice. According to King,

> At the heart of all the civilization has meant and developed is 'community'—the mutually cooperative and voluntary venture of man to assume a semblance of responsibility for his brother. ... Man could not have survived without the impulse which makes him the societal creature that he is. ... I cannot reach fulfillment without thou.[9]

Social justice scholar Andrew Fitz-Gibbon elaborated on King's dream:

> [T]he beloved community means something like a completely integrated society, a community where everyone counts simply by virtue of their humanity, a community characterized by love and justice. It was an ineluctably social vision, for King was not an individualist. Like Aristotle he assumed that by nature human beings are social animals. As social, all human beings are interrelated. What affects one ultimately affects all.[10]

The interdependence of community was an orienting notion for King—much like *ubuntu* and its notion that humanity is interlinked. This leads to the understanding that "my humanity is recognized and becomes inextricably bound to theirs."[11] King's belief in the interrelatedness of humanity resulted in his call not just for desegregation, but integration. King evoked this idea when he described the mission of the Southern Christian Leadership Conference (SCLC), "The ultimate aim of SCLC is to foster and create the 'beloved community' in America where brotherhood is a reality. ... SCLC works for integration. Our ultimate goal is genuine intergroup and interpersonal living—integration."[12]

Smith and Zepp examined King's vision against the backdrop of the civil rights struggle. The aim of desegregation was to prohibit discrimination in public spaces, schools, housing, and the workplace through legislation.[13] Integration, however, worked at a deeper level, as it called for positive acceptance and radical inclusion motivated by love. In King's view, the difference

8. Marsh, *Beloved Community*, 49.
9. King Jr., *Strength to Love*, 122.
10. See Fitz-Gibbon, "Beloved Community," 140.
11. Mother Teresa, *Love*, 3.
12. Zepp, *Social Vision*, 207.
13. Smith and Zepp, *Search for the Beloved Community*.

was clear. Desegregation could be mandated, whereas integration was a matter of the heart. King argued that desegregation without integration would result in a society "where men are physically desegregated and spiritually segregated, where elbows are together, and hearts are apart. It gives us social togetherness and spiritual apartness."[14] The beloved community, however, is a place of radical inclusivity, solidarity, and mutual sacrifice. It transforms how we behave in relation to one another because it reminds us that our destinies are intertwined.

As a Christian, King believed such an outcome was possible through *agapé* love—a Greek term for sacrificial love manifested in selfless service without precondition. It is my humble observation that this vision of mutuality is sadly missing in contemporary conversations around diversity and social justice. Without a vision of the beloved community, where all people come together as part of a collective effort, mutual gains will remain unrealized. The brilliance and beauty of King's marches, protests, and boycotts was that they welcomed people from every sphere of life—there was no bar on age, race, gender, class, educational level, or occupation; it was a true cross-section of society united against a common enemy. King viewed such unity as a "microcosm of the beloved community . . . brought together in a common cause."[15] Therefore, he called upon all people to work alongside him. King understood that humanity moves in relationship to one another,

> We must all learn to live together as brothers—or we will all perish together as fools. This is the great issue facing us today. No individual can live alone; no nation can live alone. We are tied together. . . . All I'm saying is simply this: that all mankind is tied together; all life is interrelated, and we are all caught in an inescapable network of mutuality, tied in a single garment of destiny. Whatever affects one directly, affects all indirectly. For some strange reason I can never be what I ought to be until you are what you ought to be. And you can never be what you ought to be until I am what I ought to be—this is the interrelated structure of reality.[16]

King peered through the corridors of time to see a world that was inextricably linked. He believed that segregation dehumanized not only Blacks, but Whites as well. According to Smith and Zepp,

---

14. Smith and Zepp, *Search for the Beloved Community*, 120.
15. Smith and Zepp, *Search for the Beloved Community*, 121.
16. King Jr., "Remaining Awake," para. 7.

> He attempted to make the base of the movement as broad and as universal as possible. He saw the movement as a preview of the interrelatedness of human existence that would characterize the beloved community.... Discrimination against ten percent of the population of the United States weakens the whole social fabric. The issues of race and poverty are not merely sectional problems; they are American problems. Thus it follows, according to King, that the liberation of Black people will also lead to the emancipation of White people. He took seriously the indivisibility of human existence.... King was not interested in justice for Blacks in opposition to justice for the Whites; he was concerned about justice for everyone.[17]

To King, the beloved community is society reimagined, recast, and infused with *agapé* love: "If we are to have peace on earth, our loyalties must become ecumenical rather than sectional. Our loyalties must transcend our race, our tribe, our class and our nation; and this means we must develop a world perspective."[18]

United States Senator and civil rights leader John Lewis drew a powerful word picture of the beloved community during a sermon at the National Cathedral in Washington. It was the same pulpit where King preached his final Sunday sermon on March 31, 1968:

> Consider those two words: Beloved Community. 'Beloved' means not hateful, not violent, not uncaring, not unkind. And 'Community' means not separated, not polarized, not locked in struggle. The Beloved Community is an all-inclusive world society based on simple justice that values the dignity and the worth of every human being. That is the kingdom of God.[19]

The danger today is that we treat the beloved community as either a bloodless abstraction or reduce it to a slogan. Even worse would be dismissing it as a utopian ideal. King scholar C. Anthony Hunt asserted that in the beloved community, faith and action, along with theology and ethics, are indivisibly connected and ultimately expressed. He described it as the "faith-action" and "creed-deed" dialectic."[20] With this overview of King's vision of community, we turn to an exploration of three major events where King made the beloved community visible. We begin with the Montgomery Bus Boycott.

17. Smith and Zepp, *Search for the Beloved Community*, 122.
18. King Jr., "Martin Luther King, Jr.'s 'A Christmas Sermon,'" para. 3.
19. Meacham, *His Truth Is Marching On*, 234.
20. Hunt, *Beloved Community Toolkit*, 1.

THE MONTGOMERY BUS BOYCOTT AND
THE BELOVED COMMUNITY

The Montgomery bus boycott (1955–1956) was one of the earliest expressions of the beloved community in King's leadership. The catalyst for the boycott was the arrest of Rosa Parks, a longtime member and secretary of the National Association for the Advancement of Colored People (NAACP). Parks and other local leaders were holding a series of meetings with Montgomery city officials to change Alabama's legally segregated bus system. One day after work, she seized upon an opportunity to challenge the city's discriminatory policy. According to Montgomery ordinance, the front half of a city bus was reserved for White passengers, while Black passengers had to sit in the back half of the bus. Not only this, but Blacks were required to give up their seat for Whites if the front half of the bus was full.

On December 1, 1955, Parks was heading home after her shift as a seamstress at a downtown department store. She boarded a bus and sat in the front row. Parks recalled, "I had been pushed as far as I could stand to be pushed and decided that I would have to know once and for all what rights I had as a human being and a citizen."[21] As White passengers boarded, the driver told Parks and three other Black passengers to give up their seats. While the others complied, Parks refused. She was arrested, fingerprinted, and jailed. Parks was fined $10, plus $4 in court fees for refusing to give up her seat. According to a *New York Times* article covering the incident,

> Mrs. Parks refused to yield her seat and was arrested for violation of a city segregation ordinance. Later the charge was changed to read a violation of a state law, which gives bus drivers the power to assign and reassign seating. The law makes it a misdemeanor for anyone to disobey the driver's orders.[22]

News of the incident spread quickly through the community and across the nation.

Just a year prior, twenty-six-year-old King had been installed as senior pastor of Dexter Avenue Baptist Church in Montgomery. Upon hearing of Parks's arrest, King and a number of other clergy and local civil rights leaders gathered in the church's basement and made plans to launch a citywide boycott of the Montgomery bus system. About 40 percent of Montgomery's citizens were Black, representing at least 75 percent of the city's bus riders. They launched the boycott on December 5, 1955. An estimated 90 to 100 percent of Blacks refused to use the bus system. On the evening of the

---

21. Marsh, *Beloved Community*, 21.
22. "Negroes' Boycott Cripples Bus Line," para. 8.

protest, eighteen pastors met at Holt Street Baptist and formed the Montgomery Improvement Association (MIA). They elected King as the organization's president and spokesperson. To ensure the boycott's viability, the city's Black taxi drivers charged Black riders a fare of ten cents—the same price as a bus token.[23] When the city fined the taxi drivers, Black ministers and their allies organized carpools.

The city was forced to the negotiating table under the weight of the boycott. The MIA issued a list of demands: 1) courteous treatment, 2) a first come, first served seating policy with Blacks seated from the rear and Whites from the front—no seats reserved for any race—and 3) hire Black bus drivers for predominantly Black neighborhoods.[24] Desegregation was not one of their demands. When city officials refused to meet any of their conditions, the MIA resumed the boycott. Montgomery City Lines lost between 30,000 and 40,000 bus fares each day the boycott persisted. Letters to the newspaper overwhelmingly favored the MIA's demands. When a Methodist pastor argued that a boycott was not a good look for ministers, King responded, "If one is truly devoted to the religion of Jesus, he will seek to rid the earth of social evils. The gospel is social as well as personal."[25]

King and other leaders encountered a wave of hatred for their stand. On January 13, 1956, while King was speaking to protestors at First Baptist Church, local segregationists firebombed his home. His wife, Coretta Scott King, his 10-week-old daughter, Yolanda Denise, and a family friend barely escaped with their lives. As King raced home, hundreds of protestors and local residents, armed with knives, guns, and other weapons, stood ready to battle on King's behalf. Amidst the chaos, he called for calm:

> Don't get panicky. Don't do anything panicky. Don't get your weapons. If you have weapons, take them home. He who lives by the sword will perish by the sword. Remember that is what Jesus said. We are not advocating violence. We want to love our enemies. I want you to love our enemies. Be good to them. This is what we must live by. We must meet hate with love. I did not start this boycott. I was asked by you to serve as your spokesman. I want it to be known the length and breadth of this land that if I am stopped, this movement will not stop. If I am stopped, our work will not stop. For what we are doing is right. What we are doing is just. And God is with us.[26]

23. History.com Editors, "Montgomery Boycott."

24. The Martin Luther King, Jr. Research and Education Institute, "Montgomery Boycott."

25. Smith and Zepp, *Search for the Beloved Community*, 43.

26. Sargent, *Civil Rights Revolution*, 22.

King and over eighty other leaders were indicted under Alabama's anti-conspiracy laws for participating in the boycott. He was ordered to pay $500 or serve 386 days in jail for leading the protest.

In June 1956, a federal court ruled that Montgomery's laws were unconstitutional and the Supreme Court upheld the ruling. On December 21, 1956, at 6:00 a.m., more than thirteen months after the start of the boycott, King and other civil rights leaders boarded a desegregated Montgomery city bus. The *Montgomery Advertiser* described the historic event, "The calm but cautious acceptance of this significant change in Montgomery's way of life came without any major disturbances."[27] King noted, "I rode the first integrated bus in Montgomery with a White minister and a native Southerner as my seatmate."[28]

King viewed the Montgomery bus boycott through the lens of the beloved community. The boycott was part of the larger struggle to create a new social order. King intended to cast a vision of an integrated community living together on the basis of equality, justice, goodwill, and love. King spoke directly to this hope in a speech celebrating their victory:

> But we must remember as we boycott that boycott is not an end within itself; it is merely a means to awaken a sense of shame within the oppressor and challenge his false sense of superiority. But the end is reconciliation; the end is redemption; the end is the creation of the beloved community. It is this type of spirit and this type of love that can transform opposers into friends. . . . It is this love which will bring about miracles in the hearts of men.[29]

King felt the word *boycott* failed to capture the true spirit of change he was pursuing: "Our aim has never been to put the bus company out of business, but rather to put justice in business."[30] He called for reconciliation based on mutuality, understanding, and respect. He believed that *agapé* love would win the day. King urged his followers to stay focused amidst their victory—neither gloating, nor waxing sentimental. He viewed the developments in Montgomery as an opportunity to inspire lasting change, marked by freedom, justice, and love.[31]

---

27. The Martin Luther King, Jr. Research and Education Institute, "Statement on Ending the Boycott," para. 1.

28. Marsh, *Beloved Community*, 49.

29. King Jr. et al., *Papers of Martin Luther King, Jr.*, 458.

30. The Martin Luther King, Jr. Research and Education Institute, "Statement on Ending the Boycott," para. 2.

31. King Jr. et al., *Papers of Martin Luther King, Jr.*, 458.

According to theologian and King scholar Charles Marsh, King was also transformed by the events in Montgomery. Through his servant-leadership, he gained a "new understanding of redemptive social relation: the beloved community."[32] He envisioned a picture of unity, humanity, and love that sought the transformation of the oppressed and the oppressor:

> [T]he aftermath of violence is bitterness; the aftermath of non-violence is the creation of the beloved community; the aftermath of non-violence is redemption and reconciliation. This is a method that seeks to transform and to redeem, and win the friendship of the opponent, and make it possible for men to live together as brothers in a community, and not continually live with bitterness and friction.[33]

THE BELOVED COMMUNITY AND "LETTER FROM BIRMINGHAM JAIL"

King's "Letter from Birmingham Jail" represents a second potent expression of the beloved community. King's letter rightfully holds its place as one of the most important documents in our nation's history. Indeed, the letter sparked a "critical turning point" in the civil rights movement.[34] To grasp the significance of the letter and its relationship to the beloved community, it is important to understand its historical backdrop.

As president of the SCLC, King was leading a nationwide effort to promote civil rights. He had planned a series of protests in Birmingham, Alabama, notorious for being the "most thoroughly segregated city in the country."[35] The 1963 campaign called for an end to segregation in Birmingham, particularly in the areas of transportation, dining, recreation, and employment. Eugene "Bull" Connor, the city's public safety commissioner, was an avowed segregationist. When he heard about the protest, he warned that he would enforce the city's race laws using deadly force if necessary.[36] Connor boasted that he could solve the city's racial problems with "two policemen and a dog."[37] Alabama governor George Wallace fueled the flames

---

32. Marsh, *Beloved Community*, 49.
33. King Jr., "Martin Luther King Jr.'s 'Justice without Violence,'" para. 38.
34. Sturm, "Crisis," 311.
35. Oates, *Let the Trumpet Sound*, 210.
36. Gist and Whitehead, "Deconstructing," 6.
37. Bass, "Not Time Yet," 246.

when he threatened to prevent the desegregation of public schools by personally standing in front of the doors.

In preparation for the protest, the SCLC and Birmingham's Alabama Christian Movement for Human Rights (ACMHR), led by F. L. Shuttlesworth, issued the "Birmingham Manifesto." It stated in part,

> The patience of an oppressed people cannot endure forever. The Negro citizens of Birmingham for the last several years have hoped in vain for some evidence of good faith resolution of our just grievances. Birmingham is part of the United States and we are bona fide citizens. Yet the history of Birmingham reveals that very little of the democratic process touches the life of the Negro in Birmingham. We have been segregated racially, exploited economically, and dominated politically. . . . The absence of justice and progress in Birmingham demands that we make a moral witness to give our community a chance to survive. We demonstrate our faith that we believe that the Beloved Community can come to Birmingham.[38]

As the SCLC planned their campaign, Birmingham's city-commission form of government was replaced with a mayor-council system. Though the new mayor was considered a political moderate, he supported segregation. At the request of local leaders, King agreed to postpone the protest until April 2nd in hope of a change in policy at City Hall, but it failed to materialize.

On April 3, 1963, King and the SCLC launched a campaign of nonviolent direct action. They organized a series of meetings, lunch counter sit-ins, a boycott of downtown merchants, and a march toward the county building to register voters. As the campaign gained momentum, Connor and the police force attacked protestors with fire hoses, police dogs, and nightsticks. Hundreds of activists were arrested over the course of the week. Connor obtained a court injunction banning the protests. During a Good Friday demonstration King was arrested for violating the court order and was placed in solitary confinement.

The next day a group of eight prominent Birmingham clergymen published an editorial in the *Birmingham News* criticizing the SCLC's campaign. They described it as "unwise and untimely" and suggested a more gradual approach to change—one that didn't involve protests, demonstrations, or other "extreme measures."[39] While the clergymen didn't mention King by name, they questioned the presence of "outsiders" who arrived to "incite to

---

38. King Jr., "Birmingham Manifesto," para. 6.
39. Hornsby Jr., "Martin Luther King, Jr. 'Letter From a Birmingham Jail,'" 38.

hatred and violence," rather than pursue their cause through "principles of law and order and common sense."[40]

King read the letter from his cell and understood its implications. Besides calling for a halt to the campaign, the letter carried an implicit sense of authority as it was written by members of the faith community.[41] A reply was crucial if the public was to gain an accurate understanding of their cause. King composed his message on the margins of old newspapers, random scraps of paper, and even toilet tissue until jail officials brought him a notepad. The letter was smuggled out of the jail in pieces and published as a pamphlet titled the "Letter from Birmingham Jail."[42]

In an analysis of the letter, King scholar James Colaiaco explained that King masterfully addressed each of the issues brought up by the clergy, including his right to organize in Birmingham, the nature of civil disobedience, and the necessity of direct action.[43] The enduring nature of King's letter can be attributed to his breadth and depth of vision—which stood in contrast to the myopia of his critics. King's letter not only addressed the immediate situation, but also exposed the ramifications of the clergy's advice in epistolary fashion.

King opened his letter by stating, "While confined here in the Birmingham city jail I came across your recent statement calling my present activities 'unwise and untimely.'"[44] King then addressed the charge that the protest was inconveniently timed, "I guess it is easy for those who have never felt the stinging darts of segregation to say, 'Wait.'"[45] King scholar Martha Watson contended that although the clergymen viewed themselves as "community guardians," their social status granted them a privilege the Black residents of Birmingham could not afford—infinite patience.[46] In fact, the SCLC campaign had been postponed for six months in hopes of a political solution that never emerged. King challenged the clergy's inertia,

> We know through painful experience that freedom is never voluntarily given by the oppressor; it must be demanded by the oppressed. Frankly, I have yet to engage in a direct action campaign that was 'well timed' in the view of those who have not suffered unduly from the disease of segregation. For years now

---

40. Bass and King Jr., *Blessed Are the Peacemakers*, 234.
41. Patton, "Transforming Response."
42. Colaiaco, "American Dream Unfulfilled."
43. Colaiaco, "American Dream Unfulfilled."
44. Hornsby Jr., "Martin Luther King, Jr. 'Letter From a Birmingham Jail,'" 38.
45. Hornsby Jr., "Martin Luther King, Jr. 'Letter From a Birmingham Jail,'" 38.
46. Watson, "Issue Is Justice," 13.

> I have heard the word 'Wait!' It rings in the ear of every Negro with piercing familiarity. This 'Wait' has almost always meant 'Never.' We must come to see, with one of our distinguished jurists, that 'justice too long delayed is justice denied.' We have waited for more than 340 years for our constitutional and God given rights.[47]

While it was easy for the clergymen to recommend political remedies, to those facing segregation, discrimination, arrest, physical violence, and even assassination, the city's laws represented a long-overdue problem that needed to be addressed. Indeed, by 1960, King had been jailed five times, his home was firebombed twice, his family had received daily death threats, and he had almost been stabbed to death.[48] King reminded his critics that time was not a luxury they could afford:

> Human progress never rolls in on wheels of inevitability; it comes through the tireless efforts of men willing to be co-workers with God, and without this hard work, time itself becomes an ally of the forces of social stagnation. We must use time creatively, in the knowledge that the time is always ripe to do right.[49]

Watson is helpful in analyzing the dangers of the clergy's complacency:

> From a pentadic perspective, the clergy's statements focus on scene and agency. They are concerned with preserving the peace, avoiding any civil disturbance. . . . In focusing on the Birmingham of 1963, the clergy circumscribe the angle of vision; they choose the immediate environment as a means through which to judge appropriate actions. . . . In choosing to limit their vision to Birmingham and in focusing so intently on the scene/agency ration, the clergy bind themselves to a parochial understanding of the controversy they confronted.[50]

King challenged the ministers to discern between just and unjust laws, thus elevating the discourse beyond legality to the higher issue of morality:

> A just law is a man-made code that squares with the moral law or the law of God. An unjust law is a code that is out of harmony with moral law. . . . Any law that uplifts the human personality is just. Any law that degrades the human personality is unjust. . . . An unjust law is a code that a majority inflicts on a minority

---

47. Hornsby Jr., "Martin Luther King, Jr. 'Letter From a Birmingham Jail,'" 38.
48. Simpson, "Changing the Face of the Enemy," 62.
49. Hornsby Jr., "Martin Luther King, Jr. 'Letter From a Birmingham Jail,'" 38.
50. Watson, "Issue Is Justice," 13–14.

> group that is not binding on itself. In no sense do I advocate evading or defying the law, as the rabid segregationist would do. This would lead to anarchy. One who breaks an unjust law must do it openly, lovingly, and with a willingness to accept the penalty. . . . We can never forget that everything Hitler did in Germany was 'legal' and everything the Hungarian freedom fighters did was 'illegal.'[51]

King connected the Birmingham campaign to the wider arc of history. He asked his readers to consider the brave souls who stood against injustice in the past. He cited examples of civil disobedience from the Old and New Testament, Greek history, the American Revolution, and the Civil War. He reminded the clergy that those who defied the status quo in the past had been branded as extremists too. Furthermore, King asserted that his actions could hardly be considered extreme when compared to the moral depravity reflected in the racist laws. He wondered,

> So the question is not whether we will be extremists, but what kind of extremists we will be. Will we be extremists for hate or for love? Will we be extremists for the preservation of injustice or for the extension of justice? . . . Perhaps the South, the nation and the world are in dire need of creative extremists.[52]

King also addressed the accusation that he and his fellow civil rights leaders had come to Birmingham as rabble-rousers and "outsider agitators" intending to disturb the peace.[53] King reminded the clergy that the SCLC was a regional organization advocating for civil rights across the South. Not only this, but King was in Birmingham at the request of the local ACMHR chapter—thus he was present "by affiliation and by invitation."[54] In contrast to the clergymen's shortsighted criticism, King challenged his readers to look beyond the local campaign and see the mutuality of humanity as envisioned in the beloved community. In one of the most quoted sections of the letter, King wrote,

> But more basically, I am in Birmingham because injustice is here. . . . Moreover, I am cognizant of the interrelatedness of all communities and states. I cannot sit idly by in Atlanta and not be concerned about what happens in Birmingham. Injustice anywhere is a threat to justice everywhere. We are caught in

---

51. Watson, "Issue Is Justice," 15.
52. Hornsby Jr., "Martin Luther King, Jr. 'Letter From a Birmingham Jail,'" 38.
53. Hornsby Jr., "Martin Luther King, Jr. 'Letter From a Birmingham Jail,'" 39.
54. Colaiaco, "American Dream Unfulfilled," 4.

an inescapable network of mutuality, tied in a single garment of destiny. Whatever affects one directly, affects all indirectly. Never again can we afford to live with the narrow, provincial "outside agitator" idea. Anyone who lives inside the United States can never be considered an outsider anywhere within its bounds.[55]

According to Colaico, King set forth a contrast between the American Dream and the American Dilemma, namely, "The conflict between our devotion to the American creed of democracy and our actual practice." King's presence in Birmingham served as "the conscience of an extended community, the entire human community in the scope of history."[56] Thus, the influence of King's letter lay in its ability to speak to the issues in Birmingham while simultaneously challenging his critics to consider the "beloved community whose transformative implications run to all nooks and crannies of the public realm."[57] According to Colaiaco,

> King's genius lay in his extraordinary vision. His was a vision of an America true to the sacred ideals of liberty, justice, and equality embodied in the Declaration of Independence and the Constitution. His was a vision of an America that fulfilled the promise of these ideals for all people, black and white alike.[58]

Within a matter of weeks, King's message had been reprinted in magazines across the country and nearly a million copies were distributed to churches.[59] The publication of the letter in major news outlets such as the *New York Post*, "allowed for careful scrutiny of King's position by many in mainstream America. The public was given time to contemplate King's moral argument, warm to it, and perhaps, gradually embrace it."[60] King articulated the struggle for civil rights in powerful prose as he appealed to "conscience, emotion, and moral sensibility."[61]

King's letter has been translated into more than forty languages. In an interview with bestselling author Alex Haley, King expressed confidence

---

55. Hornsby Jr., "Martin Luther King, Jr. 'Letter From a Birmingham Jail,'" 38.
56. Watson, "Issue Is Justice," 16.
57. Sturm, "Crisis," 324.
58. Colaiaco, "American Dream Unfulfilled," 18.
59. Colaiaco, "American Dream Unfulfilled."
60. Vail, "'Integrative' Rhetoric," 58.
61. Johnson, "Martin Luther King Jr.'s 1963 Birmingham Campaign as Image Event," 2.

that the Birmingham campaign and his letter helped advance the cause of civil rights in America:

> The letter helped to focus greater international attention upon what was happening in Birmingham. . . . And I am sure that without Birmingham, the March on Washington wouldn't have been called. . . . It was also the image of Birmingham which, to a great extent, helped to bring the civil rights bill into being in 1963.[62]

After spending eight days in confinement, King was released from jail on April 20, 1963. He was found guilty of criminal contempt and released on bond, pending appeal. The Birmingham campaign continued through early May and included an incident where over a thousand protestors, including children, were arrested as they sang "We Shall Overcome." As the campaign grew in strength, nearly 3,000 demonstrators were detained.

On May 7th, 1963, Birmingham's business leaders, having suffered economically and in the court of public opinion, presented the Birmingham Truce Agreement. They offered to partially desegregate the city's restaurants, provide job opportunities for Blacks, release protestors from jail, and form a Committee on Racial Problems and Employment. Despite this breakthrough, the struggle was far from over. Not only did the city delay in making good on its promises, but when King returned to Atlanta, the SCLC headquarters in Birmingham was firebombed and a riot ensued. President Kennedy dispatched federal troops to quell the unrest. On May 20th, 1963, the Supreme Court declared Alabama's segregation laws unconstitutional. One month later President Kennedy proposed comprehensive civil rights legislation to the US Congress.[63]

THE BELOVED COMMUNITY AND THE "I HAVE A DREAM" SPEECH

King's most well-known expression of the beloved community took place on August 28, 1963. His "I Have a Dream" speech followed in the wake of the historic Birmingham campaign, giving voice to the powerful words penned in "Letter from Birmingham Jail."[64] Delivered in front of the Lincoln Memorial during the historic "March on Washington for Jobs and Freedom," the

---

62. Colaiaco, "American Dream Unfulfilled," 2.
63. Colaiaco, "American Dream Unfulfilled."
64. Vail, "'Integrative' Rhetoric."

speech roused the conscience of a nation and spurred the Kennedy administration to publicly sponsor long-delayed civil rights legislation.[65]

Respected union activist and civil rights pioneer A. Phillip Randolph and a number of civil rights groups organized the march. The globally televised event drew over 250,000 participants, becoming the largest single demonstration for civil rights in American history.[66] A number of speakers challenged the nation to deliver on its promise of liberty and justice for all. Randolph introduced King as the "moral leader of our nation," setting the stage for the final address. King's message became one of the greatest speeches of the twentieth century.

King began by describing the march as an event that would "go down in history as the greatest demonstration for freedom in the history of our nation."[67] After highlighting foundational articles such as the Declaration of Independence, the Constitution, and the Emancipation Proclamation, King reminded the nation that they had drifted from the sacred promises contained within those documents. Hundreds of years after the pledge, King contended, Blacks remained shackled by the bonds of segregation and discrimination, living in poverty amidst prosperity as exiles in their own land.

King then presented the metaphor of a check written by the founding fathers, guaranteeing life, liberty, and the pursuit of happiness to all Americans. King asserted that when it came to their plight for equality, the "sacred obligation" had turned out to be a "bad check, a check which has come back marked as insufficient funds."[68] Yet, expressing faith in the promise, King declared, "But we refuse to believe that the bank of justice is bankrupt. . . . And so, we've come to cash this check, a check that will give us upon demand the riches of freedom and the security of justice."[69] King spoke of the "fierce urgency of now" and challenged the nation to live up to its promises: "Now is the time. . . . Now is the time to lift our nation from the quicksands of racial injustice to the solid rock of brotherhood. Now is the time to make justice a reality for all of God's children."[70] And for those walking the long road to freedom, King encouraged them to remain steadfast, persistent, and principled, always meeting "physical force with soul force." He quoted the Old Testament prophet Amos, "No, no, we are not satisfied, and we will not

---

65. Patton, "Transforming Response," 53–65.
66. Vail, "'Integrative' Rhetoric."
67. King Jr., "I Have a Dream," para. 1.
68. King Jr., "I Have a Dream," para. 4.
69. King Jr., "I Have a Dream," para. 5.
70. King Jr., "I Have a Dream," para. 6.

be satisfied until 'justice rolls down like waters, and righteousness like a mighty stream.'"[71]

During his sermons, King rarely spoke from notes or outlines. He made an exception for the March of Washington so the press could receive an advanced copy of his speech. At this point in the discourse, however, King spoke extemporaneously as he described his vision of the beloved community:

> And so even though we face the difficulties of today and tomorrow, I still have a dream. It is a dream deeply rooted in the American dream. I have a dream that one day this nation will rise up and live out the true meaning of its creed: 'We hold these truths to be self-evident, that all men are created equal.'"[72]

As envisioned by King, in the beloved community, people of all races, classes, and religions sit together at the table of opportunity and equality. King dreamed of a great banquet where,

> on the red hills of Georgia the sons of former slaves and the sons of former slave owners will be able to sit down together at the table of brotherhood. . . . I have a dream that my four little children will one day live in a nation where they will not be judged by the color of their skin but by the content of their character. I have a dream today![73]

Indeed, the beloved community was King's central message that day:

> I have a dream that one day every valley shall be exalted, and every hill and mountain shall be made low, the rough places will be made plain, and the crooked places will be made straight; 'and the glory of the Lord shall be revealed and all flesh shall see it together.' This is our hope. . . . With this faith we will be able to hew out of the mountain of despair a stone of hope. With this faith we will be able to transform the jangling discords of our nation into a beautiful symphony of brotherhood.[74]

As King's speech reached a crescendo, he called the nation to "let freedom ring"[75] from every valley and mountain, village and hamlet, state and city. He concluded by declaring that when we truly allow freedom to ring,

71. King Jr., "I Have a Dream," para. 13.
72. King Jr., "I Have a Dream," para. 17.
73. King Jr., "I Have a Dream," para. 20.
74. King Jr., "I Have a Dream," para. 26.
75. King Jr., "I Have a Dream," para. 30.

all of God's children, black men and white men, Jews and Gentiles, Protestants and Catholics, will be able to join hands and sing in the words of the old Negro spiritual: Free at last! Free at last! Thank God Almighty, we are free at last![76]

In a rousing speech to a fractured nation, King presented a vision of a beloved community grounded in equality, opportunity, love, and justice, where all people live together as brothers and sisters. King's dream, rooted in the American dream, called for "transforming people and relationships and creating communities grounded in reconciliation, friendship and human dignity."[77]

BUILDING THE BELOVED COMMUNITY

Robert Greenleaf referred to community as the "lost knowledge of our times."[78] Fundamental to Greenleaf's conception of community is the notion of "unlimited liability," or love without limits. The moment we limit or qualify our love for others we diminish ourselves to that same degree. Such unconditional love finds expression in "a face-to-face group in which the liability of each for the other and all for one is unlimited, or as close to it as it is possible to get."[79] We convey love without limits when we accept people without precondition, appreciating their beauty and demonstrating empathy.[80] Such an outcome requires a return to the first characteristic of servant-leadership—listening, demonstrated through authentic communication, relational vulnerability, and a commitment to stay the course.[81]

In King's beloved community, *agapé* love is expressed through unlimited liability toward the oppressed. In building community, the servant-leader rejects no one, accepts everyone, and is willing to sacrifice for the cause of justice, equality, and reconciliation. Greenleaf described this as the "feeling of total responsibility for the wider community.... The things that are good for the society please this person, and the things that harm it cause pain—deep down inside."[82] Brown summarized it well:

76. King Jr., "I Have a Dream," para. 34.
77. Pizana, "Remembering Dr. Martin Luther King, Jr.'s Beloved Community," para. 2.
78. Greenleaf, *Servant Leadership: A Journey*, 37.
79. Greenleaf, *Servant Leadership: A Journey*, 38.
80. See Lopez, "Becoming a Servant-Leader," 152.
81. See Conley and Wagner-Marsh, "Integration of Business Ethics and Spirituality," 255.
82. Greenleaf, *On Becoming a Servant Leader*, 42.

> Building beloved community offers us the opportunity to know and care for one another as human beings and to build the trust needed to successfully leap into the unknown together—to dare, to imagine, to disagree, to risk. From there, great change is possible.[83]

Servant-leadership scholar Isabel Lopez asserted that builders of community value all people and their contributions to the whole. Servant-leaders build community as *primus inter pares* ("first among equals").[84] Peter Block, echoing the ethic of *ubuntu,* reminds us of the stakes:

> But community is about coming together in the pursuit of some kind of purpose, some kind of goal that has meaning. . . . I think sooner or later all of us are going to get to the point that [we realize] 'I can't survive unless we choose 'we.''[85]

So, what can we learn from King's expressions of beloved community? In each example described in this chapter, including the Montgomery Bus Boycott, "Letter from Birmingham Jail," and King's "I Have a Dream" speech, lies an invitation to be a community builder in a broken world. King declared, "In a real sense all life is interrelated. The agony of the poor enriches the rich. We are inevitably our brother's keeper because we are our brother's brother. Whatever affects one directly affects all indirectly."[86] Greenleaf believed that this was possible if a generation of servant-leaders is willing to take up the challenge on an individual and interpersonal level:

> All that is needed to rebuild community as a viable life form for large numbers of people is for enough servant-leaders to show the way, not by mass movements, but by each servant-leader demonstrating his or her unlimited liability for a quite specific community-related group.[87]

In a 1962 address at Cornell College, King echoed Greenleaf's hope with these profound words,

> I am convinced that men hate each other because they fear each other. They fear each other because they don't know each other, and they don't know each other because they don't communicate with each other, and they don't communicate with each other

---

83. Brown, "Love in 'Beloved Community,'" para. 5.
84. See Lopez, "Becoming a Servant-Leader," 160.
85. See Wicker, "Seeking the Soul of Business," 250.
86. King, *Where Do We Go from Here?*, 626.
87. Greenleaf, *Servant as Leader*, 30.

because they are separated from each other. And God grant that something will happen to open channels of communication, that something will happen because men of goodwill will rise to the level of leadership.[88]

FINDING: BUILDING COMMUNITY

The beloved community appears in the most unexpected of places.[89] Creating the conditions for healthy and fully functioning organizations and communities begins with acknowledging our interconnectedness and interdependence. Leadership scholar Meg Wheatley spoke to this reality and offered a starting point, "Relationships are all there is. Everything in the universe only exists because it is in relationship to everything else. Nothing exists in isolation. We have to stop pretending we are individuals who can go it alone."[90]

---

88. King, "Dr. Martin Luther King's Visit to Cornell College," para. 18.
89. Deats, "Fellowship," 25.
90. Wheatley, *Turning to One Another*, 19.

Bibliography

Adjei, Paul. "The Non-Violent Philosophy of Mahatma Gandhi and Martin Luther King, Jr. in the 21st Century: Implications for the Pursuit of Social Justice in Global Context." *Journal of Global Citizenship & Equity Education* 3 (2013) 80–101.
"Adlai Stevenson: Memorial Address for Eleanor Roosevelt." https://www.americanrhetoric.com/speeches/adlaistevensoneleanorroosevelteulogy.htm.
Akella, Devi. "Satyagraha: The Gandhian Philosophy of Conflict Management." *Journal of Workplace Rights* 14 (2009) 503–23.
Aldag, Ray, and Loren Kuzuhara. *Creating High Performance Teams: Applied Strategies and Tools for Managers and Team Members*. New York: Routledge, 2015.
Anbarasan, Ethirajan. "Wangari Muta Maathai: Kenya's Green Militant." *UNESCO Courier* 52 (1999) 46–50.
Anthony, Scott D. "Why It's So Hard to Disrupt the Airline Industry." *Harvard Business Review*, April 8, 2008. https://hbr.org/2008/04/why-its-so-hard-to-disrupt-the.
Ashe, Geoffrey. *Gandhi: A Biography*. New York: Cooper Square, 2000.
Atack, Iain. *Nonviolence in Political Theory*. Edinburgh: Edinburgh University Press, 2012.
———. "Transformative Nonviolence, Power and Social Change." *Diogenes* 61 (2014) 21–29.
Autry, James. "Love and Profit: Finding the Balance in Life and Work." *Quality Progress* 29.1 (January 1996) 47–52.
Bailey, Joanna. "How Southwest Pioneered the Low Cost Carrier Model." *Simple Flying*, July 29, 2019. https://simpleflying.com/southwest-lcc-model/.
Baptist, Edward E. *The Half Has Never Been Told: Slavery and the Making of American Capitalism*. New York: Basic, 2014.
Barr, Damian. "We Are Not All in the Same Boat. We Are All in the Same Storm. Some Are on Super-Yachts. Some Have Just the One Oar." https://www.damianbarr.com/latest/https/we-are-not-all-in-the-same-boat.
Bass, S. Jonathan, and Martin Luther King Jr. *Blessed Are the Peacemakers: Martin Luther King Jr., Eight White Religious Leaders, and The "Letter from Birmingham Jail."* Baton Rouge: Louisiana State University Press, 2001.
———. "Not Time Yet: Alabama's Episcopal Bishop and the End of Segregation in the Deep South." *Anglican and Episcopal History* 63 (1994) 235–59.

Batten, Joe. "Servant-Leadership: A Passion to Serve." In *Insights on Leadership: Service, Stewardship, Spirit, and Servant-leadership*, edited by Larry C. Spears, 38–53. New York: Wiley & Sons, 1998.

"Benjamin Franklin's Anti-Slavery Petitions to Congress." https://www.archives.gov/legislative/features/franklin.

Bennis, Warren G., and Robert J. Thomas. "Crucibles of Leadership." *Harvard Business Review* 80 (2002) 39–45.

Bernanke, Ben. *Essays on the Great Depression*. Princeton, NJ: Princeton University Press, 2000.

Bete, Channing L. *How to Improve Your Listening Skills*. Deerfield, MA: Safety Concepts, 1987.

Bhargava, Rajeev. "The Importance of Listening Well." *The Hindu*, September 24, 2019. https://www.thehindu.com/opinion/op-ed/the-importance-of-listeningwell/article29492484.ece.

Biller, Karlheinz, et al. "Viktor Frankl: Opposing Views." *Journal of Contemporary History* 37 (2002) 105–13.

Black, Allida M. "Championing a Champion: Eleanor Roosevelt and the Marian Anderson "Freedom Concert." *Presidential Studies Quarterly* 20 (1990) 719–36.

———. "The First Lady of Civil Rights." *The Journal of Blacks in Higher Education* 13 (1996) 140–41.

Blanchard, Ken. "Let's Clear Up some Misunderstandings about Servant Leadership." *How We Lead* (blog), February 7, 2018. https://howwelead.org/2018/02/07/lets-clear-up-some-misunderstandings-about-servant-leadership/.

Block, Peter. *Stewardship: Choosing Service over Self Interest*. San Francisco: Berrett-Koehler, 1993.

Bondurant, Joan V. *Conquest of Violence: The Gandhian Philosophy of Conflict*. Princeton, NJ: Princeton University Press, 1958.

Bordas, Juana. "Power and Passion: Finding Personal Purpose." In *Reflections on Leadership: How Robert K. Greenleaf's Theory of Servant-Leadership Influenced Today's Top Management Thinkers*, edited by Larry C. Spears and Michelle Lawrence, 179–93. New York: Wiley & Sons, 1995.

Bose, Nirmal Kumar, ed. *Selections from Gandhi*. Ahmedabad, India: Navajivan House, 1957.

Bradberry, Travis, and Jean Greaves. *Leadership 2.0*. San Diego: TalentSmart, 2012.

Bradford, Sarah H. *Harriet Tubman: The Moses of Her People*. 1886. Reprint, Secaucus, NJ: Citadel, 1961.

Branden, Nathaniel. *The Art of Living Consciously: The Power of Awareness to Transform Everyday Life*. New York: Touchstone, 1999.

Braye, Rubye Howard. "Servant Leadership: Leading in Today's Military." In *Focus on Leadership: Servant-Leadership for the Twenty-First Century*, edited by Larry C. Spears, 295–304. New York: Wiley & Sons, 2002.

Brosi, George, and bell hooks. "The Beloved Community: A Conversation between bell hooks and George Brosi." *Appalachian Heritage* 40 (2012) 76–86.

Brown, Dorothy M. Review of *Without Precedent: The Life And Career Of Eleanor Roosevelt* by Joan Hoff-Wilson and Marjorie Lightman. *Journal of American History* 71.4 (March 1985) 896–97. https://academic.oup.com/jah/article-abstract/71/4/896/756091?redirectedFrom=fulltext.

Brown, Dwane. "How One Man Convinced 200 Ku Klux Klan Members to Give Up Their Robes." *National Public Radio*, August 20. 2017. https://www.npr.org/2017/08/20/544861933/how-one-man-convinced-200-kuklux-klan-members-to-give-up-their-robes.

Brown, Trina Greene. "The 'Love' in Beloved Community." *Move to End Violence* (*blog*), August 10, 2015. https://movetoendviolence.org/blog/the-love-in-beloved-community/.

Buechner, Frederick. *Wishful Thinking: A Theological ABC*. New York: Harper & Row, 1973.

Burgess, Gina. "Listening Is an Attribute of the Servant-Leader." *Healthy Leaders*, September 24, 2013. https://healthyleaders.com/listening-is-an-attribute-of-the-servant-leader/.

Burke, Fran. "Eleanor Roosevelt, October 11, 1884–November 7, 1962—She Made a Difference." *Public Administration Review* 44 (1984) 365–72.

Buzzanell, Patrice M. "W. Charles Redding (1914–1994): The Teacher-Scholar Model of the Redding Tradition." *Communication Studies* 50.4 (1999) 310–23.

Caroli, B. Boyd. "Eleanor Roosevelt." *Encyclopedia Britannica*, February 5, 2021. https://www.britannica.com/biography/Eleanor-Roosevelt.

Center for Ethical Leadership. "Concepts and Philosophies." https://www.ethicalleadership.org/concepts-and-philosophies.html.

Charan, Ram. "The Discipline of Listening." *Harvard Business Review*, June, 21, 2012. https://hbr.org/2012/06/the-discipline-of-listening.

Christian, William A. "Inwardness and Outward Concerns: A Study of John Woolman's Thought." *Quaker History* 67 (1978) 88–104.

Clampitt, Phillip G., et al. "Leaders as Strategic Communicators." *Ivey Business Journal* 66 (2002) 51–55.

Clifton, Donald O. *StrengthsQuest: Discover and Develop Your Strengths in Academics, Career, and Beyond*. New York: Gallup, 2006.

Clinton, Catherine. *Harriet Tubman: The Road To Freedom*. New York: Little, Brown, 2004.

Colaiaco, James A. "The American Dream Unfulfilled: Martin Luther King, Jr. and the 'Letter from Birmingham Jail.'" *Phylon* 45 (1984) 1–18.

Collins, James C., and Jerry I. Porras. *Built to Last: Successful Habits of Visionary Companies*. London: Random House Business, 2005.

"The Combahee Ferry Raid." https://nmaahc.si.edu/blog/combahee-ferry-raid.

Condé Naste Traveler. "A Conversation with Wangari Maathai." *Condé Naste Traveler*, June 15, 2008. https://www.cntraveler.com/stories/2008-01-15/a-conversation-with-wangari-maathai.

Conley, James, and Fraya Wagner-Marsh. "Integration of Business Ethics and Spirituality in the Workplace." In *Insights on Leadership: Service, Stewardship, Spirit and Servant-Leadership*, edited by Larry C. Spears, 251–57. New York: Wiley and Sons, 1998.

Cooper, Ilene. *Eleanor Roosevelt, Fighter for Justice: Her Impact on the Civil Rights Movement, the White House, and the World*. New York: Abrams, 2018.

Copeland, Camille C., et al. "Listening Skills for the Helping Profession." *ERIC* (1994) 1–16. https://eric.ed.gov/?id=ED378477.

Courses Web. "101 Zen Stories." https://coursesweb.net/blog/101-zen-stories.

Covey, Stephen R. *The Seven Habits of Highly Effective People: Restoring the Character Ethic.* New York: Simon & Schuster, 1989.
Daft, Richard L. *The Leadership Experience.* Thousand Oaks, CA: Cengage, 2018.
———. *Management.* Thousand Oaks, CA: Cengage, 2018.
Davis, Marianna W. "The Connatural Ground of John Woolman's Triangle." *College Language Association Journal* 9 (1965) 132–39.
Deats, Richard L. "Fellowship." *New York* 79 (2015) 25–27.
De La Rosa, Shawna. "New Harriet Tubman Movie Is Changing Perceptions of an American Icon." https://thehill.com/changing-america/respect/equality/472149-new-harriet-tubman-movie-is-changing-perceptions-of-an.
De Mello, Anthony. *The Heart of the Enlightened: A Book of Story Meditations.* New York: Image, 1997.
DeWine, Sue. *The Consultant's Craft: Improving Organizational Communication.* Boston: St. Martin's, 2001.
Dhiman, Satinder. *Gandhi and Leadership: New Horizons in Exemplary Leadership.* New York: Palgrave MacMillan, 2015.
———. *Holistic Leadership: A New Paradigm for Today's Leaders.* New York: Palgrave MacMillan, 2017.
Dillon, Karen. "New Managers Should Focus on Helping Their Teams, Not Pleasing Their Bosses." *Harvard Business Review*, July 07, 2017. https://hbr.org/2017/07/new-managers-should-focus-on-helping-their-teams-not-pleasing-their-bosses.
Donnelly, Gloria F. "In Praise of Harriet Tubman: Nurse, Spy, Abolitionist." *Holistic Nursing Practice* 30 (2016) 191.
Dweck, Carol S. *Mindset: The New Psychology of Success.* New York: Random House, 2006.
Edmondson, Ron. "Are You a Clueless Leader? How Would You Know?" *Church Leaders*, August 11, 2015. https://churchleaders.com/pastors/pastor-howto/259331-clueless-leader-know.html.
Egan, James. 3000 *Astounding Quotes.* Morrisville, NC: Lulu, 2015.
Egnew Thomas R. "The Meaning of Healing: Transcending Suffering." *Annals of Family Medicine* 3 (2005) 255–62.
"Eleanor Roosevelt." http://www.firstladies.org/biographies/firstladies.aspx?biography=33.
Erickson, Erik H. *Gandhi's Truth: On the Origins of Militant Nonviolence.* New York: Norton, 1969.
Ferch, Shann Ray. *Forgiveness and Power in the Age of Atrocity: Servant Leadership as a Way of Life.* Lanham, MD: Lexington, 2012.
———. "Servant-Leadership and the Interior of the Leader: Facing Violence with Courage and Forgiveness." In *The Spirit of Servant-Leadership*, edited by Shann Ray Ferch and Larry C. Spears, 21–49. New York: Paulist, 2011.
Figliuolo, Mike. *One Piece of Paper: The Simple Approach to Powerful, Personal Leadership.* San Francisco: Jossey-Bass, 2011.
Fischer, Louis. *Gandhi: His Life and Message for the World.* New York: The New American Library, 1954.
———. *Mahatma Gandhi: His Life and Times.* Mumbai: Bharatiya Vidya Bhavan, 2012.
Fisher, Roger, et al. *Getting to Yes: Negotiating Agreement Without Giving In.* New York: Penguin, 2011.

Fitz-Gibbon, Andrew. "The Beloved Community: A Neo-Aristotelian Perspective." In *The Peace of Nature and the Nature of Peace*, edited by Andrew Fiala, 139–49. Leiden: Brill, 2015.
Foner, Eric. "A Brutal Process." *New York Times*, October 3, 2014. https://www.nytimes.com/2014/10/05/books/review/the-half-has-never-been-told-by-edward-e-baptist.html.
Frankl, Viktor. *Man's Search for Meaning An Introduction to Logotherapy*. New York: Simon & Schuster, 1984.
———. *Man's Search for Ultimate Meaning*. New York: Basic, 2018.
———. *The Unheard Cry for Meaning*. New York: Simon & Schuster, 1978.
Freiburg, Kevin, and Jackie Freiburg. *Nuts! Southwest Airilines' Crazy Recipe for Business and Personal Success*. Austin: Bard, 1996.
Frick, Don M. *Robert K. Greenleaf: A Life of Servant Leadership*. San Francisco: Berrett-Koehler, 2004.
Gandhi, Mahatma. *An Autobiography: The Story of My Experiments with Truth*. Boston: Beacon, 1957.
———. *The Collected Works of Mahatma Gandhi*. New Delhi: Publications Division of the Ministry of Information and Broadcasting of the Government of India, 2015.
———. *The Essential Gandhi: An Anthology of His Writings on His Life, Work, and Ideas*. Edited by Louis Fischer. New York: Vintage, 2002.
———. *From Yeravda Mandir: Ashram Observances*. Ahmedabad, India: Navajivan, 1932.
Gandhi, Mahatma, and Bharatan Kumarappa, eds. *Non-Violent Resistance: Satyagraha*. New York: Schocken, 1961.
Gandhi, Mahatma, et al. *The Mind of Mahatma Gandhi*. Ahmedabad, India: Navajivan, 1967.
George, Bill. *Discover Your True North: Becoming an Authentic Leader*. Hoboken, NJ: Wiley, 2015.
Gettleman, Jeffrey. "Wangari Maathai, Nobel Peace Prize Laureate, Dies at 71." *New York Times*, September 26, 2011. https://www.nytimes.com/2011/09/27/world/africa/wangari-maathai-nobel-peace-prize-laureate-dies-at-71.html.
Gist, Conra D., and Karsonya Wise Whitehead. "Deconstructing Dr. Martin Luther King's 'Letter from a Birmingham Jail' and the Strategy of Nonviolent Resistance." *Black History Bulletin* 76 (2013) 6–13.
Gittell, Jody H. "Relational Coordination: Coordinating Work through Relationships of Shared Goals, Shared Knowledge and Mutual Respect." In *Relational Perspectives in Organizational Studies: A Research Companion*, edited by Olympia Kyriakidou and Mustafa F. Ozbilgin, 74–94. London: Edward Elgar, 2006.
———. *The Southwest Airlines Way: Using the Power of Relationships to Achieve High Performance*. New York: McGraw-Hill, 2003.
Goldsmith, Marshall. "Passing the Baton: Talent Management." https://www.marshallgoldsmith.com/articles/passing-the-baton/.
Goleman, Daniel. *Emotional Intelligence*. New York: Bantam, 1995.
———. "How Emotionally Intelligent Are You?" https://www.kornferry.com/insights/this-week-in-leadership/emotional-intelligence-assessment.
Goleman, Daniel, and Richard E. Boyatzis. "Social Intelligence and the Biology of Leadership." *Harvard Business Review*, September 2008. https://hbr.org/2008/09/social-intelligence-and-the-biology-of-leadership.

Gottman, John Mordecai. "A Theory of Marital Dissolution and Stability." *Journal of Family Psychology* 7.1 (1993) 57–75.

Grant, Adam M. *Give and Take: Why Helping Others Drives Our Success*. New York: Penguin, 2013.

Greenleaf, Robert K. "The Institution as Servant." Indianapolis: Robert K. Greenleaf Center, 2009.

———. *On Becoming a Servant Leader*. Edited by Don M. Frick and Larry C. Spears. San Francisco: Jossey-Bass, 1996.

———. "On Being a Seeker in the Late Twentieth Century." *Friends Journal* 21 (September 15, 1975) 452–53.

———. *The Power of Servant-Leadership: Essays by Robert K. Greenleaf*. Edited by Larry C. Spears. San Francisco: Berrett-Koehler, 1998.

———. *The Servant as Leader*. Indianapolis: Robert K. Greenleaf Center, 1970.

———. *Servant Leadership: A Journey Into the Nature of Legitimate Power and Greatness*. Mahwah, NJ: Paulist, 1977.

———. *Servant Leadership: Retrospect and Prospect*. Westfield, IN: Greenleaf Center for Servant Leadership, 2013.

———. *The Servant Leader within: A Transformative Path*. Edited by Hamilton Beazley et al. Mahwah, NJ: Paulist, 2003.

Guest, Royston. *Built to Grow: How to Deliver Accelerated, Sustained and Profitable Business Growth*. Hoboken, NJ: Wiley, 2016.

Gummere, Amelia M. "The John Woolman Memorial Association." *Bulletin of Friends' Historical Society of Philadelphia* 6 (1915) 66–70.

Gunnarson, Jan, and Olle Blohm. "The Welcoming Servant-Leader: The Art of Creating Hostmanship." In *The Spirit of Servant-Leadership*, edited by Shann Ray Ferch and Larry C. Spears, 68–85. New York: Paulist, 2011.

Guttmann, David. *Logotherapy for the Helping Professional: Meaningful Social Work*. New York: Springer, 1996.

Harriet Tubman Biography. "Harriet Tubman Myths and Facts." http://www.harriettubmanbiography.com/harriet-tubman-myths-and-facts.html.

Heifetz, Ronald A., and Martin Linsky. *Leadership on the Line: Staying Alive through the Dangers of Leading*. Boston: Harvard Business School, 2017.

Herstein, Gary. "The Roycean Roots of the Beloved Community." *The Pluralist* 4 (2009) 91–107.

Hesse, Hermann. *The Journey to the East*. New York: Noonday, 1957.

Hill, Alex, et al. "How Winning Organizations Last 100 Years," *Harvard Business Review*, September 27, 2018. https://hbr.org/2018/09/how-winning-organizations-last-100-years.

Hill, Johnny Bernard. *The Theology of Martin Luther King, Jr. and Desmond Mpilo Tutu*. New York: Palgrave MacMillan, 2007.

The Hindu. "Land of [sic] Billion Opportunities, Not [sic] Billion Problems: Mukesh." *The Hindu BusinessLine*, November 14, 2011. https://www.thehindubusinessline.com/todays-paper/tp-economy/Land-of-billion-opportunities-not-billion-problems-Mukesh/article20360141.ece.

History.com Editors. "Montgomery Buss Boycott." https://www.history.com/topics/black-history/montgomery-bus-boycott.

"History of Memento Mori." https://dailystoic.com/history-of-memento-mori/.

Hochschild, Adam. *Bury the Chains: Prophets and Rebels in the Fight to Free an Empire's Slaves*. Boston: Houghton Mifflin, 2005.
Hornsby, Alton, Jr. "Martin Luther King, Jr. 'Letter From a Birmingham Jail.'" *The Journal of Negro History* 71 (1986) 38–44.
Houston, G. David. "John Woolman's Efforts in Behalf of Freedom." *The Journal of Negro History* 2 (1917) 126–38.
Hunt, Anthony C. *Beloved Community Toolkit*. Bel Air, MD: Self-published, 2018.
Independent Television Service. "Taking Root Discussion Guide." https://cdn.itvs.org/taking_root_discussion.pdf.
Janssen, Onne et al. "How Task and Person Conflict Shape the Role of Positive Interdependence in Management Teams." *Journal of Management* 25 (1999) 117–42.
Johnson, Davi. "Martin Luther King Jr.'s 1963 Birmingham Campaign as Image Event." *Rhetoric and Public Affairs* 10 (2007) 1–25.
Johnson, Richard L, ed. *Gandhi's Experiments with Truth: Essential Writings by and about Mahatma Gandhi*. Lanham, MD: Lexington, 2006.
Jolliff, William. "The Economy of the Inward Life: John Woolman and Henry Thoreau." *The Concord Saunterer* 15 (2007) 91–111.
Jones, J. C. "Wounded Vietnam Veteran Shares His Life Journey." *Killeen Daily Heral*, July 27, 2015. https://kdhnews.com/news/wounded-vietnam-veteran-shares-his-life-s-journey/article_589caba8-340a-11e5-9f0f-53c1913783af.html.
Kastenbaum, Ben. "What, Me Lead? Don't You Think I'm Too Young?" *Tacoma News Tribune* (August 29, 2014) 15–16.
Keegan, Michael J. "Strategic Foresight and Leadership." *IBM Center for the Business of Government*, January 25, 2018. http://www.businessofgovernment.org/blog/strategic-foresight-and-leadership.
Keith, Kent M. *The Contemporary Servant as Leader*. Atlanta: Greenleaf Center for Servant Leadership, 2016.
Kellerman, Barbara. *Bad Leadership: What It Is, How It Happens, Why It Matters*. Boston: Harvard Business School Press, 2004.
———. "Insular Leadership—The Case of Barack Obama." https://barbarakellerman.com/insular-leadership-the-case-of-barack-obama/.
———. "You're a Leader? Fine. But To Whom Are You Responsible?" https://barbarakellerman.com/youre-a-leader-fine-but-to-whom-are-you-responsible/.
King, Martin Luther, Jr. "Birmingham Manifesto, April 3, 1963." https://www.crmvet.org/docs/bhammanf.htm.
———. "Dr. Martin Luther King's Visit to Cornell College." https://news.cornellcollege.edu/dr-martin-luther-kings-visit-to-cornell-college/.
———. "I Have a Dream." http://www.americanrhetoric.com/speeches/mlkihaveadream.htm.
———. "Martin Luther King, Jr.'s 'A Christmas Sermon on Peace' Still Prophetic 50 Years Later." https://www.beaconbroadside.com/broadside/2017/12/martin-luther-king-jrs-christmas-sermon-peace-still-prophetic-50-years-later.html.
———. "Martin Luther King Jr.'s 'Justice without Violence' Lecture at Brandeis." https://www.brandeis.edu/now/video-transcripts/mlk-transcript.html.
———. "Remaining Awake through a Great Revolution." https://www2.oberlin.edu/external/EOG/BlackHistoryMonth/MLK/CommAddress.html.
———. *Strength to Love*. New York: Harper & Row, 1963.

———. "Where Do We Go from Here?" In *A Call to Conscience: The Landmark Speeches of Dr. Martin Luther King, Jr*, edited by Clayborne Carson and Kris Shepherd, 165–200. New York: Grand Central, 2002.

———. *Where Do We Go from Here: Chaos or Community?* New York: Harper & Row, 1967.

King, Martin Luther, Jr., et al. *The Papers of Martin Luther King, Jr.* Berkeley: University of California Press, 1992.

Kounios, John, and Mark Beeman. "The Aha! Moment: The Cognitive Neuroscience of Insight." *Current Directions in Psychological Science* 18 (2009) 210–16.

Kouzes, James M., and Barry Z. Posner. *The Leadership Challenge: How to Make Extraordinary Things Happen in Organizations*. Hoboken, NJ: Wiley & Sons, 2017.

Kristof, Nicholas. "Where's the Empathy?" *New York Times*, January 24, 2015. https://www.nytimes.com/2015/01/25/opinion/sunday/nicholas-kristof-wheres-the-empathy.html.

Lagace, Martha. "From Tigers to Kaleidoscopes: Thinking about Future Leadership." *Harvard Business School Working Knowledge*, May 21, 2001. https://hbswk.hbs.edu/item/from-tigers-to-kaleidoscopes-thinking-about-future-leadership.

Lanzoni, Susan. "A Short History of Empathy." *The Atlantic*, October 15, 2015. https://www.theatlantic.com/health/archive/2015/10/a-short-history-of-empathy/409912/.

Lask, John S. "John Woolman: Crusader for Freedom." *Phylon* 5 (1944) 30–40.

Lee, Chris, and Ron Zemke. "The Search for Spirit in the Workplace." In *Reflections on Leadership: How Robert K. Greenleaf's Theory of Servant-Leadership Influenced Today's Top Management Thinkers*, edited by Larry C. Spears and Michelle Lawrence, 99–112. New York: Wiley & Sons.

Lee, Harper. *To Kill A Mockingbird*. New York: HarperCollins, 1999.

Leslie, Mitch. "The First Eureka Moment." *Science* 305.5688 (2004) 1219. https://link.gale.com/apps/doc/A121764072/HRCA?u=anon~4793c1d1&sid=HCA&xid=0f01b001.

Lessard, Suzannah. "The First Lady of the New Deal: How Eleanor Roosevelt Discovered Herself through Politics." *The Washington Monthly* (September 1999) 47–48.

Levernier, James A. "John Woolman (1720–1772). https://faculty.georgetown.edu/bassr/heath/syllabuild/iguide/woolman.html.

Little, Jane Braxton. "Planting Trees for Peace: The Message Brought by Kenya's Nobel Peace Prize Winner Sounds Surprisingly Familiar." *American Forests* (June 22, 2006).

Longenecker, Clinton O., et al., "Causes and Consequences of Managerial Failure in Rapidly Changing Organizations." *Business Horizons* 50 (2007) 145–55.

Lopez, Isabel O. "Becoming a Servant-Leader: The Personal Development Path." In *Reflections on Leadership: How Robert K. Greenleaf's Theory of Servant Leadership Influenced Today's Top Management Thinkers*, edited by Larry C. Spears, 149–60. New York: Wiley & Sons, 1995.

Lutkehaus, Nancy. *Margaret Mead: The Making of an American Icon*. Princeton, NJ: Princeton University Press, 2008.

Maathai, Wangari. "Be a Hummingbird." https://www.greenbeltmovement.org/get-involved/be-a-hummingbird.

———. *Unbowed: A Memoir*. New York: Alfred A. Knopf, 2006.

MacDonald, Mia. "Something Wonderful Happens When You Plant a Seed." *Sierra Magazine*, March 2005. https://vault.sierraclub.org/sierra/200503/interview.asp.

"Mahatma Gandhi." https://www.biography.com/activist/mahatma-gandhi.

Mani Bhavan. "Years of Satyagrahas of Mahatma Gandhi." https://www.gandhimanibhavan.org/about-gandhi/chrono-satyagrahasofgandhi.html.

Marsh, Charles. *The Beloved Community: How Faith Shapes Social Justice from the Civil Rights Movement to Today*. New York: Basic, 2008.

The Martin Luther King, Jr. Research and Education Institute. "Montgomery Bus Boycott." https://kinginstitute.stanford.edu/encyclopedia/montgomery-bus-boycott.

———. "Statement on Ending the Bus Boycott." https://kinginstitute.stanford.edu/king-papers/documents/statement-ending-bus-boycott.

Mayton, D. M. "Gandhi as Peacebuilder: The Social Psychology of Satyagraha." In *Peace, Conflict, and Violence: Peace Psychology for the 21st Century*, edited by D. J. Christie et al., 307–13. Englewood Cliffs, NJ: Prentice-Hall, 2001.

McGowan, James A., and William C. Kashatus. *Harriet Tubman: A Biography*. Santa Barbara, CA: Greenwood, 2011.

Meacham, Jon. *His Truth Is Marching On: John Lewis and the Power of Hope*. New York: Random House, 2020.

Mendoza, Jim. "A Grenade's Blast Left Him Disfigured. Today, His Scars Are a Message of Hope to Others." *Hawaii News Now*, February 27, 2018. https://www.hawaiinewsnow.com/story/37606497/a-grenades-blast-left-him-disfigured-today-his-scars-are-a-message-of-hope-to-others/.

Meranze, Michael. "Materializing Conscience: Embodiment, Speech, and the Experience of Sympathetic Identification." *Early American Literature* 37 (2002) 71–88.

"Merck Offers Free Distribution of New River Blindness Drug." *The New York Times*, October, 22, 1987. https://www.nytimes.com/1987/10/22/world/merck-offers-free-distribution-of-new-river-blindness-drug.html.

Misra, Bijoy. "Mahatma Gandhi's Rules for Satyagraha." http://www.lokvani.com/lokvani/article.php?article_id=13907.

Mitchell, John. "Nobel Laureate Talks at L. A. Eco-Event." *Los Angeles Times*, April 27, 2008. https://www.latimes.com/archives/la-xpm-2008-apr-27-me-nobel27-story.html.

Mitchell, Rex C. "'Framing' in Communications and Conflict." http://www.csun.edu/~hfmgt001/frameC.htm.

Mother Teresa. *Love: The Words and Inspiration of Mother Teresa*. Boulder, CO: Blue Mountain, 2007.

———. *Meditations from a Simple Path*. New York: Ballantine, 1996.

"Mother Teresa." https://www.biographyonline.net/nobelprize/mother_teresa.html.

Mouton, Phillips. "The Influence of the Writings of John Woolman." *Quaker History* 60 (1971) 3–13.

———. "John Woolman: Exemplar of Ethics." *Quaker History* 54 (1965) 81–93.

Muggeridge, Malcolm. *Something Beautiful for God: Mother Teresa of Calcutta*. New York: Harper & Row, 1971.

Nadella, Satya. *Hit Refresh: The Quest to Rediscover Microsoft's Soul and Imagine a Better Future for Everyone*. New York: HarperBusiness, 2017.

Nair, Keshavan. *A Higher Standard of Leadership: Lessons from the Life of Gandhi*. San Francisco: Berrett-Koehler, 1997.

"Negroes' Boycott Cripples Bus Line." *The New York Times,* January 8, 1956. https://timesmachine.nytimes.com/timesmachine/1956/01/08/86490725.html.

Nichols, Ralph G., and Leonard A. Stevens. "Listening to People." *Harvard Business Review,* September 1957. https://hbr.org/1957/09/listening-to-people.

Nielsen, Richard P. "Quaker Foundations for Greenleaf's Servant-Leadership and 'Friendly Disentangling' Method." In *Insights on Leadership: Service, Stewardship, Spirit, and Servant-leadership,* edited by Larry C. Spears, 126–44. New York: Wiley & Sons, 1998.

"The Nobel Peace Prize 2004." https://www.nobelprize.org/prizes/peace/2004/summary.

Nocera, Joe. "The Sinatra of Southwest Feels the Love." *New York Times,* May 24, 2008. https://www.nytimes.com/2008/05/24/business/24nocera.html.

Nouwen, Henri J. M. *The Wounded Healer: Ministry in Contemporary Society*. New York: Image, 1979.

Oates, Stephen B. *Let the Trumpet Sound: The Life of Martin Luther King, Jr.* New York: Harper & Row, 1982.

Odekon, Mehmet. *The SAGE Encyclopedia of World Poverty*. Thousand Oaks, CA: Sage, 2016.

Ornstein, Matthew, dir. *Accidental Courtesy: Daryl Davis, Race & America*. https://accidentalcourtesy.com/, 2016.

Pal, Amitabh. "Wangari Maathai." *The Progressive* 69 (2005) 35–38.

Palmer, Parker J. *A Hidden Wholeness: The Journey Toward an Undivided Life*. San Francisco: Jossey-Bass, 2000.

———. *Let Your Life Speak: Listening for the Voice of Vocation*. New York: Wiley & Sons, 2009.

———. *The Promise of Paradox: A Celebration of Contradictions in the Christian Life*. Notre Dame, IN: Ave Maria, 1980.

Pattakos, Alex. *Prisoners of Our Thoughts: Viktor Frankl's Principles at Work*. San Francisco: Berrett-Koehler, 2004.

Patterson, Kerry, et al., *Crucial Conversations: Tools for Talking When Stakes Are High*. New York: McGraw Hill, 2012.

Patton, John H. "A Transforming Response: Martin Luther King Jr.'s 'Letter from Birmingham Jail.'" *Rhetoric and Public Affairs* 7 (2004) 53–65.

Paul, W. Kohle, et al. "Advising as Servant Leadership: Investigating the Relationship." *NACADA Journal* 32 (2012) 53–62.

Pederson, William D. "Franklin Delano Roosevelt." In *The Presidents and the Constitution: A Living History,* edited by Ken Gormley, 409–26. New York: New York University Press, 2016.

Perlez, Jane. "Violence in Nairobi Draws a Warning by U.S." *The New York Times,* March 5, 1992. https://www.nytimes.com/1992/03/05/world/violence-in-nairobi-draws-a-warning-by-us.html.

Peters, Tom. "Air Travel's Greatest Show On- and Off-Earth." *Chicago Tribune,* September 26, 1994. https://www.chicagotribune.com/news/ct-xpm-1994-09-26-9409260086-story.html.

———. *Little Big Things: 63 Ways to Pursue Excellence*. New York: Harper Business, 2010.

Pink, Daniel H. "Interview with Bob Sutton." https://www.danpink.com/interview-with-bob-sutton/.
Pinsker, Matthew. "Vigilance in Pennsylvania: Underground Railroad Activities in the Keystone State, 1837–1861." Pennsylvania Historical and Museum Commission Annual Conference on Black History, Harrisburg, PA, April 27, 2000.
Pizana, Dionardo. "Remembering Dr. Martin Luther King, Jr.'s Beloved Community." Michigan State University Extension, March 19, 2018. https://www.canr.msu.edu/news/remembering_dr._martin_luther_king_jr.s_beloved_community.
Plank, Geoffrey. "The Flame of Life Was Kindled in All Animal and Sensitive Creatures: One Quaker Colonist's View of Animal Life." *Church History* 76 (2007) 569–90.
———. "Sailing with John Woolman: The Millennium and Maritime Trade." *Early American Studies* 7 (2009) 46–81.
Pradhan, Ram Chandra. "Making Sense of Gandhi's Idea of Truth." *Social Scientist* 34 (2006) 36–49.
Pytell, Timothy E. "The Man Who Would Be King: Viktor Frankl's Struggle For Meaning." PhD diss., New York University, 1999.
Questlove. "Cornel West." *Interview Magazine*, November 2, 2014. https://www.interviewmagazine.com/culture/cornel-west.
Rahman, Aziz, et al. "The British Art of Colonialism in India: Subjugation and Division." *Peace and Conflict Studies* 25.1 (2018). doi: 10.46743/1082-7307/2018.1439.
Ramchiary, Arpana. "Gandhian Concept of Truth and Non-Violence." *IOSR Journal of Humanities and Social Science* 18 (2013) 67–69.
Redding, W. Charles. *Communications within the Organization: An Interpretive Review of Theory And Research*. New York: Industrial Communication Council, 1972.
Reddy, Enuga S. *Mahatma Gandhi Letters to Americans*. Mumbai: Bharatiya Vidya Bhavan, 1998.
Redsand, Anna. *Viktor Frankl: A Life Worth Living*. New York: Clarion, 2006.
Roosevelt, Eleanor. *The Autobiography of Eleanor Roosevelt*. New York: Harper & Brothers, 1961.
———. "My Day, December 12, 1945." *The Eleanor Roosevelt Papers, Digital Edition*. https://www2.gwu.edu/~erpapers/myday/displaydoc.cfm?_y=1945&_f=md000206.
———. *Tomorrow Is Now*. New York: Harper & Row, 1963.
Rosenberg. John S. "Three Stonecutters: On the Future of Business Education." *Harvard Magazine*, October 15, 2008. https://www.harvardmagazine.com/breaking-news/three-stonecutters-the-future-business-education.
Roy, Arundhati. *Field Notes on Democracy: Listening to Grasshoppers*. Chicago: Haymarket, 2009.
Rubenstein, Richard L., and John K. Roth. *Approaches to Auschwitz: The Holocaust and Its Legacy*. Atlanta: John Knox, 1987.
Rushman, Nancy Larner. "Servant-Leadership and the Best Companies to Work for in America." In *Focus on Leadership: Servant-Leadership for the 21st Century*, edited by Larry C. Spears and Michelle Lawrence, 123–40. New York: Wiley & Sons.
Sadiq, Sheraz. "What Happens When You Put a Hummingbird in a Wind Tunnel?" *Deep Look* (*Blog*), March 31, 2015. https://www.kqed.org/science/28759/what-happens-when-you-put-a-hummingbird-in-a-wind-tunnel.
Sargent, Frederic O. *The Civil Rights Revolution: Events and Leaders, 1955–1968*. Jefferson, NC: McFarland, 2004.

Savastio, Rebecca. "KKK Member Walks up to Black Musician in Bar—But It's Not a Joke, and What Happens Next Will Astound You." *Guardian Liberty Voice*, November 20, 2013. https://guardianlv.com/2013/11/kkk-member-walks-up-to-black-musician-in-bar-but-its-not-a-joke-and-what-happens-next-will-astound-you/.

Schechter, Betty. *The Peaceable Revolution*. Boston: Houghton Mifflin, 1963.

Schmid, Karl F. *Construction Estimating: A Step-by-Step Guide to a Successful Estimate.* New York: Momentum, 2011.

Sears, Priscilla. "Wangari Maathai: 'You Strike the Woman . . .'" https://www.context.org/iclib/ic28/sears/.

Seeber, Frances M. "Eleanor Roosevelt and Women in the New Deal: A Network of Friends." *Presidential Studies Quarterly* 20 (1990) 707–17.

Shantall, Teria. *Life's Meaning in the Face of Suffering: Testimonies of Holocaust Survivors.* Jerusalem: Hebrew University Magnes, 2002.

Shepard, Mark Shepard. *Mahatma Gandhi and His Myths, Civil Disobedience, Nonviolence and Satyagraha in the Real World (Plus Why It's 'Gandhi,' Not 'Ghandi')*. Los Angeles: Simple, 2017.

Showkeir, Maren, and Jamie Showkeir. "Clarifying Intention as the Path to Servant Leadership." In *The Spirit of Servant-Leadership*, edited by Shann Ray Ferch and Larry C. Spears, 152–65. New York: Paulist, 2011.

Simpson, Gary M. "'Changing the Face of the Enemy': Martin Luther King, Jr., and the Beloved Community" *Faculty Publications* 28.1 (2008) 57–65. https://digitalcommons.luthersem.edu/faculty_articles/201.

Smith, Harold Ivan. *Eleanor: A Spiritual Biography*, Louisville, KY: Westminster John Knox, 2017.

Smith, Kenneth L., and Ira G. Zepp. *Search for the Beloved Community: The Thinking of Martin Luther King, Jr.* Valley Forge, PA: Judson, 1974.

Solomon, Brett Johnson. "On Being Maladjusted to Injustice: A Response to Cornel West." *Explore Journal.* (Spring 2015). https://www.scu.edu/ic/media-publications/explore-journal/spring-2015-stories/on-being-maladjusted-to-injustice.html.

Sparrow, Paul M. "Eleanor Roosevelt's Battle to End Lynching." *Franklin D. Roosevelt Presidential Library and Museum*, February 12, 2016. https://fdr.blogs.archives.gov/2016/02/12/eleanor-roosevelts-battle-to-end-lynching/.

Spears, Larry C. "Introduction." In *The Power of Servant-Leadership: Essays by Robert K. Greenleaf*, edited by Larry C. Spears, 1–16. San Francisco: Berrett-Koehler, 1998.

———. "Introduction—The Spirit of Servant Leadership." In *The Spirit of Servant-Leadership*, edited by Shann Ray Ferch and Larry C. Spears, 7–20. New York: Paulist, 2011.

———. "Introduction: Understanding the Growing Impact of Servant-Leadership." In *The Servant-Leader within: A Transformative Path*, edited by Hamilton Beazely et al., 13–28. New York: Paulist, 2003.

———. "Ten Characteristics of a Servant-Leader." https://www.spearscenter.org/46-uncategorised/136-ten-characteristics-of-servantleadership.

———. "Tracing the Growing Impact of Servant-Leadership." In *Insights on Leadership: Service, Stewardship, Spirit, and Servant-leadership*, edited by Larry C. Spears, 1–14. New York: Wiley & Sons, 1998.

———. "The Understanding and Practice of Servant-Leadership." Paper presented at Servant Leadership Research Roundtable at Regent University, Virginia Beach, VA, August 2005.

Spears, Larry C., ed. *Insights on Leadership: Service, Stewardship, Spirit, and Servant-leadership*. New York: Wiley & Sons, 1998.

———. *Reflections on Leadership: How Robert K. Greenleaf's Theory of Servant Leadership Influenced Today's Top Management Thinkers*. New York: Wiley & Sons, 1995.

Spink, Kathryn. *Mother Teresa: An Authorized Biography*. New York: HarperCollins, 1997.

Stevenson, Seth. "A Rare Joint Interview with Microsoft CEO Satya Nadella and Bill Gates." *Wall Street Journal*, September 25, 2017. https://www.wsj.com/articles/a-rare-joint-interview-with-microsoft-ceo-satya-nadella-and-bill-gates-1506358852.

Stewart, Margaret E. "John Woolman's 'Kindness Beyond Expression': Collective Identity vs. Individualism and White Supremacy." *Early American Literature* 26 (1991) 251–75.

Sturm, Douglas. "Crisis in the American Republic: The Legal and Political Significance of Martin Luther King's 'Letter from a Birmingham Jail.'" *Journal of Law and Religion* 2 (1984) 309–24.

Sturnick, Judith A. "Healing Leadership." In *Insights on Leadership: Service, Stewardship, Spirit, and Servant-leadership*, edited by Larry C. Spears, 185–96. New York: Wiley & Sons, 1998.

Sutton, Bob. "Of Baboons and Bosses." https://bobsutton.typepad.com/my_weblog/2009/05/of-baboons-and-bosses.html.

"Teach for America Founder Kopp Kicks Off Speaker Series." *Northwestern Business Review*, April 19, 2013. https://northwesternbusinessreview.org/teach-for-america-founder-kopp-kicksoff-speaker-series-9db7077f803a.

Terlizzi, Massimo Di. *The Women of the Nobel*. Milano: SEM Edizioni, 2004.

Terrell, Thomas E., Jr. "John Woolman: The Theology Of A Public Order." *Quaker History* 71 (1982) 16–30.

Tharoor, Shashi. *Inglorious Empire: What the British Did to India*. Brunswick, VIC: Scribe, 2017.

Tutu, Desmond. *No Future without Forgiveness*. New York: Doubleday, 1999.

UNESCO. "We Pay Tribute to Wangari Maathai, Kenya's Green Militant." *A World of Science* 10 (2012) 15.

United for Human Rights. "Champions of Human Rights." https://www.humanrights.com/voices-for-human-rights/eleanor-roosevelt.html.

United Nations. "What Are Human Rights?" https://www.un.org/en/global-issues/humanrights.

Vail, Mark. "The 'Integrative' Rhetoric of Martin Luther King Jr.'s 'I Have a Dream' Speech." *Rhetoric and Public Affairs* 9 (2006) 51–78.

Vallance, Clem, and Roger Mills, dirs. *Pole to Pole*. London: BBC Video, 2007. DVD.

Van Gogh, Vincent. "Letter from Vincent van Gogh to Theo van Gogh. The Hague, 12 or 13 May 1882." http://www.webexhibits.org/vangogh/letter/11/197.htm.

Varkey, Thomas. "The Myth and Meaning of the Gandhian Concept of *Satygraha*." *Sophia Unversity Junior College Division Faculty Journal* 35 (2014) 171–79.

Vazhapilly, S. "Relevance of Gandhian Praxis to Empowering Women." In *Gandhi: The Meaning of the Mahatma for the Millennium*, edited by Kuruvilla Pandikattu 95–118. Washington, DC: Council for Research in Values and Philosophy, 2001.

Vick, Karl. "2001: Wangari Maathai." *Time Magaine*, March 5, 2020. https://time.com/5793752/wangari-maathai-100-women-of-the-year/.

"Wangari Maathai—Nobel Lecture." https://www.nobelprize.org/prizes/peace/2004/maathai/26050-wangari-maathai-nobel-lecture-2004/.

Wangrin, Mark. "Never Let a Good Scar Go to Waste." *Texas Coop Power*, August 2014. https://www.texascooppower.com/texas-stories/history/never-let-a-good-scar-go-to-waste.

Washington, Glynn. "The Silver Dollar Lounge." *National Public Radio*, November 13, 2014. https://www.npr.org/2014/11/14/363896136/the-silver-dollar-lounge.

Watson, Martha Solomon. "The Issue Is Justice: Martin Luther King Jr.'s Response to the Birmingham Clergy." *Rhetoric and Public Affairs* 7 (2004) 1–22.

Weger, Harry, Jr., et al. "The Relative Effectiveness of Active Listening in Initial Interactions." *International Journal of Listening* 28 (2014) 13–31.

West, Cornel. "Speaking Truth to Power: A Discussion on Institutional Provincialism." Lecture to MIT School of Architecture and Planning, Cambridge, MA, February 7, 2018. Video. 2:07:17. https://livestream.com/accounts/2261474/events/8029590/videos/169920045.

Wheatley, Margaret. *Turning to One Another: Simple Conversations to Restore Hope to the Future*. Oakland: Berrett-Koehler, 2009.

Wheelock, David C. "Economic Episodes in American History: The Great Depression." Presentation given as part of an economic education workshop at the Federal Reserve Bank of St. Louis, St. Louis, MO, July 11, 2013. https://www.stlouisfed.org/the-great-depression/curriculum/economic-episodes-in-american-history-part-5.

Wicker, Christine, "Seeking the Soul of Business." In *Insights on Leadership: Service, Stewardship, Spirit, and Servant-leadership*, edited by Larry C. Spears, 246–50. New York: Wiley & Sons, 1998.

Williams, Jennifer. "What Is Empathy and Why Is It Important?" https://blog.heartmanity.com/what-is-empathy-and-why-is-it-important.

Williams, Reggie L. "Christ-Centred Concreteness: The Christian Activism of Harriet Tubman, Dietrich Bonhoeffer, and Martin Luther King Jr." *Journal of European Baptist Studies* 19 (2019) 127–42.

Wondra Joshua D., and Phoebe C. Ellsworth. "An Appraisal Theory of Empathy and Other Vicarious Emotional Experiences." *Psychological Review* 122 (2015) 411–28.

Wood, B. Dan, and Soren Jordan. *Party Polarization in America: The War Over Two Social Contracts*. New York: Cambridge University Press, 2017.

Woodson, Carter G. *The Journal of Negro History*. London: Forgotten, 2019.

Woodward, Ian C. "Three Altitudes of Leadership." *Leadership & Organisations* (*blog*) https://knowledge.insead.edu/blog/insead-blog/the-three-altitudes-of-leadership-7541.

Woolman, John. *The Journal of John Woolman*. Grand Rapids: Christian Classics Ethereal Library, 2002. http://www.ccel.org/ccel/woolman/journal.html.

———. *The Journal of John Woolman and a Plea for the Poor: The Spiritual Autobiography of the Great Colonial Quaker*. Secaucus, NJ: Citadel, 1961.

Worthington, Everett L., Jr. *Marriage Counseling: A Christian Approach to Counseling Couples*. Downers Grove, IL: InterVarsity, 2009.

Yale News. "International Environmental Leaders Named McCluskey Fellows at Yale." https://news.yale.edu/2000/05/15/international-environmental-leaders-named-mccluskey-fellows-yale.

Yeh, Raymond T., and Stephanie H. Yeh. *The Art of Business: In the Footsteps of Giants*. Olathe, CO: Zero Time, 2004.

Young, David S. "Foresight: The Lead That the Leader Has." In *Focus on Leadership: Servant-Leadership for the 21st Century*, edited by Larry C. Spears and Michelle Lawrence, 245–56. New York: Wiley & Sons.

Young, Nicholas Maurice, et al. "Even Superheroes Need a Network: Harriet Tubman and the Rise of Insurgency in the New York State Underground Railroad." *DuBois Review: Social Science Research on Race* 6 (2009) 397–429.

Yousafzai, Malala. *I Am Malala: The Girl Who Stood Up for Education and Was Shot By the Taliban*. New York: Little, Brown, 2013.

Zepp, Ira. *The Social Vision of Martin Luther King Jr*. Brooklyn: Carlson, 1989.

Index

Ambani, Mukesh D., 58
Awareness
    conscious living, 61-62
    emotional intelligence, 12, 25
    Greenleaf, view of, 56-57
    insular leadership, 60-61
    levels of, 131
    listening, 16
    obstacles to, 61
    servant leadership, xiv, 49, 56-58, 75, 139, 171
    van Gogh, Vincent, 56

Beloved community. *See* Community Building
Blanchard, Ken H., xiii, xxvii-xxviii
Block, Peter M., xiii, xv, 134, 149, 189
Bosses. *See* Management
Branden, Nathaniel, 61-62
Buechner, Frederick, 36-37

Calling (inner), xxiii, 14, 22, 34, 35-36, 37
Change making, xi, xxii, xxix, 9, 17, 27, 79, 87, 88, 90, 148
Clifton, Don O., 35
Commitment to the Growth of People
    servant leadership, xiii
Communication, 2, 4, 5, 9, 10, 11-12, 13, 15, 97, 189-190
Community Building
    beloved community, 172-175, 178-179, 183, 187
    definition, 172
    primus inter pares (first-among-equals), 189
    servant leadership, xii, xxi, xxiii-xvi, xxvii, xxviii, 149, 171-172, 188-189
    ubuntu, 170-171, 173
    unlimited liability, 188
Conceptualization
    dreams, 110
    framing, 96, 97
    servant leadership, xiv, 91-92, 109-110
Conflict, xxiii, 4, 96, 97, 107
Covey, Stephen R., xiii, 3, 28, 57
Culture (organizational), 2, 5, 7, 8, 31, 79

Davis, Daryl, 64-65
Dreams, xiv, 50, 92, 98, 110, 131, 173, 185, 187
Drucker, Peter F., 58

Emotional Intelligence, 12, 25-27, 110
Empowerment, xxvii, 4, 141, 168
Empathy
    community building, 188
    definition, 24, 28, 31
    eight dimensions of, 26-27
    emotional intelligence, 25-26
    function, 26
    Gandhi, 99
    innovation, 27-28
    listening, 6

Empathy (*continued*)
  love, 27, 29
  need for, 4, 27
  Roosevelt, Anna Eleanor, 116
  servant leadership, xiii, 20, 30–31
  Woolman, John, 75, 79, 82–83
Employees, xiii, xxvi, 4–8, 10, 27, 151, 168
Ethics, 60, 72, 73, 80, 88, 170, 175

Followers, xxi, xxvi, 60–61, 87, 148, 167, 168, 178
Foresight
  definition, 110, 112, 113, 121, 131
  clock-building, 111-113
  development of, 113, 117, 118–119
  founding fathers, 112
  Greenleaf, Robert K., 130
  kaleidoscope thinking, 131
  necessity, 131
  servant leadership, xv, 112, 130
Frick, Don M., xiii, xxvii, 130

George, William (Bill) W., 113, 116, 117
Goleman, Daniel, 13, 25, 26
Gottman, John M., xxii
Grant, Adam M., 11–12
Greenleaf, Robert K.
  career, xxv, 13, 89
  inspired by Hesse, Hermann H., xxv
  Spears, Larry C. and, xi, xiii, xxix

Healing
  forgiveness, xxiii
  forms of, 43–44
  internal wounds, 42–44
  leadership framework, 46
  love, 42, 45–47
  meaning, 155
  relationships, xii
  servant leadership, xiv, 33, 46
  wounded healer, 32–33
Heifetz, Ronald A., 56
Hesse, Hermann K., xxv, 24, 38
Hitler, Adolf, xx, xxi, 150, 153, 183
Humility, xxii, xxiii, 12, 28, 44, 85, 87, 101

Journey to the East. *See* Hesse, Hermann K.

Kanter, Rosabeth M., 131–132
Kellerman, Barbara, 60–61
Kopp, Wendy S., 59–60

Leo (Hesse character), xxv, xxvi, 24, 38
Lewis, John R., 175
Lidice Massacre, xx, xxi
Listening
  autobiographical, 3
  active listening, 3, 8, 9, 10, 13, 16, 83, 163, 188
  Barrett, Colleen C., 7
  body language, 16
  career skill, 9, 10
  cognitive biases, 6
  conflict, 4, 6, 17
  creativity, 14
  emotional intelligence, 12, 13
  empathy, 20, 30
  Greenleaf, Robert K., 2, 13, 15
  healing, 17
  inner voice, 14, 36
  organizational dysfunction, 9
  Palmer, Parker J., 14
  persuasion, 65, 71, 90
  Redding, W. Charles, 9
  relational coordination, 6–7
  respect, 12
  servant leadership, xiii
Love, xxi, xxii, 27, 29, 33, 38, 39, 40, 42, 44, 45, 46, 68, 80, 98, 99, 101, 102, 169, 173–175, 177, 178, 183, 188

Management, xxviii, 9, 13, 60, 111–112
Meaning, 97, 121, 155–157, 162, 165, 166, 168, 189

Nadella, Satya, 27–28
Negotiation, 96–97, 107, 108
Nielsen, Richard P., 89
Non-violence, 85, 95, 98–101, 102–103, 109, 179
Nouwen, Henri J.M., 32–33

Palmer, Parker J., xiii, 14–15, 36, 171
Parks, Rosa, 176
Persuasion
   contrasted, 86–87
   Davis, Daryl, 64–65
   framework, 89
   Gandhi, Mohandas K., 100, 108
   guidelines for practicing, 86, 88–89
   servant leadership, xiv, 66, 87, 134
Peters, Thomas (Tom) J., 10
Power, xxi, xxvii, 11, 100, 102, 155, 166
Primus inter pares. See Community Building

Quakers, see Religious Society of Friends

Redding, W. Charles, 9
Religious Society of Friends
   abolition, 22, 65–66, 78, 85
   doctrine, 68
   Friends Journal, xi
   Greenleaf, Robert K., xiv, 66, 85, 89
Respect, xxiii, 9, 12
Roever, Dave, 42–43
Roy, Arundhati S., 113

Self-transcendence, 24, 81, 97, 149, 157, 165–166, 175
Servant Leadership
   balance, xxi, xxvii–xxviii
   best test of, xi, xii, xvii, 167
   calling, xvi, 22, 24, 37, 70
   forgiveness, xxi
   paradox, xii, 32, 160, 164
   practice of, xiii, xxii, xiii, 167–168
   relationships, xii, xix, xx, 174, 189, 190
   ten characteristics of, xiii–xvi
   thought leaders, xiii

Servant-Leader Organizations, xii, xxviii
Spears, Larry C., ix, xi, xxvii
Stewardship
   definition, xv, 134
   servant leadership, xv, 134, 147–148
   trustees, xv, 148–149
Sturnick, Judith A., 46

Trust, xv, 4, 6, 29, 38, 79, 134, 147, 148–149, 189
Tutu, Desmond M., 16, 54, 170–171
Twain, Mark, 34, 35–36

Vagelos, P. Roy, 60
Violence (impact of), 99–101, 177, 179

West, Cornel R., 57, 169
Wheatley, Margaret (Meg) J., xiii, 17, 190

www.ingramcontent.com/pod-product-compliance
Lightning Source LLC
Chambersburg PA
CBHW062019220426
43662CB00010B/1394